ESCAPE FROM BLOOD POND HELL

ESCAPE FROM BLOOD POND HELL

The Tales of Mulian and Woman Huang

Translated and introduced by **BEATA GRANT & WILT L. IDEMA**

UNIVERSITY OF WASHINGTON PRESS *Seattle and London*

Publication of this book was supported by generous grants from the Harvard-Yenching Institute, the College of Arts & Sciences at Washington University in St. Louis, and the Chinese Popular Culture Project, University of California, Berkeley.

UNIVERSITY OF WASHINGTON PRESS
PO Box 50096, Seattle, WA 98145, USA
www.washington.edu/uwpress

LIBRARY OF CONGRESS CATALOGING-IN-PUBLICATION DATA
Escape from blood pond hell : the tales of Mulian and Woman Huang / translated and introduced by Beata Grant and Wilt L. Idema.
p. cm.
Includes bibliographical references and index.
ISBN 978-0-295-99119-1 (hardcover : alk. paper) —
ISBN 978-0-295-99120-7 (pbk. : alk. paper)
1. Bao juan (Buddhist song-tales) 2. Buddhism in literature.
I. Grant, Beata, 1954– II. Idema, W. L. (Wilt L.)
PL2368.B34E83 2011
895.1'348—dc23
2011029922

The paper used in this publication meets the minimum requirements of American National Standard for Information Sciences—Permanence of Paper for Printed Library Materials, ANSI Z39.48-1984.

Cover front: The Blood Pond, from the second of ten scrolls among the sets featured in "Taizong's Hell: A Study Collection of Chinese Hell Scrolls" (http://academic.reed.edu/hellscrolls/), courtesy of K.E. Brashier.

CONTENTS

ACKNOWLEDGMENTS

When we were working on our first coauthored publication, *The Red Brush: Writing Women in Imperial China*, we were struck by how many of our women authors turned out to have been pious Buddhists even though they grew up and lived their lives in families that otherwise were staunchly Confucian. We also noted that, while many of these writing women came from elite families, they appear to have shared many of the same religious beliefs as their less literate sisters or, perhaps to put it more accurately, they were often subject to similar popular religious notions about the nature of women and aspired to similar sorts of religious ideals. For this reason, we decided to make available in English some of the materials that shaped the religious worlds of many Chinese women of all classes in late imperial times and into the twentieth century. The result is this volume, which includes complete annotated translations of two such works, *The Precious Scroll of the Three Lives of Mulian* and *Woman Huang Recites the Diamond Sutra*. As in our other coauthored volume, each translation has been drafted by one of us and extensively revised by the other. Thus, both translations represent a truly collaborative effort, as does the introduction.

Beata Grant prepared a very sketchy draft of one of the translated texts in this volume, *Woman Huang Recites the Diamond Sutra*, a number of years ago when she was a postdoctoral fellow with the Chinese Popular Culture Project at the University of California at Berkeley. This project, directed by Professor David Johnson, has played a pioneering role in raising awareness in this country of the rich variety of popular culture in China and the extensive if scattered array of sources that are available for its study. The Chinese Popular Culture Project has further assisted in the publication of this book with a generous grant, as has the Harvard-Yenching Institute of Harvard University and the School of Arts and Sciences of Washington University in St. Louis. We are very grateful for their support.

We also wish to express our appreciation to the two anonymous readers for the University of Washington Press, who alerted us to parts of the translation in need of correction or modification and also offered useful suggestions for improving our introductory comments and our notes. We would also like to use this opportunity to thank the efficient production team at the Press, especially Laura Iwasaki, whose careful copyediting has contributed greatly to the style and consistency of this volume, and Mary Ribesky, who patiently guided it through to final publication. Needless to say, we take full responsibility for any errors or deficiencies that remain.

BEATA GRANT, *Washington University in St. Louis*
WILT L. IDEMA, *Harvard University*

NOTE ON THE TRANSLATIONS

Our primary aim has been to provide translations that are both faithful to the original and easy to read, which is why we have kept our annotations to the minimum. More detailed and more expert discussions of many of the issues and figures mentioned in the texts may be found in selected items in the bibliography.

When translating verse, we have made no attempt to reproduce the rhymes of the original, and we also have not imposed any metrical pattern on the lines. In general, one line of verse in the original is reproduced as one line of verse in the translation. Seven-syllable lines are translated as a single line; ten-syllable lines have been rendered as long lines made up of three short lines, reproducing the tripartite structure of the original lines. In extended passages of either seven-syllable verse or ten-syllable verse in the original, we have tried to give each line roughly the same length in our translations. To achieve that aim, we have admittedly on occasion made use of some minor padding. Even then, we have been far more successful in our aim in some passages than in others. When the text includes a number of songs each set to the same allometric tune, we have tried to make the songs display roughly the same pattern of long and short lines.

In Chinese names, the surname comes first and is followed by the personal name. A married woman does not take her husband's surname but is designated by her maiden family name. The months of the year are the months of the traditional lunar calendar, which starts roughly one month later than the solar calendar. Chinese seasons begin earlier, however, as the first three months of the year constitute spring, the next three months summer, and so on. A baby is said to be one year of age when he or she is born and turns two on the first New Year—in this way, a "three-year-old" child may be just over one year old according to the Western way of counting age.

ESCAPE FROM BLOOD POND HELL

Introduction

E ach of the two texts translated in this volume, *The Precious Scroll of the Three Lives of Mulian* (Mulian sanshi baojuan) and *Woman Huang Recites the Diamond Sutra* (Huangshi nü dui Jingang),[1] represents only one of numerous versions of a religious story that once enjoyed tremendous popularity all over China and is occasionally read and performed even today. The primary worldview reflected in these tales is what we might call popular Buddhism, which was quite different from the Buddhist philosophy discussed inside monastery walls or among elite clerics and literati. As early as the sixth century, Huijiao, the author of *Biographies of Eminent Monks* (Gaoseng zhuan), urged his fellow monks to adapt their message to their audience, which, should it be made up of uneducated peasants, might mean having to frighten them with vivid descriptions of the consequences of their sins before presenting them with ways of avoiding this dreadful fate. According to Huijiao, when a good preacher

> speaks about death, he makes heart and body shiver for fear; if he speaks
> about hell, tears of anxiety gush forth in streams. If he points out earlier
> karma, it is as if one clearly sees one's deed from the past; if he predicts
> the future consequences, he manifests the coming retribution. If he talks

about the joys [of the Pure Land], his audience feels happy and elated; if he discourses on the sufferings [of hell], eyes are filled with tears. At that moment the whole congregation is converted and the whole room overcome with emotion: people throw themselves down on the floor, bang their heads against the ground, and beg for grace; each and every one snaps his fingers; everybody recites the name of the Buddha.[2]

At first, it was primarily Buddhist monks who took this message of hell and damnation, sin and salvation, not only to unlettered peasants, but to society at large, high and low, men and women.[3] Beginning in the Song dynasty (960–1279), lay authors also began to create texts that conveyed similar messages of sin and salvation. Such texts only rarely ended up in the libraries of literati and even more rarely made their way into the modern academic libraries upon which scholars of things Chinese have long relied for their research. But that does not mean that these texts were not widely distributed and read in their own time. Not only did men and women with at least a basic education read these texts; many elite literati-scholars probably perused them as well, whether out of curiosity, fascination, or disgust. On the other side of the social spectrum, there were many unlettered Chinese who knew of these stories through performances of many different drama and ballad versions. Grisly and gory as these stories could sometimes be, they both reflected and informed the ethical and belief systems of countless men and women in late imperial and early modern times. They could do so only by presenting riveting narratives, stories such as those of Mulian and Woman Huang, which spoke in a particularly powerful way to universal human fears and concerns.

The histories of the Mulian and Woman Huang tales, as described in greater detail later, are quite different. The origins of the story of Mulian can be traced back to canonical Buddhist sutras dating to the sixth century at the latest, while the earliest-known textual reference to the story of Woman Huang does not appear until the late sixteenth century. There are also considerable differences in the status and gender of the main protagonists of these two tales. On the one hand, Mulian (the Chinese rendition of Maudgalyayana) is a celibate monk; he is said to have been one of the two most senior disciples of Sakyamuni Buddha and was traditionally renowned for his supernatural powers, which, among other things, allowed him to travel to other levels of existence. Woman Huang, on the other hand, is a simple laywoman, married to a butcher and the mother of his children, whose power rests solely in her pious determination to save both herself and her family by single-mindedly reciting the Diamond Sutra (Sanskrit, Vajracchedikā Prajñāpāramitā Sūtra; Chinese, Jingang jing).

Nevertheless, by the final decades of the Qing dynasty (1644–1911), when the ballad versions translated here were published and circulated, these two stories not only enjoyed great popularity but had also come to be very closely connected; in fact, at least one of the longer dramatic versions of the Mulian story includes a version of the Woman Huang story among its several subplots.[4] Also, when Woman Huang travels through the Underworld in *Woman Huang Recites the Diamond Sutra*, her ghost guides inform her that she is retracing a journey taken by Mulian much earlier. In the following pages, we offer a brief overview of the separate histories of these two legends and a discussion of some of their shared assumptions and concerns, including vegetarianism, karmic retribution (whether in the Underworld or the next life), female pollution, filial piety, and, above all, the urgent religious question of how to ensure the salvation of impure and sinful women, in particular, mothers. The differences in the gender and status of Mulian and Woman Huang, as well as the differences in the means by which they seek to resolve issues of common concern, are the reason the two stories read in conjunction offer a particularly fascinating insight into the world of late imperial Chinese popular religion and literature.

ORIGIN AND DEVELOPMENT OF THE MULIAN LEGEND

The Mulian story and the history of its development have been the subject of many excellent scholarly studies, a number of which are readily available in English. The earliest Chinese text featuring Mulian and his journey to the Underworld is the Yulan Bowl Sutra (Yulanpen jing).[5] This text, although said to have been translated by the Indian monk Dharmaraksa (fl. 265–313), was probably composed in China in the fourth or fifth century. The text is not encountered in any other Buddhist language, and the story it tells of Mulian rescuing his mother from hell has no known counterpart in any Indian source. According to the Yulan Bowl Sutra,

Desiring to save his parents to repay the kindness they had shown him in nursing and feeding him, he used his divine eye to observe the worlds. He saw his departed mother reborn among the departed ghosts; she never saw food or drink, and her skin hung from her bones. [Mulian] took pity, filled his bowl with rice, and sent it to his mother as an offering. When his mother received the rice, she used her left hand to guard the bowl and her right hand to gather up the rice, but before the rice entered her mouth, it changed into flaming coals, so in the end she could not eat. [Mulian] cried out in grief and wept tears. He rushed back to tell the Buddha and laid out everything as it had happened.[6]

The Buddha then tells Mulian:

"The roots of your mother's sins are deep and tenacious. It is not within your power as a single individual to do anything about it . . . You must rely on the mighty spiritual power of the assembled monks to obtain her deliverance."[7]

The Buddha then proceeds to instruct Maudgalyayana to provide bowls of food to the monastic community on the fifteenth of the Seventh Month, and indeed this results in the salvation of his mother. The Buddha finally adds that all people may in the same manner save their parents from hell and that offerings to monks and nuns on the fifteenth of the Seventh Month are the highest expression of filial piety.

By the Tang dynasty (618–907), Yulan Bowl Sutra had become the foundation text for what was known as the Yulan Bowl Festival (Yulanpen hui) or, more popularly, the Ghost Festival, which was celebrated on the fifteenth of the Seventh Month.[8] This was a ritual ceremony, conducted by Buddhist monks and sponsored by the laity on behalf of deceased family members as well as the many hungry ghosts who might lack surviving family who could care for their restless and unhappy spirits. Traditionally, this date also marked the end of the monks' strenuous summer retreat, when their spiritual powers were believed to be at their peak. This meant that offerings dedicated to the well-being of one's ancestors made to the monastic community on this date would be particularly efficacious. The Yulan Bowl Festival was to become one of the most popular of all Buddhist religious festivals, not only in China, but also in Japan, where it is known as the Obon Festival.[9]

The legend of Mulian also became the basis for other types of literary and religious texts, many of which were likewise intended for performance during the Yulan Bowl Festival. Among the many important manuscripts from the Tang dynasty discovered in the caves of Dunhuang in northwest China in the early twentieth century were various prosimetric versions of this legend, including a "transformation text," or *bianwen*. This text, *Transformation Text of Maha-Maudgalyayana Rescuing His Mother from the Realm of Darkness* (Da Muqianlian mingjian jiumu bianwen), has been dated to around 800 and is preserved in a number of copies.[10] Transformation texts were written in a combination of prose and rhymed verse (usually seven syllables per line) and, with their combination of overt didacticism and entertaining descriptions and dialogue, were intended for a wide audience of varying degrees of literacy.[11] In the transformation text adaptation of the legend of Mulian, the story is greatly developed. While Mulian's father is described as the perfect lay patron of Buddhism, his mother turns out to be a weak-willed woman who abandons her pious lifestyle soon after the death of her husband. Upon her death, Mulian becomes a monk and then discovers that his father has been reborn in heaven but that his mother has been condemned to hell. Mulian travels through the various hells, each characterized by a particular (and horrific) punishment for sinners, and eventually locates his mother in the Avici Hell, the deepest of them all. When she is freed from the Avici Hell through the intervention of the Buddha, she is first reborn as a hungry ghost and then as a dog; she is reborn in heaven only after the Buddha institutes the Yulan Bowl Festival.[12]

Beginning in the Song dynasty, the legend of Mulian saving his mother was also adapted for the stage, again primarily for performance on the occasion of the Yulan Bowl Festival. In the early years of the twelfth century, the play was said to have been performed in the Northern Song capital of Kaifeng during the seven days preceding this festival—it is not clear whether the same play was performed seven times or whether the full performance of the play took seven days. No text of this early play has been preserved, but the Japanese scholar Kikkawa Yoshikazu has suggested that the vivid dialogues in a thirteenth-century (or even earlier) prose account of the legend, *Sutra Spoken by the Buddha of Mulian Rescuing His Mother* (Foshuo

Mulian jiumu jing), which has survived in Japanese and Korean reprintings, may well derive from the play.[13] The earliest text of a Mulian play, however, dates to the late sixteenth century, when Zheng Zhizhen in 1582 published his *Mulian Rescues His Mother: An Exhortation to Goodness* (Mulian jiumu quanshan ji), which was composed of one hundred scenes. Performances of Mulian plays were often quite spectacular, boasting a wide variety of subplots and filled with acrobatic displays and vivid costuming. These performances continued to be popular both at court and in the countryside well into the twentieth century.[14] The eighteenth-century version of the Mulian play as performed at the Manchu court in Beijing ran to 240 scenes and took ten days to be performed in full. Numerous scripts of local performance traditions have been recovered in recent decades.

During the decade of the Cultural Revolution (1966–76), Mulian plays were seen as both feudal and superstitious, and their performance was strictly prohibited. Today, Mulian plays are being performed again, although on a much reduced scale. In particular, they seem to be experiencing a limited revival as part of the efforts of various localities to promote their regional cultural heritage. That this regional association is not entirely new can be seen from the case of Anhui, the home province of the late-sixteenth-century literatus Zheng Zhizhen, where the staging of this play, which lasted for a full seven days and nights and required a considerable amount of financial backing from local elites, especially the merchants of Huizhou, has long been a vital component of community and ritual life.[15] While today the staging of the Mulian play no longer fills this function in quite the same way, and its performance takes three days and three nights instead of the original seven, it is still performed regularly in places in Anhui such as Mashan village, near Huangshan.[16]

The story of Mulian was also a popular subject of the prosimetric literature of the later dynasties, especially the genre known as "precious scrolls" (baojuan).[17] Precious scrolls were usually written in a combination of prose and seven-character rhymed verse, but the genre also allowed for the inclusion of lyrics based on popular tunes. This genre appears to have emerged in the Yuan dynasty (1260–1368), and it became particularly popular during the Ming (1368–1644) and Qing dynasties, when precious scrolls were often used by various new religions (often pejoratively designated as "sectarian") to propagate their ideas in a simple and entertaining manner.[18] Whether "sectarian" or not, precious scrolls as a rule were performed in a ritual context. It is worth noting that even today in certain areas of mainland China, one finds precious scrolls being performed in a ritual context, whether in a temple or at home.[19] This is also suggested by the opening verses of the *Precious Scroll of the Three Lives of Mulian* translated in this book, which reads:

> *Raising high in my hands this single stick of true incense,*
> *I ascend the platform, preach the Law, and open the sutra.*
> *All men and women in this hall, please listen quietly, as it*
> *Brings blessings, extends longevity, and frees from disaster!*

The earliest prosimetric ballad on Mulian explicitly titled a precious scroll is the *Precious Scroll on Mulian Rescuing His Mother from Hell and Her Rebirth in Heaven* (Mulian jiumu chu diyu shengtian baojuan). This text must have been in circulation during the Yuan dynasty, as a beautifully illustrated manuscript dating from 1337 (or 1371) has been partially preserved.[20] In this version, Mulian's mother is reborn in the Hell of Darkness before she is reborn as a hungry ghost. Various precious scroll adaptations of the Mulian legend circulated in the Ming and Qing dynasties,[21] but by the second half of the nineteenth century and the first half of the twentieth century, two precious scrolls on the legend of Mulian appear to have enjoyed considerable popularity: *The Precious Scroll on Mulian Rescuing His Mother and Visiting the Underworld* (Mulian jiumu youming baozhuan),[22] which circulated in Hebei, and *The Precious Scroll of the Three Lives of Mulian*, which was popular in Zhejiang. The first, which is written in an alternation of prose and ten-syllable verse, has been studied in detail by David Johnson.[23] This text includes a prologue set in the reign of Emperor Wu (r. 502–49) of the Liang dynasty (502–56), who is well known for his patronage of Buddhism and even became the protagonist of his own precious scroll. The prologue is followed by accounts of the lives of Mulian's great-grandfather, grandfather, and father and then proceeds to the sins of Mulian's mother and Mulian's journey through hell in order to save her from suffering. The earliest-known printing of this precious scroll dates from 1881, and there are also five other known Qing dynasty printings.

The earliest-known printing of the precious scroll version translated here, *The Precious Scroll of the Three Lives of Mulian*, is dated 1876; more than ten later printings are known.[24] This version comprises three parts, corresponding to the three lives of Mulian (Mulian, Huang Chao, and He Yin). The text is composed using alternating prose and verse. As is common in precious scrolls, the verse passages are written mostly in rhyming seven-syllable lines or in rhyming ten-syllable lines. The first part, however, also includes a number of verse passages that have a different structure as well as a number of songs. As in the better-known Dunhuang transformation texts on Mulian saving his mother, the main body of the narrative is devoted to Mulian's journey through the hells of the Underworld in search of the mother who has been sent there for her sins. In the precious scroll translated here, that narrative is preceded by a description of the miraculous birth of Mulian, which also provides an account of the origin of his peculiar personal name, Luobo (Radish). As the concept of the Blood Pond Hell (discussed in detail later in this introduction) developed over the course of the eleventh and twelfth centuries, the Dunhuang versions of the legend provide no account of this hell. The Precious Scroll of the Three Lives of Mulian, however, features not one but two Blood Ponds, one designed exclusively for women and the other for male and female sinners alike. The Precious Scroll of the Three Lives of Mulian also provides an extended description of the Wheel of Rebirth, which is not found in the Dunhuang transformation text. In its description of the Six Paths of Rebirth, this precious scroll would appear to be highly original, as it includes neither the path of the demigods nor that of the hungry ghosts, both of which feature prominently in the earlier Chinese written accounts and pictorial representation of the Wheel of Rebirth as described by Stephen Teiser.[25]

Yet another difference between the Dunhuang versions of the legend of Mulian and The Precious Scroll of the Three Lives of Mulian is the appearance of the bodhisattva Guanyin and her acolytes. The widespread veneration of the bodhisattva Guanyin in China goes back to the fifth century. Although initially depicted as a handsome young prince, from the tenth century onward, Guanyin was increasingly venerated as a lovely young woman, and it is in this female form that the bodhisattva became probably the most widely venerated Buddhist deity in all of East Asia.[26] There are numerous popular stories and tales in which Guanyin makes use of her feminine beauty and charm to seduce sinners into virtue. In The Precious Scroll of the Three Lives of Mulian, however, she prefers to have her acolytes take female form in order to test the resolve of the monk Mulian as he sets out on his journey. Guanyin and her acolytes again test the resolve of Mulian, who at this point has been reborn into the body of the butcher He Yin, near the end of the third part of the text.[27]

ORIGIN AND DEVELOPMENT OF THE LEGEND OF WOMAN HUANG

Although not as well known as the Mulian story, the tale of Woman Huang (sometimes also referred to as Woman Wang) appears in a wide variety of versions and genres, including dramas and prosimetric ballads such as precious scrolls.[28] While it is difficult to ascertain its origins with any precision, the story appears to date back to at least the Song dynasty (960–1279), when the Tiantai Buddhist master Fakong composed a text titled "The Spiritual Rewards of [Reciting the] Diamond Sutra: After Three Lifetimes of Religious Cultivation, Woman Wang Ascends to Heaven in Broad Daylight."[29] By the early Ming dynasty (1368–1644), the story is mentioned by Luo Menghong (1442–1527), also known as Luo Qing or, simply, Patriarch Luo. Luo's teachings were extraordinarily influential in the later development of many different types of the new religions that, as noted earlier, are often referred to as "sectarian religions" and made use of precious scrolls in order to propagate their teachings.[30] Luo's reference to Woman Wang (Huang) appears in one of the precious scrolls associated with him and reads "The Patriarch Limitless Comes to Liberate the Wise Woman Wang [Huang]; About to Depart, She Takes Her Leave and, Weeping, Exhorts Sentient Beings to Salvation."[31]

During the Ming dynasty, the Woman Huang story continued to be associated primarily with the precious scroll genre, which was often read or recited in a ritual context. It would also appear that many times the primary audience for such ritual recitations was female, and, as described by Richard Shek, the recitations "often took place at nunneries and temples, but more frequently in the homes of the devout. Surrounded by women and the children of the household, the principal reciter would, with the help of partner[s] or acolytes, recite and enact various [precious scrolls] upon request, with appropriate intermissions for rest and refreshment."[32] A fascinating description of this sort of ritual recitation is found in chapter 74 of the famous Ming novel *Plum in the Golden Vase* (Jin ping mei), which was written around the end of the sixteenth century. In the novel, we find the ladies of a fairly well-off household gathered around a Buddhist nun, Nun Xue, to hear her recount the admonitory story of Woman Huang, an abridged version of which is provided.[33]

New religious movements such as the one established by Patriarch Luo often made use of precious scrolls. One such movement was the Way of Former Heaven (Xiantian Dao), sometimes also called Great Way of Former Heaven (Xiantian Dadao). This sectarian group was founded by the lay preacher Huang Dehui (1644–1662) and not only enjoyed great popularity during the Qing but continues, in modified form, to attract adherents even to this day. The Way of Former Heaven represents a conscious effort to combine elements of all of the so-called Three Teachings—Confucianism, Daoism, and Buddhism—in a way that would be meaningful to ordinary people. As one source succinctly puts it, the idea was to instruct its followers how to "maintain the ritual propriety (*li*)" of Confucianism, "accept the moral precepts (*jie*)" of Buddhism, and "cultivate the Way (*dao*)" of Daoism.[34] Included among the religious texts that the Way of Former Heaven used to propagate its messages was a precious scroll that appears under various different titles, including *The Precious Scroll of Woman Huang's Religious Cultivation over Three Lifetimes*, *The Precious Scroll of Reciting the Diamond Sutra*, and *The Woman Huang Precious Scroll*. The earliest extant version of this precious scroll is dated 1848, but there are numerous other editions that were published in various locations up through the Republican period (1911–49). Of particular interest is the fact that in this version, Woman Huang, like Mulian, is provided with "three lives," all of which are described in considerable detail.

According to this version, in her previous lifetime, Woman Huang was not a woman or even a layperson: she was a monk named Chan Master Dequan. Master Dequan had led a holy life: he had began chanting sutras from the age of seven and for the rest of his life spent the daylight hours assiduously reciting the Diamond Sutra and sitting in deep meditation at night. One day a layman by the name of Huang Lingda came to the temple where Master Dequan resided in order to make a generous donation and was converted by Master Dequan. Worried because he was getting on in years and his wife had not yet borne him any children, Huang Lingda was also hoping that his meritorious action would bring him an heir. Not long after this, the seventy-five-year-old Master Dequan began to make preparations for his death. Given his life of piety, Master Dequan should have been entitled to final liberation; however, seven lifetimes earlier, he had been a disciple of the famous Daoist immortal Lü Dongbin and, taking advantage of Bodhidharma's state of trance, had stolen the Chan patriarch's sandal. Despite Dequan's many years of religious cultivation, he had not yet made full amends for this crime and was thus fated to come back to the world yet again. Thus, the story goes, not long after the master's death, the childless wife of the generous lay donor Huang Lingda becomes pregnant and subsequently gives birth to Dequan's reincarnation, the child that would grow up to be Woman Huang.

As in the other versions, after Woman Huang dies and is called down to the Underworld, she is reborn as a male and subsequently achieves success as a high official, leaves the worldly life to engage in further intensive spiritual cultivation, and, ultimately, attain liberation. The assumption, presumably, is that the teachings of the Way of Former Heaven provide this final course of instruction. Traces of this connection with the Way of Former Heaven can be seen in the ballad version of the Woman Huang story translated in this book, although here the emphasis is placed as much on the entertainment value of the story as on the religious message behind it.

Precious scrolls based on the story of Woman Huang continued to circulate widely in the late Qing dynasty, not all of them necessarily directly associated with sectarian religious groups. The Japanese scholar Sawada Mizuho describes in some detail several versions of precious scrolls in different editions dating from the late nineteenth and early twentieth centuries.[35] Despite certain differences in details, such as the names and number of some of the minor protagonists, the story in all of these precious scrolls is fairly similar, and many although not all of the elements can be found in dramatic as well as prosimetric ballad versions of the story, including the one translated in this book.

All of the precious scroll versions are set in the Nanhua district of Chaozhou prefecture, in Shandong, where a fairly well-off villager surnamed either Huang or Wang finds that he and his wife are getting on in years and are still childless. They go to various temples to make offerings and pray for a child, and eventually the gods (in some cases the Jade Emperor, in others the bodhisattva Guanyin) take pity on them and arrange for an elderly monk to be reincarnated as their daughter after his death. The girl is born on the fifteenth day of the Seventh Month, which is also the day on which Buddhist monks celebrate the Yulan Bowl Festival for the benefit of the souls of the dead, especially those of one's parents.

While this book's ballad version begins the story with Woman Huang as a married woman, some of the precious scroll versions reveal a bit more about her life before marriage. The exact details differ from version to version, but one of the more common plots relates that Woman Huang took up the pious recitation of the Diamond Sutra at the early age of seven. She is also just a young girl when her mother dies, and her father marries a widow with a son by the name of Houqi. She is mistreated by her stepmother, however, and Houqi harasses her sexually. In the end, Houqi plots to kill his father-in-law but ends up killing his own mother by mistake. When Woman Huang's father is falsely accused of the crime, the young Woman Huang offers to be executed in his stead, and as she is taken to the execution ground, the God of Thunder comes to her rescue, striking Houqi dead. After this, she is married to the Zhaos' son and thus begins another stage of her life. Those familiar with the famous Yuan dynasty drama *The Injustice to Dou E* (Dou E yuan) by Guan Hanqing will recognize the plot, and it may be that this play was the inspiration for this particular addition to the Woman Huang story.[36] Although the version of the Woman Huang story translated here mentions only that Woman Huang's parents were devout Buddhists and that she learned to recite the sutra from her mother, Woman Huang's extended warnings to her husband, to be very careful about taking a second wife after she dies, and to her children, to be careful not to provoke the anger of their stepmother should their father remarry, hark back to these other versions.

Not surprisingly, the Woman Huang story also found its way into many different sorts of dramatic genres, including a long *chuanqi*, a form of romantic drama often composed of as many as thirty or more scenes, which enjoyed great popularity in the Ming and Qing dynasties. Although the *chuanqi* version of the Woman Huang story, which dates to the late Ming and early Qing, is no longer extant, a summary of the plot of this play, clearly based on the precious scroll versions described above, includes the reincarnation of the elderly monk and the sufferings of Woman Huang at the hands of her stepmother and stepbrother. There are also several Beijing opera versions as well as many regional dramatic versions of the Woman

Huang story, especially from Hubei and Shandong. While many of these plays focus on her sufferings as a young girl at the hands of her evil stepmother and stepbrother, they also elaborate on her life as a married woman and her tour of the Underworld.[37] During the nineteenth and twentieth centuries, these operas were performed widely in both city and countryside, often for temple festivals. With the establishment of the People's Republic of China, performances of operatic versions titled *Woman Huang Tours the Underworld*, along with other works regarded as being "superstitious," were prohibited. Even when this ban was temporarily lifted in 1957, the play was harshly criticized as backward, not only by public officials, but by artists and intellectuals as well. The playwright and film director Wu Zuguang, for example, decried the Woman Huang play as being unnecessarily violent and fatalistic, lamenting that if it were to be seen by a "foreign friend," that person would have "plenty of reasons to conclude that ours is a backward, uncivilized, and ignorant country."[38] What these criticisms failed to note, however, is that while the descriptions of the Underworld are certainly grim and gruesome, ultimately Woman Huang emerges victorious over the forces of sin and suffering, and achieves liberation for both herself and her family.

It is in the prosimetric and verse ballads, which are long enough to allow for a fuller psychological exploration of emotions and states of mind, that the Woman Huang story would seem to receive its fullest and most poignant treatment. One such ballad is a version of the Woman Huang story, in this case titled "Fifth Daughter Wang," which was part of the repertoire of long songs written in "women's script" (*nüshu*) of Jiangyong in southern Hunan. This version, the Chinese transcription of which has been translated into English, also includes an account of Woman Huang's journey through the ten courts of the Underworld and her rebirth as a male, after which she goes on to become a high official and then to convert and save her former husband.[39] Several versions of the Woman Huang story are from the Bai ethnic minority in Yunnan. One, at 2,300 lines long, is considered to be the longest ballad in the Bai folk literature repertoire. More than a decade ago, Wang Mingda, who belongs to the Bai minority, gathered together a number of stories and ballads about Woman Huang from various locations in Yunnan. Apparently unaware of the history of this story-cycle, Wang Mingda considered Woman Huang to be a tragic figure of Bai religious folklore.[40] As the observant reader will notice, in this book's translated version, when Woman Huang is reborn as a male and eventually becomes a high official, he is sent to an official post in Yunnan. This would indicate a connection between Shandong and Yunnan, perhaps associated with the religious networks established by the Way of Former Heaven sectarian movement. It would appear, then, as in the case of the Mulian story, that there has been a renewed interest in the story of Woman Huang in recent years, although, officially at least, for its cultural and entertainment value rather than any religious message.

One of the most fully elaborated of the many ballad versions of the Woman Huang story is the one translated here, *Woman Huang Recites the Diamond Sutra*, published in Shanghai by the printing house Chunyin shuzhuang, probably in the first decade of the twentieth century, although no publication dates are given. A rare copy of this edition is kept at the Fu Ssu-nien Library of the Academia Sinica in Taiwan, where it is cataloged as a "plucking rhyme" (*tanci*), a popular form of performance literature usually designed to be sung to the accompaniment of instrumental music, often by women for a female audience. Plucking rhymes represent one of the wide variety of prosimetric texts that enjoyed great popularity from the late Ming onward and, as such, belong to the same general category as precious scrolls. Thus it would be no surprise that they share stories such as that of Woman Huang. As noted earlier, the emphasis this book's version places on the importance of adhering to a vegetarian diet as well as occasional references to the Way of Former Heaven might indicate that this text may be loosely based on the precious scroll used by this sectarian group to propagate its teachings. These references appear only occasionally, however, and mostly toward the end of the text, suggesting that they were added later. In any case, the publisher of the version translated here felt no need to specify the genre, perhaps because the text was printed primarily for reading rather than for performance, and the text refers to itself only as a "morality book" (*shanshu*). In short, all that can be said with complete confidence is that this version of the Woman Huang story belongs to the general generic category of prosimetric ballad, and that it was probably designed not to be recited or performed in a ritual context but simply to be read for personal enjoyment and edification, perhaps largely by a female audience, as by this time, many more women were literate and could read it for themselves.

As ballads go, the version translated in this book is quite long, and like the Yunnan ballad mentioned above, with the exception of a single short passage in prose, is composed in rhymed verse of seven syllables per line.[41] Its exceptional length allows for a greater elaboration of inner worlds of feeling and emotion rather than mere narration of plot. This version of the story of Woman Huang offers a vivid portrayal of the psychological and emotional aspects of the spiritual crisis Woman Huang suffers when she is called down to the Underworld because of her religious piety and must leave behind her family, particularly distressing for her because of her three young children. The length of the text also allows for the introduction of new characters, such as Woman Huang's sister-in-law, a conventional woman whose lack of piety makes her a perfect foil to Woman Huang. (This sister-in-law is surnamed Liu and may have been inspired by the character of Mulian's mother, Liu Qingti.) As Woman Huang travels through the Underworld, guided and protected by the Golden Lad and the Jade Maiden, she witnesses her sister-in-law being subjected to various sorts of painful tortures in punishment for her sinful lifestyle. Woman Huang is then reborn as a male in a rich family and proceeds to pass the metropolitan examination and be appointed to a high official position. Then, after making sure that her sons are well-established in their own careers, and her daughters married off, Woman Huang, or rather, Zhang Jinda, leaves behind the life of an official and, in the company of her parents, goes off to find a teacher who will show them the way to enlightenment.

THE SINFUL NATURE OF WOMEN

As noted earlier, both the Mulian and the Woman Huang story share certain basic religious assumptions and concerns. One of the most important of these is the conviction that women are more prone to sin and thus in greater need of salvation from the torments of hell. The notion not only that women are of weak character and particularly susceptible to sinful behavior but that their female bodies are inherently polluting can be found in many of the world's religious traditions, both East and West. Buddhism is no exception. Although there is a diversity of views to be found in the early texts of Indian Buddhism, there is no dearth of misogynist attitudes, some of which are traditionally attributed to the Buddha himself.[42] In the larger Buddhist context, sex and sexual desire are closely associated with attachment, which is regarded as the source of all suffering and the greatest impediment to salvation or, in Buddhist terms, liberation. By extension, sex is what leads to procreation, that is, to being born into the very karmic round of suffering that the Buddhist strives to transcend once and for all. Because of a woman's biological capacity to give birth, it was assumed that she was inherently prone to emotional attachment, sensual desire, and, ultimately, sin. Thus she came to represent, particularly in the eyes of monastic males—who, after all, were both the primary authors and the audience for most Buddhist texts—all that they had to reject if they were to achieve liberation. For men, rejecting women and everything they supposedly represented was a matter of rejecting the Other; for women who aspired to liberation, it meant rejecting the Self, that is, their own female embodiment. One way to do this was to cultivate enough merit in the present life to assure rebirth, either in this world or, preferably, in a Buddhist Pure Land, as a male.[43] Failure to do so would mean, at the very best, continued rebirth into the inferior body of a woman. At the very worst, and especially if she not only failed to cultivate merit but actively indulged in sinful behavior, a woman would be condemned to suffer the excruciating pains of hell, sufferings that, while not thought of as eternal as such, are described as truly terrible and sometimes of almost unimaginably long duration.[44]

There was, however, a problem with this outright condemnation of women, sex, and marriage. For one thing, Buddhism offered a cosmic vision of many lifetimes as well as many different realms of existence. Traditionally six in number, these realms included those of the gods, the demigods, animals, hungry ghosts, hell-beings, and, of course, humans. This last realm was considered both the rarest and the most fortunate. Thus, while men dedicated to a celibate life of monasticism might find it convenient to avoid, if not condemn, women and their wily ways, they could not avoid the fact that without mothers they would never have been born, and for that if for nothing else, they owed women a great debt of gratitude. Thus, even in India, although a man might "leave the household," it was not always so easy to shrug off deeply ingrained notions of filial duty toward his parents, including and perhaps even particularly, his mother, since it was she who endured the suffering of pregnancy and childbirth and took primary responsibility for the crucial early years of child-rearing.[45] As the Buddha himself reputedly said: "Moreover, monks, if he should establish his parents in supreme authority, in the absolute rule over this mighty earth abounding in the seven treasures—not even with this could he repay his parents. What is the cause for that? Monks, parents do much for their children: they bring them up, they nourish them, they introduce them to this world."[46]

When Buddhism came to China in the first century, it almost immediately found itself confronted with widely accepted Confucian norms according to which woman's natural destiny was marriage and motherhood. Once married, a woman's paramount duty was to give birth to children, preferably male, who would carry on her husband's family line and ensure the continuation of the ancestral sacrifices. If she accomplished this, she could expect to rely on her children's filial obligation to respect and care for her, both in life and, perhaps even more important, after death. These ideas on the duties and joys of marriage and motherhood were dominant throughout the imperial period and well into the twentieth century.[47] This is not to say that women were not regarded as hierarchically subordinate: while the notions of yin and yang may have been complementary in theory, in practice, yang was largely regarded as being hierarchically superior to yin, just as the sky was always located above the earth. In short, while indigenous Chinese religion did not lack its own notions of female impurity, with the coming of Buddhism, they came to be both emphasized and elaborated upon to a far greater degree than ever before.

According to scholars such as Alan Cole, this emphasis on female impurity was in large part perpetuated by Buddhist monastics who, by persuading women of their sinfulness, and in particular, by persuading sons of the sinfulness of their mothers, could then assure them of the possibility of ameliorating, if not completely avoiding, the consequences of this sinfulness. They could do this by engaging in religious activities such as vegetarianism, scripture recitation, and, not incidentally, rituals that could be conducted only by Buddhist monks and monasteries. In so doing, argue these scholars, these monks (and later lay believers as well) were able to apply deeply rooted indigenous notions of filial piety to the greater Buddhist goal of liberation from suffering, whether in this world or, more especially, in the Underworld.

THE HELLS AND THEIR BUREAUCRATS

The Chinese Underworld represents an amalgamation of indigenous and Indian Buddhist ideas and images. In many ways, its infernal punishment and pain resemble those described in other religious traditions. However, the Chinese Underworld is relatively distinctive in its portrayal as a bureaucracy, which, like its earthly counterpart, has officials of varying ranks, with their records and documents, mistakes (such as condemning the wrong person because of confusion over an identical surname), and occasional cases of corruption. This notion of a bureaucratic underworld appears in early Chinese tomb documents and was already well established by the time Buddhism came to China around the first century.[48] Buddhism added several important elements to this Underworld, one of which was a more fully developed notion of many hells (according to one version, eight cold and eight hot), located at different levels, each with specific forms of torture designed for specific types of sins.

The sufferings in these hells were excruciating and might last for an extremely long time, but none lasted forever. In other words, hell was more of a purgatory, or rather, to use the Chinese term, it was an "earth prison" (diyu) from which one would be released (into a hoped-for human rebirth, although rebirth as an animal was also a possibility) after one had undergone one's punishment. If the Underworld was thought of as a prison, this required the presence of judges (not to mention secretaries and security guards) who were qualified to determine the punishment appropriate to the sin. By the Tang dynasty, an indigenous Buddhist scripture titled Sutra of the Ten Kings (Shiwang jing) had emerged, which provided a description of the Ten Courts of Hell, each presided over by a king, who, with the help of his aides, studied the ledgers of life and death, considered the crimes, and meted out the punishment.[49] Souls of the deceased who had to appear before these kings were sometimes, although not always, allowed to plead their own cases. The most important of the Ten Kings is King Yama (Yanluo Wang), based loosely on one of the most ancient of Indian Vedic gods, said to have been the first mortal to die and find his way to the otherworld, of which he was then declared the de facto ruler. (In the Woman Huang story, the ten kings are referred to as Yama Kings, to be distinguished from King Yama, who is their overlord.) Both the Mulian and Woman Huang stories translated here place particular emphasis on the sins and punishments corresponding to each of the Ten Courts. When she comes to the Seventh Court, for example, Woman Huang sees:

> *The sinners were all stripped of all their clothing,*
> *And their bodies were covered with bloody slashes.*
> *Their sinews were pulled out, their stomachs cut open;*
> *Fainting and reviving, they were tortured yet again.*

When she asks her guide what sin these hapless souls committed to deserve this punishment, she is told that they all had eaten meat and in some cases had been butchers who not only ate meat but slaughtered living creatures and sold them in the marketplace. Woman Huang, whose husband is a butcher, is appalled and bursts into heartrending tears. Chinese literature is full of such descriptions of karmic retribution, many in the form of tales that describe an actual journey to the Underworld by a person who died but then comes back to life in order to inform the living about what he has seen.[50] Such accounts of descents into the Underworld feed the universal curiosity about life beyond the grave and provide an opportunity for those who read or hear these stories, or watch one in performance, to be both entertained and instructed about the many types of activities that will bring painful retribution in the afterlife.

VEGETARIANISM

Both men and women could and did sin, of course, but women were often regarded as the "weaker sex" and thus particularly susceptible to immoral behavior. Not only that, by late imperial times, even the most virtuous of women was popularly believed to be committing a terrible sin by the very act of being a woman, that is, by "polluting" the world through her menstrual blood and the blood shed in childbirth. While the belief in the polluting power of female blood may well be older, it was first made explicit in the Blood Bowl Sutra (Xuepen jing), a very brief and noncanonical text discussed in more detail below, which emerged in the Song dynasty and would continue to enjoy wide circulation throughout the past millennium. Women, then, were placed in a religious double bind to which men were not subject. Not only that, it was a bind from which usually (although not always) they could be freed only by the filial actions of their sons.

Among the varieties of immoral behavior, lust, greed, and gluttony play the leading roles. In the early versions of the story of Mulian, for example, the primary reason given as to why his mother is condemned to suffer the horrific torments of hell is that she had broken the precepts against eating meat and imbibed alcohol. Her sin is compounded in these versions by the fact that she had broken her vow to abstain from eating meat.[51] For many Buddhists in late imperial China, vegetarianism—and, by implication, refraining from taking the lives of sentient beings—was absolutely essential for salvation.[52] But for many, this call to avoid taking life and eating meat represented a real dilemma. Many social occasions in family and community life called for people to make offerings of meat to the ancestors, offerings that they would then consume themselves. Vegetarianism thus implied not only refusal to eat meat oneself but also refusal to offer the ancestors or local deities the offerings to which they were entitled.

At the same time, vegetarianism had deep roots in Chinese culture, preceding the introduction of Buddhism. Early Daoism also distinguished itself from local cults by its absolute refusal of "bloody sacrifices," and as early as the fourth century B.C.E., the philosopher Mencius noted that, while sacrifices were essential, a true gentleman should do his best to avoid witnessing the slaughter of the animals involved. Although Mencius by no means went so far as to advocate the substitution of vegetarian sacrifices, later advocates of vegetarianism would use his comment precisely for this purpose. This indigenous Chinese tradition of aversion to "bloody sacrifices" was further strengthened following the introduction of Buddhism and its teachings on rebirth, which held out the frightening prospect that in killing animals—whether ants, fish, chicken, or pigs—one might actually be slaughtering one's own deceased parents or more distant ancestors. In fact, by carrying this reasoning to its logical conclusion, one could say that to eat meat was to engage in familial cannibalism![53] This sin only becomes greater if one does so knowingly, that is, if one takes a vow to keep a vegetarian diet but then fails to keep it. In this way, the consumption of meat could end up standing for sinful depravity as such. It goes without saying that men as well as women could and did break the precepts. Indeed, Woman Huang is married to a butcher, a figure that in popular Chinese Buddhist texts often represents the very personification of sin. This sinfulness of the occupation of butcher is also underlined in *The Precious Scroll of the Three Lives of Mulian*, in which Mulian himself must be reborn as a butcher in order to work off negative karma created by his overeagerness to rescue his mother, perhaps an indication that he was originally motivated more by personal attachment rather than by pure and simple filial piety. In the *Three Lives of Mulian*, however, Mulian's stint as a butcher is temporary and is far overshadowed by his mother's failure to give alms to monks and, even worse, her willingness to brazenly break the precepts against killing and eating meat (although a modern reader cannot help but wonder if this sin, as horrible as it is, truly warrants punishment in the Avici Hell, the deepest and most ghastly of the Buddhist hells). It is important to note, however, that Mulian's mother sins only after the death of her pious husband and in the absence of her pious son, who is away on a business trip, and, even more significantly, at the urging of her brother (also a butcher), who persuades her that she has no hope of success when so many others have failed at adhering to a vegetarian diet. In other words, it is her "emotional weakness" that makes her more susceptible to both suggestion and sin. In the case of Woman Huang, it is worth nothing that she is far more worried than is her husband about the karmic consequences of his livelihood, and it is she who, in some versions of the legend at least, works off his negative karma and thus makes it possible for him to achieve salvation.

POLLUTION AND THE BLOOD POND

Deliberate misbehavior is one thing; sinfulness as a result of having been born with the body of a woman, whose menstrual and childbirth fluids were said to defile the world and pollute the gods, is another. This notion of female pollution is elaborated with particular force in the story of Woman Huang, which offers the following description:

> *When you gave birth to your children, you also committed a sin:*
> *How many bowls of bloody water, how many bowls of fluids?*
> *For every child, there were three basins of fluids,*
> *Three children, and thus nine basins of fluids.*
> *   The bloodied waters were dumped into the gutters,*

And in so doing, polluted the Sprite of the Eaves.
Three mornings and you were already back in the kitchen,
And in so doing, polluted the Lord of the Kitchen God.
   And before ten days were up, you went into the front hall,
And in so doing, polluted the family deities and the ancestors.
And before a month was up, you went out of doors,
And in so doing, polluted the sun, the moon, and the stars.

By this description, it seems it was nearly impossible for a woman, in the normal course of her duties as a wife and mother, to avoid polluting, not only her immediate surroundings, but all the gods and even the "sun, moon, and stars"![54] The Buddhist hells, especially as elaborated upon in Chinese iconography and narrative, were filled with specific sites and punishments designated for specific sins. There was one site, however, that does not appear to have been part of the original Indian Buddhist scheme but became increasingly important in Chinese texts. This was the Blood Pond Hell, which was reserved simply for those who had committed the sin of having been born women, and it is here that all women must go after their deaths. By the Ming dynasty, the notion of the Blood Pond had become very widespread,[55] so much so that it was also incorporated into popular religious Daoist texts.[56] Interestingly, in some of these popular texts, the Blood Pond is reserved for women who *fail* to give birth, often because they had died in the effort to do so. Thus, the blood that fills the Blood Pond is nothing less than menstrual blood, "the blood that she had failed to give life to by transforming it into a child."[57] In other words, that a woman was damned if she did bear a child, and damned if she didn't. In the version of the Mulian legend included in this volume, for example, Mulian's mother is first sent to this frightening place when she is consigned to hell. Although her ostensible sin may have been to break the precepts of vegetarianism, she is consigned to the Blood Bond Hell as punishment for having been a woman and, especially, a mother.[58]

Mulian's close connection with the Blood Pond is demonstrated by a text, composed anonymously in China probably sometime in the twelfth century, the full title of which is Blood Bowl Sutra of the Correct Teaching of the Great Canon as Preached by the Buddha (Foshuo dazang zhengzhao xuepen jing). The first part of this short text begins as follows:

Once, some time ago, Venerable Mulian was traveling in the Zhuiyang district of Yuzhou prefecture when he saw a Blood Bowl Pond Hell that was eighty-four thousand leagues wide. In the pool there were 120 implements of iron beams, iron pillars, iron yokes and iron chains. He saw many women of Jambudvipa (the human world)— their hair in disarray, their necks in cangues, and their hands in fetters—suffering for their sins in this hell [lit. "earth prison"]. The demon in charge of the punishments three times a day takes the blood and makes the sinners drink it. If the sinners are not willing to submit to him and drink, then he takes his iron rod and beats them as they scream.[59]

When Mulian saw this, he sadly asked the hell warden, "I do not see any men from Jampudvipa here suffering these torments. [Why] do I only see women here suffering this cruel retribution?" The warden answered him, "Master, it is not something that involves men. It only has to do with women, who every month leak menses or in childbirth release blood which seeps down and pollutes the earth gods. And, what is more, they take their filthy garments to the river to wash, thereby polluting the river water. Later, an unsuspecting good man or woman draws some water from the river, boils it for tea, and then offers it to the holy ones, causing them to be impure. The Great General of heaven takes note of this and marks it in his ledger of merits and sins. After a hundred years, when their lives are over, [these sinful women] undergo this retribution of suffering [that you see before you]."[60]

Placing a woman, and especially a mother, in this excruciating and seemingly untenable position makes for a far more effective story, both in narrative and didactic terms: the more drastic the punishment, the more glorious and commendable the achievements of the filial child who seeks the parent's release from such unbearable suffering. Filial piety, although by no means absent in Buddhist India, was and still is the root virtue in Chinese culture. And, as many scholars have noted, it is largely by more fully and explicitly incorporating these deeply ingrained notions of filial piety into its teachings and rituals that the Buddhist worldview eventually became so widely accepted in China. Indeed, the legend of Mulian, which holds out the promise that a mother may be saved from the torments of hell by the efforts of her son, is often pointed to as a prime example of this process of accommodation.

The story of Mulian is also the classic expression of this tension between the notion of female impurity and the demand for filial piety: Mulian's resolve to rescue his mother from the sufferings of hell is seen as an expression of his exemplary filial piety. Although present in the early versions of the story, it is in the later narrative versions that this often excruciating tension finds its fullest and most elaborate expression and, in the minds of believers at least, its religious resolution. In many parts of traditional China, for example, funeral ceremonies for a woman included a ritual that reenacted Mulian's deliverance of his mother from hell. Taiwanese funerary rituals described by anthropologist Gary Seaman included the rite of the son drinking out of a cup of blood-colored liquid, the symbolic equivalent of the blood shed by his mother in giving birth to him. In Seaman's descriptions, these rituals often featured a scene in which Mulian, on his journey to the Underworld, is reminded in a flashback of the sufferings undergone by his mother on his behalf.[61] Needless to say, it is not only Mulian who is reminded of the immense debt he owes his mother but the mourners as well and, in particular, the children of the deceased. Such reminders would appear to have been considered very necessary. The emergence of the legend was accompanied by the proliferation of a large body of popular texts that stressed all the sufferings and sacrifices that parents, especially mothers, had made in the course of bearing and raising their children, thus impressing on sons and daughters both the need for filial piety and the near-impossibility of ever fully repaying that enormous debt. This same body of literature also reveals a deep anxiety on the part of mothers, perhaps because children only too often neglected their duties toward their mother, both when she was alive and after her death.

SUFFERING MOTHERS AND FILIAL SONS (AND DAUGHTERS)

One of the most vivid examples of such texts (and one that in Seaman's account was often read in its entirety as part of the funerary ritual) is "The Ten Months of Pregnancy,"[62] which provides a graphic and quite detailed month-by-month description of the pains and fears suffered by a pregnant woman. As it happens, a version of the very same text is also included in this book's version of the Woman Huang story. The last section describes the final months of pregnancy:

In the eighth month, the child can hardly move,
And the child weighs ten tons inside the womb.
The mother wants to move but finds she cannot,
And she becomes cranky and angry in her speech.

In the ninth month, it is all painful beyond words,
And the mother's thoughts start to wander away.
She fears that she will give birth to a monster,
Or that she will give birth to a child deformed.

In the tenth month, to do anything becomes hard;
The mother carrying the child is choked with fear.
She is so frightened that she cannot even speak,
Overcome by a depression she does not express.[63]

In the absence of advanced scientific and medical knowledge, childbirth in the premodern world (and even in today's world, in places where such medical advances are not readily available) was always a risky proposition. When used as part of a religious ritual, this description of the difficulties of pregnancy, in many ways quite realistic, is intended primarily to remind sons and daughters of all that they owe their mothers. We find similar sorts of descriptions of the trials and tribulations suffered by parents, and in particular mothers, in a constellation of related Buddhist texts, one of the most popular of which is Sutra on the Impossibility of Repaying the Great Favors of One's Father and Mother as Spoken by the Buddha (Foshuo fumu en zhong nan bao jing). Although said to have been rendered into Chinese by the great translator Kumārajīva (344–413), this text would appear to be entirely a Chinese creation.[64] It became very popular, and today one can even find somewhat modified cartoon versions in print and online for use in educating children in their filial duties. Here is a section from this text:

When the mother is carrying her child for ten months in a row, she is ill at ease. She stands and sits [with difficulty] as if she were carrying a heavy load and, like a chronically ill person, cannot hold down any food or drink. When at the completion of the [ten months] she gives birth, she suffers from all sorts of pangs and pains. When she is about to deliver the child, she fears she may die, and the blood that flows across the floor is like that from a goat when it is slaughtered.[65]

The comparison of a mother giving birth to a goat being slaughtered is meant, one assumes, to induce profound guilt in children for having caused their parent such terrible suffering.

In the Blood Bowl Sutra, when Mulian asks what can be done to repay one's mother for all that she had endured, he is given very explicit instructions.

> Master, you only need to take care to be a filial son or daughter, respect the Three Jewels, and, for the sake of your mother, hold Blood Bowl Feasts for three years, including organizing Blood Bowl gatherings to which you invite monks to recite this sutra for a full day, as well as ceremonies of repentance. Then there will be a *prajñā* (enlightened wisdom) boat to carry the mothers across the River Alas, and they will see five-colored lotuses appear in the blood pond, and the sinners will come out happy and contrite and they will be able to take birth in a Buddha Land.[66]

Here one sees quite clearly the basis for the argument that this notion of sinful mothers and filial children worked very much to the benefit of Buddhist monks and monasteries, whose services are obviously essential if these women are to be saved.[67]

In *The Precious Scroll of the Three Lives of Mulian*, and indeed in many other popular religious tales, it is a filial son who seeks to save his mother from the gruesome consequences of having indulged in greed and gluttony or of simply having been born a woman. This makes sense in the Confucian context, given that it is the son who remains responsible for his parents for their entire lives, while a daughter's filial loyalties are transferred to her husband's family. It is important to note, however, that the Blood Bowl Sutra expands the discourse to include mothers and daughters as well as mothers and sons. The Blood Bowl Sutra does indeed explicitly describe ways in which women can create merit for the sake not only of their mothers but of their grandmothers and great-grandmothers as well, which may explain why even today one finds groups of elderly women gathering in local temples to chant this scripture with great devotion.[68]

> The Buddha again told women, saying: "As for the Blood Bowl Sutra, if you copy and keep this sutra with a believing mind, then you will be causing,

as far as possible, the mothers of the three worlds to gain rebirth in heaven, where they will receive pleasures, clothes, and food naturally; their lives will be long, and they will be rich aristocrats."[69]

Sutra on the Past Vows of Dizang Bodhisattva (Dizang pusa benyuan jing), ascribed to the seventh-century Khotanese monk Śikṣānanda and most likely composed either in Khotan or China, also contains stories of filial daughters who play roles similar to that played by Mulian. The setting of this sutra is the Trāyastriṃśa Heaven, where the Buddha is spending the rain retreat preaching to his mother, Maya, who died seven days after giving birth to him and then immediately was reborn in this heavenly realm. In this sutra, the Buddha elaborates on four of the previous lifetimes of the bodhisattva Ksitigarbha, who would in China become the bodhisattva Dizang (in Japan, where he is also very popular, he is known as Jizō), associated primarily with the task of assisting the souls of the dead in the Underworld.[70] In two of these lifetimes, Dizang is born as a woman, and in both of these existences, her primary acts of devotion are motivated by filial piety. In the earliest of these lifetimes, the bodhisattva is a devout Brahmin girl whose mother was much like Mulian's mother in that she had indulged in evil behavior and blasphemed the Buddhist teachings, as a result of which she fell into the Avici Hell. The daughter is filled with grief at the thought of her mother's suffering and seeks the assistance of a buddha whose name is Sovereign Lord of the Flower of Enlightenment (Juehua ding zizai wang rulai). Moved by her piety, both religious and filial, he allows her the following vision of the Underworld:

> After one day and one night she suddenly found herself on the shore of a raging ocean. The waters swirled and swelled, and fearsome iron beasts swooped and galloped back and forth above the waters. She saw hundreds and thousands of men and women rising and sinking in the waves, chased and pecked by the beasts. Again she saw demons of strange appearance, with many hands, many eyes, many limbs, or many heads, with teeth sharp as swords protruding outside their mouths. The demons herded the sinners toward the iron beasts and fought among themselves head to head and foot to foot. There were ten thousand such apparitions, too frightful to look upon. But the Brahmin woman, protected by the power of Buddha, was not afraid.[71]

The horrified (although unfrightened) Brahmin girl then meets a demon king who provides her with more information about the hells and their suffering inhabitants. When the girl asks him about the whereabouts of her deceased mother, he reassures her and tells her that, thanks to her filial piety and cultivation of religious merit, not only has her mother been released from the hells but infinite numbers of other suffering souls have as well.

In a subsequent lifetime, the future Dizang again is reborn as a woman. Named Bright Eyes (Guangmu), she is again a filial daughter who, after the death of her mother, provides food and other offerings to a holy man. The holy man then goes into trance and finds out that her mother, who indulged in sinful behavior when she was alive, is now undergoing unspeakable suffering in hell. Bright Eyes then recalls how her mother used to take such special pleasure in eating fish and turtles, and that if one were to calculate how many such creatures she had consumed, it would add up to many tens of thousands, if not more. Bright Eyes is then told to recite the name of the Clear-Eyed Lotus Blossom Tathagata and to have an image of him made. This she does, and one night she is granted a vision of this buddha, who informs her that her mother will be reborn into her household. Shortly afterward, a maidservant gives birth to a male infant, who, when not yet three days old, sobbingly describes the terrible sufferings that he, as Bright Eyes's mother, had endured in hell. The child then tells Bright Eyes that unless she is able to help him, in thirteen years he will die and again be sent to hell. Hearing this, Bright Eyes cries out:

> "Buddhas of the ten directions, have compassion and listen to the great vow
> I make for the sake of my mother. If my mother can attain eternal liberation
> from the unhappy paths of hell (fire, blood, swords), lowly birthright, and
> woman's body, I vow before the image of the Clear-Eyed Lotus Blossom
> Tathagata, from now onward, to save and raise from rebirth the suffering
> beings from all of the worlds of hundreds of ten thousands millennia,
> from all of the earth prisons and three evil paths. I shall enter rightful
> enlightenment only after all such beasts, hungry ghosts, and people who are
> paying for their sins have achieved buddhahood."[72]

In response to this fervent vow, the Clear-Eyed Lotus Blossom Tathagata promises Bright Eyes that her mother, after a series of auspicious births, will in the end "achieve buddhahood and deliver [from suffering and rebirth] sentient beings as numerous as the sands of the Ganges."[73]

There are some clear parallels between the stories of the Brahmin girl and Radiant Eyes on the one hand and the legend of Mulian on the other, not the least of which is the focus on filial piety and the salvation of a mother from the sufferings of hell. There is also an emphasis on vegetarianism: both the mother of Radiant Eyes and the mother of Mulian are said to have been sent to hell because of their indulgence in nonvegetarian foods.[74] Moreover, underlying all of these stories is the notion that the real sin is not so much the failure to adhere to a vegetarian diet but, ultimately, birth into a female body. In other words, while vegetarianism is clearly an important theme in both of these texts, it is not the only, or even the primary, source of their emotional and narrative power. For while one can make a conscious choice to refrain from eating meat (or, as in the case of Woman Huang's butcher husband, to ignore the precepts against killing altogether), one cannot so easily, in this lifetime at least, choose not to be a woman or, especially in traditional China, a wife and mother. All one can do is seek to be reborn in a male body: this is what Radiant Eyes aims to attain for her own mother, and it is also what Woman Huang in the end achieves for herself.

THE RITUAL POWER OF WOMEN

In the story of Woman Huang, a woman, instead of relying on a son or even a daughter to save her, takes it upon herself to ensure her own salvation as well as that of her husband and children. She urges her husband to abandon his sinful trade of butcher, and when he not only refuses to do so but argues that she as a woman and mother is far more sinful than he can ever be, she immediately breaks off all sexual relations with him in order to devote herself to a life of religious austerities and the recitation of the Diamond Sutra.[75] Like Mulian, Woman Huang ends up taking a journey to the Underworld, when she is summoned by the king of the Underworld, who is impressed by her faultless recitation of the sutra. While trekking through the numerous hells, she is filled with alternating horror and compassion. She is provided with not only a vision of the suffering of its inhabitants, in particular, its women, but also an opportunity to relieve some of their suffering. (It is worth noting that, while there is no explicit mention of the Blood Pond

Hell in the version of the Woman Huang story translated here, Women Liu is consistently described as being covered with blood. Thus, in effect, all of hell has been turned into the Blood Pond.) Finally, Woman Huang is brought into the presence of King Yama, and it is there that she is able to defend and demonstrate both her piety and her ability to recite the Diamond Sutra, earning a release from the Underworld, among other rewards. The interrogation covers many different areas, including an extended section on the origin and history of the Diamond Sutra and its efficacy.

One may ask why it is that Woman Huang is reciting the Diamond Sutra, which is more commonly associated with the so-called Prajñāpāramitā, or Great Wisdom literature, of Mahayana Buddhism that deals not with pollution and sin but rather with the ultimate emptiness of such concepts.[76] This is probably because, as Stephen Teiser has pointed out, the earliest extant versions of *The Scripture of Ten Kings* are more often than not found bound together with a Chinese translation of the Diamond Sutra attributed to Kumārajīva (350–409) that differs from other versions in that it closes with a series of three dharani, or ritual chants. This would indicate that these two scriptures, although they had little in common contentwise, were often recited together in the context of a funerary service.[77] It is also clear from the story translated here that one of the primary benefits thought to derive from the recitation of the Diamond Sutra was a long life, which, in traditional China, was considered to be, along with wealth and many sons, one of the greatest blessings one could possibly hope to enjoy. In any case, the close connection between the two texts may explain why Woman Huang is called to the Underworld and the Courts of the Ten Kings to demonstrate her ability to recite the Diamond Sutra. In the story, Woman Huang calmly answers all the questions put to her by King Yama, breaking down only when she notes that one of the rewards of a faithful recitation of the Diamond Sutra is supposed to be a long life (another indication that it was the actual practice of reciting the sutra, rather than the philosophy it expounded, that was deemed efficacious.)

"Although the Diamond Sutra can still be found in the world,
One who chants sutras and the Buddha's name is hard to find.
I began reciting the sutra at the tender age of seven years,
So why has King Yama cut my life short to call me here?"

When King Yama heard this, he gave a little smile
And said, "Good woman, how little you know!
To die early is actually the much better thing—
You'd rather remain forever in a woman's body?"

Woman Huang is asked to ascend a tall platform built expressly for the purpose and recite the Diamond Sutra. Before she has finished reciting it, however, she is asked to stop, since the combined power of her piety and the Diamond Sutra itself is causing havoc in the Underworld by liberating its sinners before they have served the time to which they were justly sentenced.[78]

Anthropologists such as Gary Seaman and Emily Ahern have pointed out that because of the belief in female pollution, women are generally disqualified from participating in formal ritual activities, and "as a result they must depend on men to act as their representatives or intermediaries in most important religious matters."[79] It is also often pointed out that although women have little ritual power in the world of the living, they often have great power indeed in the world of the dead. Thus, in China, spirit mediums and those who make contact with the dead are often women. The story of Woman Huang displays clear evidence of this female ritual competence and power that can be demonstrated only in the Underworld. It is first seen when Woman Huang's zealous reciting of the sutra "startles and alarms" King Yama, and he sends his messengers to go and fetch her—he is both impressed by her piety and alarmed by it. In the end, this female power is contained by having Woman Huang return to the world of the living, not as a woman, but as a man.

It is interesting to note that in the version of the Mulian story translated here, Mulian, who after all is an ordained monk well on his way to spiritual liberation, also exercises religious power but, unlike Woman Huang, is punished rather than rewarded for it. He is required to undergo two additional lifetimes, which represent significant detours on his path to liberation. His crime? In his overeagerness to save his mother, Mulian opens the gate of the Avici Hell so wide that eight million sinful souls manage to escape and be reborn as humans or animals, thus upsetting the law of karmic retribution. As punishment, Mulian is first reborn as the rebel Huang Chao, an historical figure whose rebellion lasted from 875 to 884, when he was killed or committed suicide. Huang's armies wreaked great destruction as they crisscrossed China from north to south and east to west, and the once-flourishing Tang dynasty never fully recovered from its effects.[80] Curiously, Mulian's rebirth as Huang Chao, responsible for the slaughter of thousands and perhaps millions, is described only very briefly: the focus instead is on the well-known tale of Huang Chao's accidental killing of the monk Liaokong at the start of his rebellion, an anecdote encountered in a number of earlier stories.[81] The story of Mulian's rebirth as a butcher named He Yin is told in more detail, in part as it allows for development of a didactic theme of conversion: in this case, the butcher He Yin, although a terrible sinner, turns out to be amenable to conversion, while Man of the Way Wang, seemingly a holy man, turns out to be a hypocrite who, unlike the converted butcher, is unable to withstand the seductions of sex. The point, however, is that Mulian cannot resume his former identity as monk until all the souls he allowed to escape from the Avici Hell have been returned to complete their terms of punishment. Many of these souls have already taken rebirth as humans or as animals, meaning that they all have to die or be killed off in order to return to the Underworld. In this way, the story may also be read as an explanation of violence and arbitrary killing in this world.

Despite their emphatically didactic intent, both the Mulian and the Woman Huang story are filled with such tensions, contradictions, and paradoxes. This is understandable if one considers the fact that they are attempting to reconcile so many different ideas and deeply held notions: Buddhist salvation and Confucian filial piety, the love of sons and daughters for loving but sinful mothers, women's biological impurity and women's religious power, the pleasures of this life and the (all too likely) sufferings of the next. Perhaps this explains why these stories held such sway over the imaginations of women and men from all levels of society.

The Precious Scroll
of the Three Lives of Mulian

Count on your fingers: light and shadow are like a thrown shuttle;
As long as your killing mind does not die, what can you hope for?
This world of dust and its madness in the end are but an illusion—
Make sure to carefully polish and brighten this mysterious secret!

Never say that Our Buddha resides only in the Western Paradise;
If you want to see the Western Paradise, it's right before your eyes.
If you ask for the road, the distance is ten times a myriad of miles—
If you wish to get it by merits accomplished, it's like hazy clouds.

PART 1

Raising high in my hands this single stick of true incense,
I ascend the platform, preach the Law, and open the sutra.
All men and women in this hall, please listen quietly, as it
Brings blessings, prolongs life, and frees one from disaster!

Once upon a time there lived, in Guanxi of Nandu, a certain gentleman Fu
Xiang, whose personal name was Yuanwai.[1] From his earliest days he had
practiced self-cultivation. His wedded wife, who was called Liu Qingti, had
not yet borne him a child. Fu Xiang practiced goodness and kept the fast;[2]
he read the sutras and recited the name of the Buddha. All on his own, he
had built a Myriad Cause Bridge and a Myriad Buddha Hall, where a great
number of monks congregated and which came to be called the Hall for
Feeding Monks. He also had made a pond for the release of live fish, and
he would buy live fish and release them in this pond.[3] He treated monks to
vegetarian meals and provided them with donations. In this way he was able
to extensively accumulate good karma. One day when Fu Xiang was walking
outside, he saw his servants harvesting radishes. Suddenly there appeared a
monk, who begged for a radish. Fu Xiang immediately gave him one, and
as soon as the monk held it in his hands, he wolfed it down. Fu Xiang said:
"Monk, you must be very lazy; you didn't even take this radish down to the
river to wash it but just swallowed it, mud and all!" When the monk heard
Fu Xiang say these words, he composed the gatha[4] that follows:

Allow me to express my gratitude to you, good Fu Xiang,
For having given this radish to me, a poor monk. But if
I'd walked to the riverbank to wash it clean, Impermanence[5]
Might well have showed up, leaving me no time to eat it!

Fu Xiang said: "This lazy monk could not even find a little time to go
and clean this radish!" But then he saw the monk fall down and die right
after having eaten the radish! This created quite a commotion among his
neighbors and town elders, and a big crowd gathered to have a look. Fu
Xiang heaved a sigh and spoke the following gatha:

"Alas! How pitiable, you old monk, so advanced in years!
In what township might your monastery have been located?
Instead of reciting the sutra scrolls in your dhyana-forest,[6]
You went running around in the world, and then you died.

You knew that you didn't have much light and shadow left;
So why didn't you stay in your temple and wait for Death?
Today, by dying right here in front of the gate of my house,
You've implicated me in the law, and I will suffer disaster."[7]

Once Fu Xiang was done sighing, his neighbors and the town elders said to him: "Given that you have a reputation as a good man who provides monks with vegetarian meals and makes donations, this monk had probably come to you to beg for a coffin. There is no need for you to report this to the magistrate and bother the authorities. Why don't you buy him a coffin and bury him?" When Fu Xiang heard this, he expressed his gratitude to his neighbors. He then bought a coffin, after which he had the corpse dressed and buried.

That night as Fu Xiang lay sleeping, around midnight he saw the monk entering his house, and immediately he said: "Monk, you died in front of the gate of my house, and I bought you a coffin and had you buried. That should do it! Why then are you coming back to my house again?" "I have come to return the favor," said the monk, "and also return the favor to your wife." Saying this, he went into the inner apartments and suddenly disappeared. Fu Xiang woke up with a start when he heard the maid, who came in to announce that his wife had given birth to a baby boy and wanted her husband to give the child a name. "It must be that monk who has come to take rebirth here," Fu Xiang said to himself. "Because it all began with a radish, I'll call the boy Radish Fu." He then got up immediately, lit some incense to thank Heaven and Earth, and composed the following gatha:

I, Fu Xiang, light a candle and burn this incense;
I thank the Honored Lord Buddha, the Tathagata.[8]
The name I choose for him will be Radish Fu;
The name by which he'll be known is Mulian.

One day two monks arrived at Fu Xiang's house. After coming forward to greet him, they praised him, saying: "Because you have now loved goodness for a long time, we have come with the express purpose of bringing peace to your heart." Fu Xiang was extremely pleased and asked the monks: "What are your religious names?" "My name is Have-Karma (Youyuan)," replied the eldest monk, "and my younger brother is called Meet-Karma (Yuyuan)." Hearing this, Fu Xiang thought: "Today I have met my karma!" He told the maid to go to the inner apartments and ask his wife to come out and greet the monks and listen to their discourse on the Buddha's Dharma.⁹ Hastily, they set down a Dharma-seat and set out an incense table. He then invited the monks to ascend the platform and preach the Dharma, as described by the following gatha:

"It's rare to be born as a human, but in this life you were;
It's rare to be born here in China, but in this life you are.
It's rare to meet an enlightened teacher, but now you do;
It's rare to hear the Buddha's Dharma, but now you can!"

When Fu Xiang heard him recite this gatha, he laughed heartily and achieved enlightenment in his heart: "Today I have met my karma!" He then asked the monk for yet another instructive gatha, and the monk replied: "Listen to me!

"A human existence in this world cannot last long,
But lost in flowers and wine,¹⁰ people are clueless!
A hero of a hundred years is like the dew at dawn;
A long-lived stalwart brave is like morning frost."

Fu Xiang said: "If even a long-lived stalwart brave resembles morning frost, then all this heroic behavior, glory and wealth, fields and riches are of no use at all." "Listen to me!" said the monk.

"Husband and wife have always been birds sharing a grove,
But when the Final Moment arrives, each goes its way.
Not even your wife and children can die in your stead;
Never have sons or daughters gone in place of their parents.
    You won't be able to take your savings of many millions:
With two empty hands, you'll stand before King Yama!¹¹

I urge you to search for the gate as soon as possible,[12]
Because time is in short supply—the finale is near!"

Fu Xiang said to his wife: "With all my heart I would like to practice cultivation. To our great fortune we have met today with these two enlightened teachers. The two of us, man and wife, today should respectfully accept them as our teachers, take refuge in the Three Jewels, and strictly observe the Five Precepts."[13] They then knelt down facing Heaven in a westerly direction and pronounced the following great vow: "If we ever neglect to keep the fast or violate the precepts, may we fall eternally into the earth prison and not be allowed to be reborn!"[14] They rose to their feet and took refuge in the Three Jewels and promised to abide by the precepts. They then prepared a vegetarian meal for the monks, who, after they had eaten, took their leave and went on their way.

Once Fu Xiang had accepted these monks as his teachers, his devotion to the Way only became firmer and more solid. He added merits to merits, day and night practicing cultivation. He built two Buddha-halls, one called the Hall for Feeding the Monks, and one called the Hall of the Three Officials.[15] All day long he read the sutras and recited the name of the Buddha, fed monks and made donations, restored bridges and repaired roads, and assisted the poor and needy far and near. He extensively accumulated good karma and engaged in all kinds of good works. Practicing meditation and self-cultivation, he realized the Way and nurtured his Nature and was able to know past and future. One day, realizing that his amount of merit was full and complete, he spoke to his wife, saying: "Tell our child to come here, because today I will be returning home.[16] My only instructions concern the three thousand strings of cash that I am going to leave you. One thousand strings are for reading sutras and reciting the name of the Buddha. One thousand strings of cash I leave to you to feed monks and make donations and support people in need. And one thousand strings of cash are to assist my son in the business of buying and selling. I have here a small collection of books about the Way, which I leave to the two of you, mother and son. Earnestly I exhort the two of you in the future never to neglect the fast or violate the precepts. Be firm and solid in your devotion to the Way, and diligent in your practice both day and night!" He then recited the following two gathas:

"When people break the fast and precepts, they anger the buddhas,
Who then take the sinners and cast them down into the pit of fire.
Separated from humans and gods, they will suffer there forever;
Falling into the deepest earth prison, they will never be reborn.

Meditate on the Great Way even among wolves and tigers,
And persistently accumulate merits amid swords and lances.
Even when sabers and swords threaten to cut off your head,
In the face of death, never indulge in wine, meat, and spices."[17]

Even before Fu Xiang had done speaking, and before his gathas were finished, an extraordinary fragrance suddenly filled the room. Seated on a lotus, he returned to the Void; riding a phoenix and straddling a crane, in broad daylight he ascended to heaven, where Golden Lads and Jade Maidens, bearing banners and pennants and precious parasols, welcomed him into the halls of heaven. Thus he left behind a fine reputation for all eternity.

Mulian invited some monks to say masses for the benefit of his deceased father. Then one day, after the merits of the Sevens had been completed,[18] he took leave of his mother and entered the Monastery of Repaying Favors, where he shaved off his hair, became a monk, and took the monk Future-Fruition (Laiguo) as his teacher. Back at home Madame Liu read the sutras and recited the name of the Buddha. One day her brother Liu Jia came to her house to visit her. After he had greeted his elder sister, they sat down to talk. Liu Jia thought to himself: "Since her husband has passed away, let me try encouraging her to break the fast and abandon the precepts and see how she reacts." So he said: "When it comes to life here on earth, there is nothing real except for food and clothing. If you have ten thousand strings of cash and cannot enjoy your life, it is all in vain. I have something I would like to tell you, so please listen!

"In front of the gate of the earth prison, there is no wine house,
So it makes sense to eat well, drink well, and dress well now.
If you don't believe me, just open a coffin and have a good look:
The eyes filled with yellow earth and the mouth filled with mud!
    If you cannot enjoy your capital of ten thousand strings of cash,
You've passed through this human existence completely in vain.

Those who practice the Way are as numerous as buffalo hairs;
Those who realize the Way are as rare as the horns on a hare!"

Then Liu Jia said: "Sister, why should a human being living in this world keep the fast and observe the precepts? Mencius says: 'When people reach the age of seventy, they will not be warm unless they are dressed in brocade, and they will not be sated unless they eat meat.'[19] The world's pigs and sheep, chicken and geese, fishes and turtles, shrimps and crabs are there to be eaten by humans. So why do you pretend that you can't stand to eat them anymore?" "My dear brother, you are wrong," Qingti replied. "The glory and riches we enjoy in this life are the result of having engaged in religious cultivation in a former existence. The people in this world all know the letter but rarely understand the principle. They all act like people in a dream. The Sage also said: 'If one has seen an animal when it is alive, one cannot bear to see it die; if one has heard its cry, one cannot bear to eat its flesh.'[20] The Sage had a heart filled with compassion, and God on High[21] also loves all living beings. Now you listen to me:

"Inside the character for 'meat' there are two human beings,[22]
So I urge you never in your life to kill any sentient beings.
When in this life you eat a pound of of an animal's flesh,
You must pay it back with twice that much in your next.
    In market and square, human beings eat the meat of dogs,
But in the public graveyard, it's dogs that eat human bodies.
If you do not understand the deeper meaning in all of this,
Consider carefully these three simple words: man eats man."

Madame Liu said: "For those who practice cultivation, it is a basic duty to eat only vegetarian food and to observe the precepts; meditation is also very important. As soon as one no longer keeps the fast and observes the precepts, one has failed to be a good person." Liu Jia said: "If I look at all those people in this world who eat only vegetarian food and practice cultivation, there are only a few who can keep it up to the very end. Here you have this Man of the Way Chen: following his teacher, he protected the Dharma, he ate only vegetarian food, and he recited the name of the Buddha. But when he turned seventy, he broke both the fast and the precepts. There you have this

Man of the Way Ma. He explained the sutras and preached the Dharma and acted as a teacher to others. He would also pay back debts and return favors on behalf of those who could not: by dissolving disasters and reciting the name of the Buddha, he reached the age of eighty. But then he too broke the precepts.[23] Of all the many people I have seen who eat only vegetarian food, there is not a single one who could keep it up to the very end. So I urge you to stop being stubborn and just forget about it." Liu Qingti didn't say a word, but in her heart she thought: "What he says is true. He now urges me to break the fast. If I don't break the fast, I will always be filled with the fear of not being able to keep it up to the end, in which case he would make fun of me. Why don't I just give it up?"

As soon as people vow to keep the fast, the Buddha worries,
As he fears they will not be able to keep to a permanent fast:
On the day such people decide to break both fast and precepts,
On that very day, they toss away the merits of a thousand days!

Liu Qingti had allowed that Liu Jia to stir her blood-heart.[24] She immediately ordered her servant Jinnu to go straight to the market and buy meat and wine with which to prepare a banquet and break the fast. The next day she slaughtered pigs and sheep. Performers came to play and dance, and beggars came to sing their songs. From the moment she broke her fast, she went on to slaughter sentient beings every day. She cared for nothing except the next tasty morsel, and she spared no thought for the lives of others. She buried the white bones in the dry well in the flower garden behind the house; her pleasure knew no limits, and she gave no thought to future distress.

Liu Qingti did not have the determination to maintain her fast;
She broke the fast and the precepts, slaughtered pigs and sheep.
Persuaded to break the fast, she was destined to be a hungry ghost:[25]
Once this woman had broken the fast, this could not be avoided.

Our story goes that once Madame Liu had been persuaded by Liu Jia to break the fast, she drank wine and ate meat and forgot about reading the sutras, reciting the name of the Buddha, burning incense, and making donations.

Nor did she venerate the Buddha and practice goodness, and her evil karma piled up as high as a mountain.

Liu Qingti accumulated evil karma as deep as the ocean
By breaking fast and precepts, slaughtering pigs and sheep.
Each day she enjoyed lamb and mutton and the finest wines
And never again gave any thought to the reading of sutras.

Let's speak no further of Madame Liu committing sins but rather tell of Yili,[26] who said: "Madame, please allow me to inform you that the young master will be returning home today." As soon as Qingti heard this, she immediately ordered the servants to sweep the Buddha-altars, light candles, and burn incense. When the sutra hall had been prepared, she began to read the sutras and recite the name of the Buddha. When Mulian arrived home, he went first to the sutra hall to pay his respect to the ancestors. Then, after he had made his bows, he went to his mother to ask her how she was doing.

Every day Mulian recited the sutras. But before many days had passed, the neighbors spoke to him, saying: "Sir, after you left this house, your mother broke the precepts by slaughtering sentient beings and indulging in wine and pungent foods." When Mulian heard this, he was very displeased and greatly annoyed. He immediately spoke to his mother, saying: "During his lifetime my father accomplished his full count of merits, and he has gone to heaven. On his deathbed he left us his books of the Way and exhorted us so earnestly to never in the future break the fast or violate the precepts. You can't say you have forgotten those words! When I was away from home and left you here, how could you have slaughtered pigs and sheep, broken the fast, and violated the precepts?" His mother did not know how to answer him. There is a gatha that speaks to this:

"Mother, you broke the precepts, slaughtered sentient beings,
And failed to follow the deathbed instructions left by my father!
Instead you believed the foolish and baseless words of my uncle:
This is what will send you through the gates of the earth prison."

When Madame Liu heard her son say these words, she cursed him loudly: "I don't know what kind of scoundrel has been spreading rumors about this family, creating dissent between mother and son! Since you don't believe me, my son, I will have the servant and the maid set up an incense table in the flower garden behind the house, and there I will swear, with Heaven as my witness, this oath: May I die this very instant if I have ever broken the fast and violated the precepts!" But she had forgotten that there are gods and ghosts coming and going in the heavens, and that Oxhead and Horseface had been waiting for some time at her side![27] And so, before Liu Qingti could even finish pronouncing her vow, blood spurted from the seven holes of her body, and she collapsed in the dust. She was still alive when the hosts nabbed her; she was still alive when they grabbed her and locked her in iron chains. As Oxhead took her away, Horseface covered her with blows, yanking at her arms and twisting her legs. Liu Qingti got such a beating that her skin was torn and her flesh was reduced to a rotten pulp, and she was covered all over with blood. She screamed and hollered and wept in pain in a truly heartrending way! There was no road for her to ascend to heaven; there was no gate through which she could vanish into the earth. At this moment she could not live even if she begged for life, and she could not die even if she begged for death.

By the time they arrived at the Blood Pond, it was already late. Oxhead and Horseface were both tired and wanted to take a rest, so they carried Madame Liu to the edge of the Blood Pond and tossed her in. She screamed and hollered and wept in pain as the red waves rose up as high as heaven, covering the top of her head. She saw that the women in this pond were all stark naked, their bodies completely exposed: the skin on their bodies was ripped away, and their flesh had been reduced to a rotten pulp. Madame Liu then asked these women: "What crime did we commit to have been sentenced to endure such suffering in this Blood Pond?" "You have just arrived," replied the women, "so you don't know. We will recite a gatha for you:

"Before one month had passed,[28] you walked into the hall,
So polluting the family's ancestors and the household gods.
Before one month had passed, you walked into the kitchen,
So polluting the Lord of the Stove and the visiting deities.
    Before one month had passed, you went to the riverbank;
With your washing, you polluted the Dragon King's palace,[29]

And by drying your blood-stained clothes in the open air,
You also polluted the sun, moon, and stars up in the sky!"

After the women recited this gatha, together they screamed and hollered and wept in pain. But then suddenly, the watchtower announced the first watch of the night.

To the tune of "Yinniuxi"[30]

By the first watch[31] our suffering is unbearable,
And the tears coat our cheeks.
In this Pond of Blood we weep in a piteous way,
Our hearts all deeply wounded.
The skin and flesh of our bodies are ripped and torn all over.
We remember how, during our lifetimes,
We were pregnant and heavy with child.
Our faces were sallow, our flesh shriveled because of the baby.
Who would have thought that after death our distress would be greater still?
If our sons don't come and save their mothers,
How will we be released from this disaster?
Oh, dearest Buddha,
What son repays the favors shown by his mother?
Make haste to keep both the fast and the precepts!

By the second watch our suffering is unendurable,
And tears course down in confusion.
In this Pond of Blood the water is even colder than ice,
And there is no bottom at all!
Soaked through, our skin dissolves, and we're covered in blood.
We remember how, when were living
And that child in our belly was born,
The pain of those contractions, again and again, was unbearable!
Who would have thought that, after death, disaster would strike yet again!
If our sons do not come and save their mothers,
How will we be able to be reborn in heaven?
Oh, dearest Buddha,

What son maintains the fast and the precepts
And saves his mother's damaged life and fate?

By the third watch our suffering knows no end,
And still our eyelids begin to droop.
In this Pond of Blood we fall sound asleep
Even as the pain wounds our hearts,
And the pain our bodies suffer is like the piercing of nails.
We remember how, when we were alive,
We suffered because of these children;
We fretted and worried whenever they had smallpox or measles!
Who would have thought that after death we'd be punished for these crimes?
If our sons do not come and save their mothers,
Even if we sprouted wings, we could not escape.
Oh, dearest Buddha,
What son maintains the fast and the precepts
And takes on the crime for his mother's sake?

By the fourth watch we suffer from the painful hurt,
And we are awash in tears.
In this Pond of Blood our suffering is truly unbearable,
Truly so sad and miserable.
Stark naked, our bodies exposed, we are tossed by the waves.
We remember how, when we were alive,
We were constantly busy for the children—
Not even once could we eat a mouthful of soup at our ease.
Who would have thought that after death disaster would strike yet again!
If our sons do not come and save their mothers,
We will never obtain permission to be released.
Oh, dearest Buddha,
What son maintains the fast and the precepts
In order to save his own dear old mother?

By the fifth watch our suffering is beyond all endurance,
And tears gush from our eyes.
In this Pond of Blood, our suffering is impossible to endure,

And there is no one to grant us pardon—
Who even has any idea of the hunger pangs in our bellies?
We remember how, when we were alive,
We raised sons to provide against old age
And would burn paper money on the first day of the four seasons.[32]
But if our sons do not come and save their mothers,
How will we ever be able to escape and run away?
Oh, dearest Buddha!
You must be sure to maintain the fast and precepts
In order to dissolve the great sins of your mothers!

Beaten by iron cudgels,
　　This multitude of women
　　　　Screamed and hollered and painfully wept:
"We beg you, Sir Demon,
　　To show some compassion
　　　　And please save our miserable lives!
We are stupid and foolish people
　　Who, while in the World of Light,
　　　　Clung to our sons and our daughters.
Who among us could have known
　　That we were committing a sin
　　　　That later would cause us such trouble?
A filial and obedient son
　　Maintains the fast and the precepts
　　　　And so will come and save his mother,
But a disobedient and rebellious son,
　　By slaughtering sentient beings,
　　　　Implicates ancestors and parents in his crime."

Our story goes on to tell how the yakshas[33] and demons escorted Liu Qingti to the earth prison, where she suffered suffering upon suffering. She painfully wept in a most piteous way—truly a most heartrending sight! Suddenly she thought to herself: "My son lives in the World of Light, and my husband dwells in the halls of heaven, but I find myself in the World of Darkness, where I am experiencing such suffering—but how could they know of it?

Even the heart of a man made of iron or stone would be shattered! While in the World of Light, I committed violence and accumulated evil; I slaughtered sentient beings and indulged in music and song and dance, thinking that there was no problem. How did I know that when I arrived in the World of Darkness, I would have to walk bareheaded and barefoot, with only a pair of short trousers to cover me, and that I would be beaten over all my body until it was pulverized and could not move even an inch?" Weeping and wailing, she called out: "My dear son!" And she wailed: "My dear husband!" And she cursed: "What a slut I was! When I was alive in the World of Light, I did not believe in self-cultivation, so I broke the fast and violated the precepts, pummeled monks and cursed priests. But what one's self creates, one's self suffers, and the law of retribution is clear. In truth, remorse always comes too late."

The chill wind made one shiver,
    And the black vapors rose—
        With nowhere a single friend in sight,
The lady Liu Qingti
    Was alone and lonesome,
        All by herself and filled with gloom.
She wept: "My dear husband,
    My darling son,
        When will we be able to meet again?
While in the World of Light,
    I, nothing but a woman,
        Failed to grasp the Way and Principle.
Slaughtering sentient beings,
    I robbed them of their lives,
        And drinking wine, I broke the fast.
So now it has come to this day:
    The count of my evil has been fulfilled,
        And the wronged souls demand their lives."
If one takes one life,
    One must return one life:
        There is not the slightest discrepancy;
If one eats eight ounces,

One must pay back half a pound:
    Not the slightest mistake ever happens.
When old King Yama
    Pronounces his verdict,
        He does not care for family connections.
You will be tied with ropes,
    You will be shackled with chains,
        And you will be locked in an iron cangue.
Your arms will be yanked up;
    Your legs will be tortured
        Such that you cannot walk even half an inch.
Beaten up by the Oxhead Demon,
    Pulled forward by the Horseface Demon,
        You have no road to ascend to heaven;
Whipped by big ghosts,
    Hammered by little ghosts,
        You have no gate through which to enter earth.
When they escort you
    To the Hall of Transformation,[34]
        And the documents of your case are studied,
The judges make the decision:
    You will become an animal,
        For all eternity never allowed to change its shape.
The lady Liu Qingti,
    There in the earth prison,
        Screamed and hollered and painfully wept,
Filled with remorse
    Because, at an earlier moment,
        She had taken a stand that was utterly wrong.

Then Oxhead and Horseface took Madame Liu to the Senluo Hall.[35] The chilly wind made one shiver, and black vapors rose up in the air. When the [demons escorting Liu Qingti] appeared before King Yama, they submitted to him their iron plaque[36] and then took up position on both sides. King Yama, pronouncing his sentence, submitted her to questioning. When this Lord of Darkness saw Madame Liu, his anger turned to rage.

Striking his table in a terrifying way, the judge interrogated her:
"Destroying images and deceiving the gods: your sins are many.
Breaking and destroying bridges, you robbed people of their road;
Beating monks and cursing priests—your words lack all reason!

"Who told you to break the fast and offend against the precepts? If you slaughter sentient beings, you have to repay their lives!" When Madame Liu lifted her head to have a look, she saw King Yama seated in the Senluo Hall. The civil and military judges in attendance on either side of him held in their hands the ledgers of life and death, and in front of the steps Oxhead and Horseface, yakshas and minor demons were arranged in two groups. Some of them held swords, and others held lances; some of them held iron cudgels, and others held pitchforks. Each and every one of them looked like wolves and tigers, with faces that were evil and mean. Madame Liu Qingti was so terrified that her guts[37] and heart began to quake and shiver, and she fell to her knees, awash in tears and weeping piteously.

She begged King Yama: "My younger brother, who is called Liu Jia, urged me to break the fast. He said that our food and blessing are predetermined by our karma from an earlier life. That's why I slaughtered sentient beings all day long. I never thought that I would create sins and suffer punishment in the earth prison." She begged King Yama: "Please spare my miserable life!" When King Yama heard this, he only flew into a greater rage and immediately ordered the attending judges to look up Liu Jia in the ledgers of life and death. After the assistant judges had checked the ledgers carefully, they reported: "Your Majesty, during his lifetime Liu Jia committed every kind of evil and took an excessive number of lives. His life on earth has come to its end." Hearing this, King Yama then promptly took an iron plaque and dispatched Oxhead and Horseface with the order to immediately go and fetch Liu Jia. As soon as Oxhead and Horseface had received this iron plaque, they left the Senluo Hall, carrying their iron cudgels, pitchforks, and chains.

Once they had left the World of Darkness and arrived at Guanxi in Nandu in the World of Light, they ordered the local god of the soil to go with his minor devils and arrest Liu Jia, who was in his shop busily killing pigs and selling pork when Oxhead and Horseface blocked him with their pitchforks, locked him in iron chains, and set off with him in tow. Once they had entered the World of Darkness, arrived at the Senluo Hall, and appeared before King Yama, the demons submitted their iron plaque, and then both brother and sister were questioned, as described in this gatha:

The Son of Heaven[38] King Yama showed no mercy at all;
The Three Bureaus compared the cases to find out the truth.
Although brother and sister still wanted to deny their guilt,
The karmascope in the front hall clearly showed their sins.[39]
    Liu Jia was sentenced to be reborn in the form of a beast
And undergo suffering in all forms of animal existence,
While Madame Liu was flung down into the Avici Hell,[40]
For thousands and ten thousand years never to be reborn.

The woman Madame Liu
    Was flung down into hell,
        So she hollered and screamed and wept,
Now filled with remorse,
    Because in the World of Light
        She refused to practice self-cultivation.
"Had I known earlier
    That here in this hell
        I would have to undergo such suffering,
I would never have dared
    Slaughter sentient beings
        And kill and harm their lives and their fates!"

Let's not talk about how Madame Liu cried and wept in the earth prison but rather tell about Mulian. After his mother had passed away, he had purchased a coffin, dressed her corpse, and seen to her burial. At home he paid respects to her ancestral tablet and recited the sutras in order to ensure her rebirth in a higher realm. When he thought about the fact that he had not yet repaid the favors she had shown him by toiling wearily to feed him and rear him, he cried and wept day and night.

"Oh Mother,
Your son Mulian is dressed in mourning beside your coffin,
And, weeping and crying, he is reciting the Diamond Sutra.

Oh Mother!

When one's life comes to an end, one goes back to heaven,

But I do not yet know in which region you currently reside.

Oh Mother!

When your son calls you to mind, his guts are all shattered,

And he can't stop his tears from coursing down his cheeks.

Oh Mother!

I've no desire to eat any rice or drink any tea at the three meals,

So you can imagine how gaunt and sallow my face now looks.

Oh Mother!

In this life we will not be able to meet each other, because

You are now in the World of Darkness, I in the World of Light.

Oh Mother!

When I call your face and voice to mind, you seem to be alive,

But I can no longer see my own dear mother before my eyes.

Oh Mother!

In the morning I call you to mind, in the evening I do the same;

All through the night I cry and weep and weep and cry till dawn.

Oh Mother!

When I sleep on the Yang Terrace, I imagine that I meet you,[41]

But when I awake with a start, it all is a Southern Branch dream.[42]

Oh Mother!

How I hate this sword that showed no mercy, and with one blow

Cut us apart, mother and son, so that we were separated into two.

Oh Mother!

With each day you go farther away, with each day go still farther;

The road grows more distant whenever I call my mother to mind.

Oh Mother!

Please walk as slow as you can on the road to the World of Darkness;

Please wait for your son before you appear before King Yama.

Oh Mother!

With a golden needle you've poked a hole in the gauze of heaven;

I will meet with you, Mother, in the Western Heaven's Pure Land.[43]

Oh Mother!

Because it is impossible to repay the favors of feeding and rearing,

Every word I say is in memory of you, as my weeping guts shatter."

Now Mulian had always been filial and obedient toward his parents. After his father and mother had returned to the World of Darkness, he recited the true sutras each day, in order to assist them with their rebirth in heaven. Awash in tears, he could not stop thinking about his dear mother, as the favors of feeding and rearing are impossible to repay.

"These favors are as deep as the blue ocean, and are hard to imagine.
So let me explain the ten kinds of bitter sufferings a mother endures.

The first kind of favor
For which to thank Mother:
She carried me in her womb;
While I lived in her belly,
She had no yen for tea,
She didn't care for rice—
Her face was sallow, her flesh so gaunt.
Whatever she would eat
Would fill her with fear,
Feeling the pangs of hunger,
Hunger that shattered her guts.
This kind of favor and love
Must have caused my mother
Such suffering in those years long ago!

The second kind of favor
For which to thank Mother:
When I was to be born,
She tossed and turned.
One bout of contractions,
One more bout of pain:
The pain of the contractions unbearable!
One more bout of pain,
One bout of contractions:
She fainted for pain and
She about died of pain—
This favor and love

Must have caused my mother
Such suffering in those years long ago!

The third kind of favor
For which to thank Mother:
When the child is still in the belly
And wants to be born,
The nails on its fingers cause pain;
It stamps on the placenta.
When the child appears,
The mother faints, and
Her breath is stuck in her throat.
She has lost consciousness
But comes back to life,
Having almost gone
To meet King Yama.
I must have caused
Much suffering to my mother back then!

The fourth kind of favor
For which to thank Mother:
She did not feel relief
Until I had been born.
On behalf of her son
She chose a milk-name,
Carefully memorizing the eight characters.[44]
Within a full month
She left her chamber,
When the foul stench
Was most unbearable!
This favor and love
Must have caused Mother
Such suffering back in those days long ago!

The fifth kind of favor
For which to thank Mother:

She cleaned shit and piss
And my pair of pants too;
When the water became ice,
The cold pierced her marrow,
Her ten fingers all frostbitten.
Heat may be endurable,
But cold is unbearable.
Undeterred by the smell,
Undeterred by the dirt—
This favor and love
Must have caused Mother
Such suffering back in those days long ago!

The sixth kind of favor
For which to thank Mother:
Each and every day, she'd
Feed me with breast milk;
If her child cried or wept,
Mother would panic and
Hurry to pick me up, take me in her arms.
Comforting her child,
She would go outside
And buy some candy
For a copper penny—
I must have caused
My mother much suffering way back then!

The seventh kind of favor
For which to thank Mother:
When evening would come,
She'd press me to her breast.
She'd sleep together with me,
Lying in a puddle of piss.[45]
The mattress was soaked.
Was it soaked on this side?
She'd sleep on this side.

Was it soaked on that side?
She'd sleep on that side.
If both sides were soaked,
I would sleep on her body.
I must have caused
My mother much suffering way back then!

The eighth kind of favor
For which to thank Mother:
When 'heavenly flowers'[46]
Appeared on my body,
And she saw those signs,
She didn't starch my clothes.
My parents, full of fear,
Promised the God of Pox
They would burn incense for him;
They called for a doctor,
To ask for a prescription—
How can I ever forget
How my dear mother suffered?

The ninth kind of favor
For which to thank Mother:
When I went out to play
And got into mischief,
She'd watch from the door
And call me back home.
When my body was cold,
She'd give me warm clothes;
When my belly was hungry,
She would feed me soup.
This favor and love
Caused my mother much suffering!

The tenth kind of favor
For which to thank Mother:

She paid for a teacher
So I could go to school;
She cajoled her child
Into going to class
And not wasting his time in play.
If I wrote my characters well,
My mother had a reward,
Or she would even make me
A new set of clothes.
This favor and love
Must have caused my mother
Such suffering in those days back then!

I truly hoped and expected
That my father and mother
By their great good fortune
Would live to a ripe old age,
Enjoying wealth and status,
Enjoying riches and glory,
Living forever and never growing old!
Who could have known
That their lives would end,
My father dying first,
My mother dying after?
Which of their favors
Had I ever paid back?
Alas, my dear mother truly did suffer!

Gone to Spirit Mountain,[47]
She offers her veneration.
I cry out: 'Dear Mother!'
I call: 'Dearest Mommy!'
I weep when I walk, and
I weep when I sit down.
In what region do you currently reside?
My hands beat my breast, and

My feet stamp the earth.
Writhing, I dig myself a hole
That is big enough for a pool!
Now I wail: 'Dear Father!'
Then I wail: 'Dear Mother,
In what region do you currently reside?'

My father and my mother
Must together have gone
To the Western Paradise,
The Land of Great Bliss,
To venerate the Buddha,
Bow to the Dharma King—
They have gone to the best place of all!
They have left their child
Back in their hometown,
Reading the sutra chapters,
By the side of their coffins.
Let me go to the West
And there find my mother,
The place where she has found her rest!

When I am able to meet
My father and my mother,
I'll tell them how much
I miss them all the time.
I will repay my mother
For the favor of feeding,
And there we will pass the time together.
Only then will I stop
Thinking of her all the time,
Not wanting any tea,
Not wanting any rice.
I long for her early, and
I long for her till late—
I long for my mother, but she does not come.

But I on the other hand
Know no way to stop:
I weep while walking;
I weep while waiting;
I weep while sitting.

When lying down, I weep, weeping until my innards shatter;
I weep for my mother till both heaven and earth grow dark.
I weep so much that sun and moon no longer shine bright,
Weep so much that somber clouds stretch in all directions.
     I weep so much that a thick fog blankets the Western Paradise;
I weep so much that raven and crow do not flap their wings.
I weep so much that fleet-footed beasts all run to the hills—
There is no end to the weeping of longing for one's parents."

But let's now stop for a while and not talk about this any more.

Our story goes that from the time Mulian's mother passed away, he wept and
wailed day and night, unable to let her go. He did not know whether or not
his mother had indeed made it to the Western Paradise and there found her
rest, which is why his heart was filled with worry and sorrow. So one day he
bowed in front of the Buddha, and let Him know that he wanted to go to the
Western Paradise—since only by meeting with his mother could he put his
mind at ease. After he had dressed himself in the proper outfit, he prepared
two bundles: in one of them he packed the sutras, and in the other he packed
his mother's ancestral tablet. Then he bowed and said good-bye to his fellow
monks. While on the road, at dawn he would set out, and at night he would
stop at an inn; he would eat when he was hungry, and he would drink when
he was thirsty. These thousands and myriads of sufferings are described in
the following gatha:

Mulian departed for the Western Paradise to find his mother,
Walking from early till late, carrying his pole on one shoulder.
Enduring all kinds of wind and frost, he never once grumbled,
All for his mother's favor of wearisome toil, feeding and rearing.
     Carrying the sutras in front, he feared soiling his mother's tablet;

Carrying his mother's tablet in front, he feared soiling the sutras.
Considering the matter from all perspectives, he saw no solution
Except to walk on ahead with the pole across both his shoulders.[48]

Let's not talk now about how Mulian traveled, seeking his mother, but instead recount how the bodhisattva Guanyin in her Purple Bamboo Grove of the Southern Sea[49] saw that Mulian was headed to the Western Paradise to find his mother. "I don't know whether his intention is sincere. Let me put him to the test!" Guanyin then summoned Good-in-Talent and transformed him into a girl[50] while transforming herself into the girl's mother. Leaving Incense Mountain, the two of them arrived at a spot about midway, where Guanyin transformed a grotto on a wild mountain into a nice house. Mulian was walking along, and since it was getting to be evening, when he caught sight of this house, he knocked at the door and asked whether he could stay there for the night. The mother immediately asked the monk: "Where are you from? And where are you going?" Mulian replied: "I hail from Guanxi in Nandu. All his life my father practiced goodness. My mother also kept the fast, but she has passed away. I performed the rituals that would assure her rebirth on a higher level, but I would like to know whether she made it to the Western Paradise. I cannot get my mother out of my mind, which is why I want to go to the Western Paradise to find her." The girl's mother said: "So you are a filial son! Rare indeed! I have been looking for a filial and obedient son to be the husband of my daughter, but so far I have failed to find one. So you have come at just the right time! Why don't you stay here and be my son-in-law?"[51] When Mulian refused the offer, the girl's mother said: "Please listen to me!

(A Daoist song)[52]

"Oh you, you little monk,
> You're stupid and foolish:
If your dear mother truly
> Kept strictly to the fast,
She must have met with the Tathagata upon her death.
> When after a hundred years you go up to heaven too,
You will see your mother and can tell her of your love,

But how can you ascend to the world of gods right now?
　　　But when you marry my girl and become my son-in-law,
You soon will have fine sons to continue the family line!"

When Mulian heard this, his anger turned to rage:
"Old woman, what you are saying makes no sense!
When very young, I shaved my head to be a monk,
To read the sutras, to recite the name of the Buddha.
　　Because the favor of feeding is impossible to repay,
I will go to the Western Paradise to find my mother.
Tonight I came here to seek lodging for the night,
Only to have you make this outrageous proposition!"

When the girl saw that Mulian was not amenable to their suggestion, she also stepped forward and said to him: "If you want to go from here to the Western Paradise, you will find your way blocked by the Heavenly River. How could a mortal person get there? It would be much better if you would stay here and be a son-in-law, you cute little monk!" Then the girl sighed and said:

(*A Daoist song*)

"You cute little monk,
　　Please listen to me,
Because you and I
　　Are meant to marry
And be husband and wife, as predestined in an earlier life.
　　Five hundred years ago, this bond of marriage was settled.
If destined by karma, people a thousand miles apart will meet;
If not, they will never meet, even when they stand face to face!
　　Don't go to the Western Paradise to find your mother,
But stay here with us, and we can be united in wedlock!

Enjoy wealth and status, and pleasure and joy without end!"[53]

When Mulian heard this, his anger boiled over again:
"You silly little girl, you really have no shame at all!

You are a young girl and live in the inner apartments,
But now in the vilest manner you try to make me stay.
 I will go to the Western Paradise and find my mother—
Who wants a female skeleton dolled up with makeup?
If you make one more attempt to charm and seduce me,
You'll forfeit the human body your parents gave you."[54]

When the girl's mother saw that Mulian was determined to refuse her offer—let's not recount idle talk—she immediately said: "It's getting late. Monk, you go and sleep in that room over there." When Mulian heard this, he went to the room to sleep and, because of all his exertions on the road, immediately fell sound asleep. Now that the bodhisattva had determined that Mulian was sincere in his intention to look for his mother, she and Good-in-Talent returned to Incense Mountain.[55]

When Mulian woke up from his sleep, the sky was already bright. When he opened his eyes, there was not a house to be seen, and it turned out he had been sleeping in a mountain grotto. He got up greatly angered: "Which monster came here to fool with me?" Hoisting his carrying pole onto his shoulders, he once more walked on. There's no need to recount the idle talk of his journey on the road. One day he arrived at the banks of the Heavenly River[56] and was unable to continue his journey. He then composed this gatha:

Mulian, on his way to the Western Paradise to find his mother,
Was blocked by the Heavenly River and so could not walk on.
There was no bridge across the river, so he could not walk on,
And neither was there a ferryboat waiting for him at the bank.
 Standing on the riverbank, he hollered and screamed and wept;
He wanted to walk on even if it meant drowning in the river.
He considered the matter from every angle but found no solution—
How he hated not being able to ride the clouds into the sky!

On the riverbank Mulian wept for a while. Then, saying, "I never thought that the Heavenly River would block my way! But even if it means shattering my bones and pulverizing my body, I still want to go and find my mother!" he plunged in! His soul was so frightened by this that it fled his body, but not recognizing that it was his own corpse, Mulian took it for some dead monk.

Standing there in the water, Mulian thought to himself: "So be it. Why don't I use this corpse to cross the river!"

After Mulian had crossed the Heavenly River, he climbed up the bank and walked on and, after who knows how many days, arrived at the Western Paradise. From a distance, he saw Spirit Mountain and heard the clap of the thunder.[57] Bells and drums resounded together, and filled with great joy, Mulian composed this gatha:

I now hear the clap of the thunder, as bells and drums resound:
Spirit Mountain is not far but rises up here in front of me.
The rare shrubs and new grasses bloom and blanket the earth,
And the wind-borne fragrance of the flowers is overwhelming!
　　Immortal peaches and divine fruits of all kinds are found here;
Antelopes and deer, gibbons and monkeys are running around.
Let me walk up to Spirit Mountain's Thunder-Clap Monastery,
To pay my respects to Sakyamuni, the World-Honored Buddha.

Mulian paid his respects and, kneeling down in the dust in front of the Buddha, begged him to show compassion. "I, Mulian, have come here looking for my father and mother, since I have not yet been able to repay their favor of wearisome toil. But why don't I see them here?" The Buddha said: "When your father died, the Teaching Lord of the World of Darkness, King Ksitigarbha,[58] kept him at his side as a protector of the Dharma, so he was not sent to the Western Paradise." Mulian beseeched the Buddha to show his compassion: "But where is my mother?" The Buddha explained: "Wasn't your mother Madame Liu?" When Mulian replied that she was, the Buddha said: "While she was alive, she broke the fast and violated the precepts, she deceived the gods and destroyed their images, she beat up monks and cursed priests, and she broke down bridges. So King Yama dispatched Oxhead and Horseface, who locked her in chains and a cangue and threw her into the earth prison to undergo suffering." When Mulian heard this, he hollered and screamed and wept most painfully. A gatha describes this:

When Mulian heard this, pain wounded his heart;
He wailed and wept painfully, loudly raising his voice.
"I only thought that my mother would find a good place.

Who could have known she would suffer in this prison?

In vain she raised a son—what was the use of my birth?
I have failed to repay my mother for all her many favors.
So I beseech the Buddha to show me some compassion:
Enable me to save my mother from that joyless world!"

The Buddha said: "Mulian, the sins committed by your mother are too heavy, so she cannot be pardoned and released. But considering that you practice goodness and want to save your mother, you must be a person of exceptional filial piety. So I will gift you with my gown, my begging bowl, and this meditation staff with nine rings. When you go to the World of Darkness, you only have to tap once very lightly with this meditation staff on the gate of hell to save your mother. In this bowl you have water and rice to give to your mother to relieve her hunger." When Mulian heard this, his heart was filled with joy. After he had received the gown, the bowl, and the meditation staff, he took his leave of the Buddha with a bow.

After he had left Thunder-Clap Monastery, he arrived in the World of Darkness and got down from his cloud.[59] He stood atop Ghost-Gate Pass,[60] and his feet walked in the realm inside the earth of the Court of Shade. The piteous sound of his weeping and crying, crying and weeping, moved the prison lord, who dispatched minor demons to find out who the person crying and weeping was and to report back to him once they had an answer. When these demon-soldiers arrived before Mulian, they asked him: "Monk, why are you here crying and weeping?" Mulian replied: "At the behest of the Buddha I have come here to look for my mother, and I am filled with sadness because I don't see her." The demon-soldiers reported this to the prison lord, and he ordered them to invite Mulian in. When Mulian arrived at the prison, the prison lord rose from his seat to welcome him and immediately asked him: "Where are you from, sagely monk? What is your religious name and that of your teacher? How many years ago did you leave the family to become a monk? Whom do you serve as your teacher? Which method of practicing the Way have you mastered? And which school of Buddhism do you practice?" Mulian replied as follows:

"My original name was Radish Fu, and now I'm the monk Mulian;
From my earliest youth I left the family and recited the sutras.

The monk Future-Fruit transmitted to me his method of the Way;
What I practice is the Highest Vehicle of Emptiness Spirituality."

When the prison lord heard this, he was very pleased. "I also left the family early in my youth, but I have not yet met with an enlightened teacher. Today I have the good karma to meet with one. So I had better, in a soft voice and with bated breath, ask him for an explanation of the Way." So he stepped forward, bowed deeply, and asked:

"May I ask you, my teacher, how the root of the Way sprouts?
May I ask you, my teacher, how the Way opens its flowers?
May I ask you, my teacher, how the Way forms its fruit, and
May I ask you, my teacher, how the Way returns to its home?"

Mulian said: "If you ask for the method and rules for returning home,[61] you first have to strictly maintain the Five Precepts and firmly uphold the Threefold Refuge. Please listen to me:

"The root of the Way sprouts from the teacher's single sign.[62]
The Way opens its flowers upon penetrating the Three Passes.[63]
The Way forms its fruit if the enlightened mind sees its nature,[64]
And the Way returns home by each single movement and step."

When the prison lord heard this, he realized Mulian was indeed a true monk, so he immediately thanked him for this favor of guidance and instruction. And then he said: "A few days ago there was this sinning soul, Liu Qingti, who said she had a son who in early youth had left the family to practice the Way. I am sure that son must be you, dear reverend." Mulian said: "Yes, you are right. But is she still here?" "She isn't here anymore. She has been taken away together with her younger brother."

Mulian then asked the demon-soldiers: "What is this place here?" The demon-soldiers told him: "This is Ghost-Gate Pass, the border between darkness and light. When the people in the world die, they have to go through this pass. There is a gatha that describes this, so please listen:

"How cold and desolate the atmosphere of Ghost-Gate Pass—

All alone, all by oneself: you're now without any assistance!
You've abandoned your hometown, your sons and daughters;
You're far from the wife and concubines who shared your bed.

Your eyes cry tears of blood because of a thousand vexations;
Inside your belly your innards are twisted ninefold for grief.
And those many friends of the bordello and the wine house
Have gone their own way by the time you reach this place."

Having heard this, Mulian entered the pass to seek his mother, and the demon-soldiers dared not block his way.

As he was walking along, Mulian suddenly saw a high terrace, which was guarded by demon-soldiers, so he asked: "What is the name of this terrace?" The answer he got was: "This is called Karmascope Terrace, which brings to light a person's heart and gall. Please let us explain:

"On Karmascope Terrace
    A mirror is hung high
        To shine on all the people of the world:
Good and evil,
    Merit and misstep,
        All are shown without any discrepancy.
Reflected in this mirror
    You well may have
        A mouth of steel and teeth made of iron,
But you cannot negate
    And you cannot deny
        The obvious facts: as the form, so the image!
When filial sons
    Or virtuous daughters
        Come and arrive in the World of Darkness,
Our lord King Yama
    Descends from the hall
        And goes out to welcome them in person.
They do not have to ascend
    This high terrace,
        As their faces are reflected fully on their own,

And instantly,

> There will be a virtuous light
>> That pervades the entire World of Darkness.

Those who practice goodness,

> Once they have been reflected,
>> Are filled with joy and pleasure in their hearts.

While in the World of Light

> They established good karma
>> Because they didn't care for money and silver.

At every opportunity

> They practiced good deeds,
>> Not willing to stop for even a single moment:

A hundred turned thousand,

> A thousand, ten thousand:
>> Their good virtues accumulated more and more.

When they come here,

> The Star of Misfortune leaves:
>> They are lucky people with heavenly features.

We show them each hall,

> Where they roam for a while,
>> And then they're reborn again in human form.

Those who practiced evil

> Ascend the terrace in chains
>> In order to observe the many sins they committed.

These are the people in the world

> Who committed evil deeds,
>> Day in and day out, and also month upon month.

The first category includes

> Disobedient, rebellious sons
>> Who never respected their fathers and mothers.

Elder and younger brothers,

> True flesh-and-bones relatives,
>> They consider no better than complete strangers.

But wives and concubines,

> Their own sons and grandsons—
>> Those they cherished like the rarest of treasures!

They fight over the inheritance
    And steal their brothers' fields,
        Never showing the slightest feeling for anyone else.
They always follow their own desires
    And never care about others:
        They're haughty and proud, stubborn and arrogant;
In their breasts they harbor
    A myriad of evil schemes,
        Filled with vile jealousy, filled with greed and rage.
How could they know
    That above their heads
        Gods record each of their sins, each of their crimes,
To be stored in this mirror—
    So when they arrive here,
        They'll have to confront each and all of them clearly?
If their sins and crimes are minor,
    They will be reborn as animals—
        From a womb, from an egg, from moisture, by miracle.[65]
However, if their evil karma is heavy,
    They will sink down into the hells,
        Never again for all eternity to be reborn in any form."

After the demon-soldiers had provided this explanation, they asked: "Where do you come from? And what are you looking for?" Mulian said: "I hail from the World of Light and have come here at the behest of the Buddha to find my mother. Could she be here?" The demon-soldiers replied: "Some days ago there was someone called Madame Liu. Her hair was in disarray, her feet were bare, and she was wearing a cangue and shackled in chains. Oxhead and Horseface were beating her so much with their iron cudgels that she was crippled. Crying and weeping, she left." This gatha may serve as description:

When Mulian heard this, pain wounded his heart;
Weeping painfully, he loudly hollered and screamed.
"Mother, while in the world you were keeping the fast,
Who told you, Mother, to eat spicy dishes once again?
    With fish and meat you'll never be able to extend your life;

Today your sufferings here in hell are beyond description!
Oh, how I hate my uncle, your brother, for his vile guts,
For involving you in the sins that created this evil karma!"

After Mulian had said this, he wept as he entered the pass in search of his mother. When the demon-soldiers saw that he was carrying a begging bowl and a meditation staff, they dared not block his way.

He had not gone very far when he saw a high mountain. Mulian immediately asked its demon-soldiers: "What kind of place is this?" The demon-soldiers replied: "In the World of Light, stupid and foolish people do not believe in the Dharma of the Buddha but instead slaughter sentient beings, drink wine, and eat spiced dishes. But when death approaches, they are overcome by fear and urge their sons and daughters to burn paper money, believing that it will go to the World of Darkness and there redeem their sins. Little do they know that it is of no use at all. It just piles up here, which is why this place is called the Wasted Money Mountain. There is a gatha that describes this, so please listen:

"The Wasted Money Mountain towers ten thousand feet;
When souls arrive here, they weep and holler and scream.
Even if you had burned a thousand sheets of paper money,
It would not diminish the karma of your sins in any way.
   If the World of Darkness could be swayed by paper or cash,
The poor would all perish and only the rich get away.
The endless ocean of suffering that is the earth prison —
The only thing that works is to pile up merits sky high!"

When Mulian heard this, he asked the demon-soldiers: "Has a certain Madame Liu been here?" The demon-soldiers said: "Indeed, she has. A few days ago we saw her. Her hair was in disarray, her feet were bare, and she was wearing a cangue, shackled in chains. Oxhead and Horseface were beating her so much with their iron cudgels that she was weeping and wailing, wailing and weeping."

When Mulian heard this account, pain filled his bosom;
He hollered, screamed, and painfully wept, venting his grief.

Hearing that his dear mother suffered such pain, the child
Hurried on ahead to catch up with her and take her place.

After Mulian had done weeping, he continued on his way. He then caught sight of a pavilion that was open on all four sides and guarded by yakshas and little demons. On each side there were a countless number of men's and women's clothes piled up high. Immediately Mulian asked: "What kind of place is this?" The demon-soldiers said: "This is the Pavilion for Stripping Off Clothes." He then asked further: "What sort of people have their clothes stripped off like this?" They replied: "The people who have their clothes stripped off are those who captured frogs and snakes, chopped off their heads, and stripped off their skins as well as those who liked to hunt winged birds and fleet-footed beasts, remove their pelts, and chop off their legs and then day after day put them out for sale in the marketplace, after which they would buy wine with the money they made—those sorts of sinners! Little did they know that in the World of Darkness, where not the slightest mistake is made, they would have to suffer punishments without number. There is a gatha that describes this, so please listen:

"The Pavilion for Stripping Off Clothes is full of wronged ghosts:
Badness is requited by badness, all without the slightest discrepancy.
They're punished by being reborn in the World of Light as animals,
Simply because of the many evils they committed in an earlier life.
  Not daring to challenge people, they indulge in catching critters,
Skin stripped off, legs chopped off—how painful that must be!
Now they are waiting for you, here in this pavilion, where they will
Strip off your clothes and your skin: it is an exchange that is equal."

When Mulian heard this, he asked: "Has a certain Woman Liu been here?" The demon-soldiers replied: "There was such a woman. Her hair was in disarray. Walking barefoot, she was wearing a cangue, and she was shackled in chains. Oxhead and Horseface were beating her so much with their iron cudgels that she was weeping and wailing, wailing and weeping."

When Mulian heard the story of how his mother suffered,
He could not stop the tears from gushing from his eyes.

"If only you would not have listened to my uncle back then,
You wouldn't have to suffer this punishment for your sins."

After Mulian had done weeping, he continued on his way. What he saw next was a pond piled high with ice, in which the souls of men and women were wailing and weeping. On the bank of the pond stood demon-soldiers, guarding them. Immediately he asked them: "What pond is this?" The demon-soldiers replied: "This is Cold Ice Pond." He then asked: "What kind of sin did the people in this pond commit?" They replied: "These are men and women from the World of Light who did not provide clothing for their fathers and mothers and their parents-in-law. Even if they had the money, they refused to give them clothes against the cold, and not only did they not spare any expense to dress themselves in flashy garments, but they didn't take care of the clothes they had. They also cut through dikes, committed arson, and killed people. That is why, after they died, they were sent to undergo suffering in this pond. There is a gatha that describes this, so please listen:

"In Cold Ice Pond they are pierced by the freezing air;
If you don't take care of your clothes, you will end up here.
Although they wore the most beautiful clothes themselves, they
Didn't even give their fathers and mothers simple[66] clothes to use.
    Although rich, they are stingy and did not make any donations;
They didn't make any clothes to help the poor and the needy.
Cutting dikes, flooding fields, and committing arson as well—
These are the sins for which people go to Cold Ice Pond."

When Mulian heard this, he immediately asked: "Has a certain Madame Liu been here?" The demon-soldiers replied: "A few days ago there was such a woman. Her hair was in disarray. Walking barefoot, she was wearing a cangue, and she was shackled in chains. Oxhead and Horseface were beating her so much with their iron cudgels that she was weeping and wailing, wailing and weeping, as she was led away."

Now when our Mulian
        Had heard them recount
            The many sufferings of his mother,

He could not stop
>   His tears from gushing
>   Down from his eyes like a flood.
He beat his breast
>   And stamped the earth,
>   Screaming and hollering and weeping.
He wept so painfully
>   That even those demons
>   Were deeply saddened at this sound.
"I cannot wait
>   To go another stretch,
>   And in a single moment, a minute or less,
To catch up with
>   My suffering mother
>   And share the road she must travel.
And in the case that there is
>   Some kind of punishment,
>   I, as her son, will take her place,
And in this way spare
>   The mother who raised me
>   From suffering the penalties of hell."

After Mulian had done weeping, he continued on his way. In front of him he saw a high mountain. On that mountain there were countless roosters who, with their bronze bills and iron spurs, were pecking out people's eyes while demon-soldiers stood guard. Mulian asked: "What kind of mountain is this?" The demon-soldiers replied: "This mountain is called Divine Rooster Mountain. There are people in the world who although they have eyes that see perfectly clearly don't use them in the right way: they are always leering at the wives of others and always reading obscene books and lewd songs, and day and night they engage in gambling. Then there are geomancers who, although they have two eyes, are unable to identify the veins of the earth and thus make mistakes when siting graves for people—in minor cases this results in decay and misfortune, in more serious cases in lack of heirs.[67] And then there are women who are always using their eyes to flirt. Upon their deaths they all are condemned to this mountain, so these bronze-billed iron-spurred roosters can eat their hearts and peck out their eyes, so that for all eternity these people will not be able to see anything. There is a gatha that describes this, so please listen:

"His road took him by the base of Divine Rooster Mountain:
Roosters with bronze bills and iron spurs—rare in the world!
They peck out only the eyes that while alive leered at women,
They eat just the eyes that when in the world looked for men,
     Those who read lascivious books, are addicted to gambling,
And habitually deceive others by misreading the earth's veins:
When those kinds of sinners arrive in the earth prison,
They are punished there by blindness in both of their eyes."

When Mulian heard this, he immediately asked: "Has a certain Madame Liu been here?" The demon-soldiers replied: "She has been here. Oxhead and Horseface were beating her so much with their iron cudgels that she was weeping and wailing, wailing and weeping, as she was being led away."

When Mulian heard how his mother had been taken away,
Unable to stop himself from crying, his tears flowed down.
"How I hate my uncle, my mother's brother, for his evil heart!
He persuaded my mother to break the fast and again eat meat.
     The bodily sufferings that my mother is now forced to endure
Make me feel as if a fierce fire is burning inside my chest.
I must catch up with my mother so that I can take her place
And repay her a little bit for the favors of feeding and rearing."

After Mulian was done weeping, he continued on his way. He next saw a large farmstead. Inside the farmyard were many grated pens, and the chilly air made one shiver. Countless souls had been transformed into donkeys and mules and other animals, and demon-soldiers stood guard all around. Mulian asked them: "What kind of place is this?" The demon-soldiers replied: "This place is called the Turning-into-Beasts Depot. All those people in the world who as officials enjoyed their salaries but failed to show any loyalty, craved riches and accepted bribes, and treated the common people cruelly, and those who as common citizens did not pay their taxes in full, wrongfully seized the property of others, cheated and deceived both openly and secretly, beguiled and bamboozled their own hearts, used tampered balances and altered measures in order to give too little and demand too much, defaulted on debts and did not repay them, and collected interest beyond measure, those who in every possible way harmed others to benefit themselves—they come to this place upon their deaths and are turned into animals so as to pay back their debts. Then you have those people in the world who refuse to keep to the fast and love to kill sentient beings—they too are punished by being turned into animals, that they may suffer the retribution of being chopped up by a knife! There is a gatha that describes this, so please listen:

"Those people who upon their deaths are turned into animals
Are so reborn because of karma accumulated in an earlier life.
Those who enjoy a salary but show no loyalty, acting cruelly,
Those who default on taxes and loans and profit themselves,
　Those who harm others to profit themselves, full of deceit,
Those who refuse to keep to the fast, killing sentient beings,
Are punished by being sent to this place to become a beast—
Retribution is as clear as day and the rationale is most true."

When Mulian heard this, he immediately asked: "Has a certain Madame Liu been here?" The ghost soldiers replied: "Indeed. But the demons Oxhead and Horseface took her away."

When Mulian came to this place but did not find his mother,
He could not keep himself from wailing at the top of his voice.
"If only I would be able to find my old mother in person,
I would be happy to suffer all these punishments in her place."

After Mulian had done weeping, he continued on his way, looking for his mother. He saw a place where vats of oil had been set out. Oxhead and Horseface were pushing sinners into these vats of oil with their pitchforks, so that their flesh would dissolve and their bones would melt—a thousand kinds of painful sufferings! Mulian immediately asked: "What kind of evil did these sinners commit during their lifetimes?" The demon-soldiers replied: "In the World of Light they delighted in buying fishes, turtles, and animals with fur or feathers, cutting them up and flaying them so that their blood poured out all over, washing and cleaning their white flesh, and then dumping them in a pan of oil to cook and roast so they would smell nice and taste good. All they cared about were their own tongues and stomachs, and they gave no thought to High Heaven's virtue of loving life. As punishment they are sent to this place in order to pay back the lives of those creatures. Retribution is truly exact! There is a gatha that describes this, so please listen:

"Because of the many evil sins committed during their lives,
Now they can't escape being thrown into vats of boiling oil.
The flavor that delights your tongue and tastes so wonderful
All comes from pigs and goats, chicken, ducks, and geese!

  While it pleased your palate to cook them while you lived,
Now in the Underworld you're fried yourself—how about it?
If as a human being you refrain from eating spices and meat,
After you die you will go to a place of contentment and peace."

Mulian heaved a sigh and then asked the demon-soldiers: "Has a certain Madame Liu been here?" The demon-soldiers replied: "Indeed. But she was led away."

  Mulian continued on his way, looking for his mother. He then saw a large pond whose red-colored waves reached up to heaven. Countless male and female souls were immersed in this pond, while demon-soldiers stood watch on the banks. Mulian immediately asked them: "What is the name of this pond?" The demon-soldiers replied: "This is the Pond of Filth and Blood. All those people in the world, whether men or women, who do not abide by the Right Way but crave only wine, sex, riches, and honor are sent to this place after they die to suffer punishment. There is a gatha that describes this, so please listen:

"Those who during their human lives created much evil karma,
Those who did not practice the recitation of Amitabha's name,
Those who craved wine and sex, as well as riches and honor,
Those who disobeyed their parents and their parents-in-law."

When Mulian heard this, he heaved a sigh—

Now our Mulian
    Sighed at the Pond of Blood:
        "Alas, the condemned sinners in this pond
All are people
    Who in the World of Light
        Were men and women who lacked goodness.
When they were still daughters
    Living in their parents' home,
        They had been pampered and spoiled and
Did not understand
    A proper woman's
        Fourfold virtue and threefold obedience.[68]
They were willful and
    Had a cranky character,
        Creating all kind of problems and scandals,
And having developed
    This weird and strange character,
        They had no self-restraint and got into fights.
When just a few words
    Failed to strike their fancy,
        They'd create a ruckus as high as heaven:
Their hair in disarray,
    Walking barefoot,
        They did not care if they risked their lives!
When they left home to marry
    And became wedded wives,
        They showed their husbands no respect;
They disobeyed their parents-in-law,
    Angered their sisters-in-law,
        And cursed and reviled all the neighbors!
If there was only the slightest
    Event that displeased them,
        They would threaten to commit suicide—
Cheating their brothers-in-law

And bullying their husbands,
>> They showed no concern for propriety.
They craved fine foods, and
>> They loved beautiful clothes
>>> And painted their faces with rouge and powder,
And once they had finished
>> Their bewitching makeup,
>>> They would seduce and entice other men,
Disregarding their parents'
>> And parents-in-law's
>>> And their own husbands' status and honor!
In this way a family wasted all its money
>> And ended up bringing home
>>> A wife who only shamed and disgraced them!
Then there is another kind:
>> While the parents-in-law,
>>> By eating little and spending almost nothing,
Had been able to accumulate
>> Houses and money and fields
>>> To leave in turn to their sons and grandsons,
She, once they had brought her
>> Home as their daughter-in-law,
>>> Ate without any restraint and spent like a fool,
Bringing completely to ruin
>> Houses and money and fields
>>> And giving them all a bad reputation!
There is yet another kind:
>> Those unchaste women
>>> Who, no sooner do their husbands die,
Than they immediately start to flirt
>> With romantic ne'er-do-wells,
>>> Bringing them to their rooms to have affairs.
Of course their husbands'
>> Sentient souls will
>>> Be roused to indignation and gnash their teeth,
And when they arrive at

The courts of King Yama,
They are bound to accuse their wives of their crimes.
The Oxhead Demon
And the Horseface Demon
Will be ordered to arrest and shackle the women,
Who will sink into the Pond of Blood
And swallow its bloody fluids,
Never in all eternity to be reborn again!
Female sinners for
All of their crimes
Are sent to this place to undergo suffering,
But there are men
Who have committed sins
And are punished here in just the same way.
There is a kind of person
Who loves to drink wine
And fails to care for his father and mother,
But with a few friends and
Together with some buddies
He is drunk like a skunk from early till late.
Once he gets drunk,
He runs his mouth,
Talks nonsense and make outrageous remarks.
Little does he know
That his drunken talk
Easily hurts and offends many other people!
It may go so far that
Under the influence of alcohol
They kill a man in a drunken brawl,
With the result that
All members of their families
Will suffer fear and consternation!
Then when they sober up,
They feel remorse
About not strictly upholding the precepts—
If only he had done so,

He would have avoided
    The disastrous fate he is suffering this day!
And they also resent
    The owner of the brewery
        For not doing anything considered useful,
For he does nothing but take
    The beneficial five grains
        And brew them into a source of evil karma.
Looking back, they resent
    That Yidi of old,[69]
        Who presented his fine brews to Emperor Yu—
Ever since that day
    This line of business
        Has continued on down to the present age.
Once in the World of Darkness
    Yidi was sent
        For punishment to the Opulent Metropole,[70]
And to this very day
    He has yet to take rebirth
        In the form of a human being!
Then there is another kind:
    The men who love romance
        And are filled with the most obscene desires.
When they see a beautiful girl
    Or a beautiful wife,
        They are bound to want to have sex with her.
They use a thousand tricks,
    Come up with a hundred schemes,
        To seduce her and get their hands on her,
And even virtuous women
    May for one moment
        Be moved and aroused by 'springtime lust,'
But then later they are
    Overcome by remorse
        And hang themselves from a rafter.
There also are unmarried girls

Who first awaken to love
		And are talked into sex before marriage—
In the beginning these men
		Promise them
			A union of a hundred years, until old age,
But when some time later,
		When they are pregnant,
			The full extent of their situation is revealed,
These men will then circulate
		Their ugly reputations,
			Causing these poor girls to commit suicide.
There are Buddhist monks
		And also Daoist priests
			Who look for sex and seek out whores—
They concoct 'spring recipes'[71]
		And mix cinnabar pills
			To strengthen potency and spread obscenity.
These kinds of people
		Are sent to this place
			To suffer their punishment here in this pond.
Those people who love riches,
		And when seeing silver and cash,
			Do not hesitate to risk their own lives,
Those people who have money
		And still are unwilling
			To use it to assist the poor and the needy,
Who demand high interest rates
		And want to fleece people,
			Making relatives and neighbors their victims—
Their foolish aim in life is
		To build a luxurious house,
			Regarding even a thousand rooms as too few,
Yet little do they know
		That when the construction is finished,
			They have lost their lives and left for the shades,
Leaving the empty building

To serve as a burrow for animals and rats,
>> Haunted by ghosts and haunted by apparitions.
Even though your
> Money be a million,
>> It cannot affect the World of Darkness below,
So you had much better
> In this World of Light
>> Amass and accumulate good virtuous karma.
There is also a kind of people
> Whose honor is easily rankled
>> To the extent they do not care about their fate,
And in a single moment
> This may cause them
>> To bring ruin to their families, forfeit their own lives.[72]
Those who stand on their honor,
> Neglect their own wives,
>> And do not take care of their fathers and mothers—
Since they cannot suppress
> The rage in their breasts,
>> They are condemned to death and executed.
Among those who are easily rankled
> There are indeed many
>> Who fall ill because of this raging breath.
Once this raging breath is stuck
> Inside their hearts and their bellies,
>> Their bodies feel bloated and completely blocked.
Their hearts and stomachs are in pain,
> Their heads feel all dizzy and dazed,
>> Their kidneys are empty, their blood runs fast.
And then when later
> This disease slowly grows worse,
>> They lose their lives, leaving for the World of Darkness.
These kinds of people
> Refused in the World of Light
>> To devote themselves to the study of goodness,
And so, down in the earth prison,

They suffer the retribution
Of being soaked and soiled in this Blood Pond."
Now our Mulian
Pitied these many souls,
But it was impossible for him to take their place,
So he went on ahead,
Looking for his mother,
Unable to stay there, not even for a short while.

After Mulian had heaved a sigh, the souls all wailed, but their remorse came too late! Mulian asked the demon-soldiers: "Has a certain Madame Liu been here?" The demon-soldiers replied: "Indeed. But she was taken away."

When Mulian heard this, he continued on his way. As he was walking, he saw a mountain. No grass or tree was growing on that mountain; instead it was covered in oily sand and oily gravel, making it slippery beyond compare. He saw how Oxhead and Horseface were forcing some sinful souls to climb this mountain. These souls couldn't make any headway, but when they slid backward, they got a beating, and their wailing and weeping was too terrible to hear. Mulian asked: "What kind of mountain is this?" The demon-soldiers replied: "This is called Slippery Oil Mountain. All those people who in the World of Light had plenty of money but refused to build bridges and repair roads or to donate oil for the lamps used to light the roads, and those people who were poor but refused to accept their lot and stole the stones meant for paving the roads and the oil meant for the lamps used to light roads to make oil cloth, and also those people who, when they were walking on the road, refused to yield to elderly and handicapped persons, and those who took land meant for public roads and who leveled grave mounds—after they die, all such people are punished by being forced to undergo the suffering of having to climb this mountain. There is a gatha that describes this, so please listen:

"Slippery Oil Mountain is so slippery you can't walk—
It's because during their lives they were not fair-minded.
They refused to build bridges, neglected to repair roads;
Too stingy, they were unwilling to donate oil for lamps.

They leveled grave mounds, took land meant for roads,
But the gods and ghosts up above saw everything clearly.

And so, once their souls arrived in this World of Darkness,
They were forced to climb up this Slippery Oil Mountain."

When Mulian heard this, he immediately asked: "Has a certain Madame Liu been here?" The demon-soldiers replied: "Indeed. But she was taken away."

Mulian once more continued on his way, looking for his mother. In front of him he saw a high terrace, and on the terrace were countless sinners. At the top of the terrace were inscribed the four characters meaning "All cares and worries turn out to be empty." At the base of the terrace there were countless iron pillars, to which sinners had been tied so that their hearts could be ripped out. Demon-soldiers were standing guard, so Mulian asked them: "What kind of place is this?" The demon-soldiers replied: "This is the Hometown-Gazing Terrace, at the base of which you have the Place for Ripping Out Hearts. After mortal men die, they come here, and we make them ascend the terrace, from which they can look around. From there they will see, as if before their very eyes, their wives and daughters, riches and fields, and sons and grandsons, but one glance will be enough to show that they are all insubstantial. Although they may have left a fortune of ten thousand strings of cash to their sons and grandsons, the latter, craving pleasure and buying smiles,[73] will fritter it away until nothing is left. They have no thought of repaying their parents for their favors; all they care about is good food and fancy clothes, whoring and gambling, or getting together with friends and buddies to slaughter sentient beings—and they create nothing but evil karma. After seeing this, these souls are deeply pained in their hearts; wailing and weeping, they are then filled with remorse, regretting they did not accumulate virtue, practice cultivation, and in this way amass many merits during their lifetimes and by so doing alleviate their punishment after death. As it is said:

"Your chests may be filled with coins and silks;
However, you cannot take them with you,
But your evil karma will follow after you,
And it will be impossible to shake it off!

"Once they have had a look back at their hometowns and come down from the terrace, those who practiced goodness can leave without any further ado, but those who committed evil are tied to an iron pillar and their hearts are ripped out. The only hearts that are ripped out are the hearts that are disobedient and rebellious, the hearts that are treacherous and thieving, the hearts that are filled with lascivious lust, the hearts that slandered the Right Path and adhered to perverse teachings, the hearts that slandered monks and cursed priests, the hearts that were filled with vicious hatred, and the hearts that were filled with foolish longing: every heart that was filled with inequity is ripped out. There is a gatha that describes this, so please listen:

"Now, on the fifth Seven,[74] one ascends the terrace to have a look,
And as soon as one sees one's hometown, pain fills one's heart.
One wants to have a discussion or to chitchat with one's wife,
But the World of Light and the World of Darkness are far apart.

Even if one's compassionate grandsons have rituals performed,
The sure way to end enmity is not to slaughter sentient beings.[75]
Little do they know that the way to repay the favor of parents
Is to cultivate virtuous causes and accumulate good karma.

I urge all people to be ever attentive and never commit adultery:
Foolish longings and deceptive schemes only create evil karma.
Upon your death, the Son of Heaven King Yama will judge you:
Any heart that is filled with inequity is bound to be ripped out!"

When Mulian heard this, right away he asked: "Has a certain Madame Liu been here?" The answer was: "Indeed. But she was taken away."

Mulian continued on his way, so as to catch up with his mother. As he was walking, he saw a walled city. Above the gate of that city were displayed the three characters saying "City of Those Who Died Unjustly." Inside that city a chilly wind blew that made one shiver. Again there were demon-soldiers standing guard. Mulian asked: "Which souls are housed in the City of Those Who Died Unjustly?" The answer was: "The souls in here are all wronged souls who have been hindered by their karma. Some of them were killed by others, some of them were the victims of a flood or a fire, some of them died of rage and frustration, and some of them for some reason or another committed suicide. These souls are all brought together in this city, and only after the cycle of enmity and revenge has been cleared are they taken from here to have their cases decided on. There is a gatha that describes this, so please listen:

"The karma of souls in the City of Those Who Died Unjustly is heavy;
Caught up in karmic causes, they were brought to the World of Darkness.
When all wrongs have been revenged and all feuds are played out,
Only then will they appear before King Yama, whose laws are strict.
     However, if what we are dealing with is a loyal minister or a filial son,
After he dies, he will immediately be raised to the ranks of the gods,
And he will be spared having to dwell and linger in this somber city,
Proving that retribution in the World of Darkness accords with deeds."

Mulian asked: "Has a certain Madame Liu been here?" The answer was: "Indeed. A few days ago she passed by. But Oxhead and Horseface immediately took her away, beating her with cudgels and whips."

Upon hearing this, Mulian continued on his way. He then saw a place where people had been tied to pillars by yakshas and little demons who were sawing them in half! Mulian asked: "What kind of crime did these sinners commit in the World of Light that they are tortured like this?" The demon-soldiers replied: "When they were alive, they liked to compose lewd lyrics and sing racy songs. When having a play performed in honor of the gods, they refused to choose plays about loyalty, filial piety, chastity, and righteousness but instead would always pick plays about romantic affairs and perverse adulteries. Because the men and women who watched these plays were moved and deluded and mistook illusion for reality, they could no longer uphold their chastity and keep their righteousness intact. After they die, those sorts of people come here to suffer this torture. There is a gatha that describes this, so please listen:

"The punishment of dismemberment by sawing is truly heartrending;
Those who are sawed in two are people who while alive did wrong.
When putting on plays in honor of the gods, they used obscene songs,[76]
And the men and women who were watching were moved and deluded.
     Also, widows who did not uphold their chastity but married once again:
Such women are taken here so we can saw their bodies into two halves.

Know that the best way to avoid suffering the punishment of the saw
Is never once to talk of perverse adultery or lewd passions and desires."

Upon hearing this, Mulian immediately asked: "Has a certain Madame Liu been here?" The answer was: "Indeed. But she was led away."

Mulian again hastened on to find his mother. He then saw demon-soldiers who were opening the chests and cutting up the bellies, extracting the tongues and ripping out the guts of sinners who had been tied up or shackled—it was too frightful for words! Mulian asked: "What kind of sins did these people commit in the World of Light?" The demon-soldiers said: "Those whose tongues are extracted and whose guts are ripped out in the World of Light are ones who used their talent at writing with the brush to deceive officials and bamboozle superiors. With their smart mouths and glib tongues they could argue both sides of a case, turn white into black, and spread lies and slander, and by so doing, they created the evil karma of the mouth. They slandered the virtuous and the good, and with their sweet and honeyed words, they tricked people out of their money. Those whose chests are opened and bellies cut up, in the World of Light were single monks and unattached priests who deluded people with their perverse Way. They refined red mercury,[77] treating it as their greatest treasure, and indulged in their lewd desires. They falsely claimed to be founding teachers, but their heterodox teachings ruined people's lives. Others were bandits and robbers who committed arson and robbery, and yet others burned down mountain forests, causing the sentient beings in them to perish at their hands. As punishment they are sent down here to undergo this torture. There is a gatha that describes this, so please listen:

"The evil karma created in the world comes from their mouths
Because they could talk black into white as well as true into false.
They slandered the virtuous and good, seduced and tricked them,
So it is fitting that their tongues be extracted, their guts ripped out.
They called themselves teachers and founders, deceiving people,
And practicing as well the Chan of unattached monks and priests.
Engaging in sexual combat, they realized their lascivious desires:[78]
Which is why we open their chests, cut up their stuffed bellies!"[79]

Upon hearing this, Mulian asked: "Has a certain Madame Liu been here?" The demon-soldiers said: "Indeed. But she has been taken away."

Upon hearing this, Mulian hurried on to find his mother. He next saw a place ahead of him where demon-soldiers were binding up female sinners, putting them in a press, and squeezing them until their blood flowed out in all directions. Mulian asked: "What sin did these women commit?" The demon-soldiers replied: "In the World of Light they were filled with lewd desires. Even though they could not themselves produce sons or daughters, still they were jealous and prohibited their husbands from taking a concubine.[80] After they died, they were sent down here to undergo this torture. There is a gatha that describes this, so please listen:

"This hell of iron plates truly wounds the heart with great pain:
Women who were wives in the World of Light are crushed here.
Filled with lascivious desire but unable to give birth to children,
They were jealous and refused to let their men take a concubine.
    Not to continue the ancestral sacrifices is a crime against filiality;[81]
That's why they undergo this punishment in the World of Darkness.
If you want to avoid the pain of being crushed in hell by this press,
Rid yourself of all forms of jealousy and cultivate the heart-mind."

Upon hearing this, Mulian asked: "Has a certain Madame Liu been here?" The demon-soldiers replied: "Indeed. But she was led away by Oxhead and Horseface, who were beating her so much that she wept and wailed, wailed and wept."

Now when our Mulian
    Heard them say
        That his mother had been taken away,
He could not stop
    His tears
        From gushing from his eyes in a flood.
He beat his breast
    And stamped the earth,
        Weeping and crying without any end.
He cried out:

"My dear mother,
    How overwhelming is my sadness and pain!
Your son has failed
    To catch up with you,
        And he cries out from the pain in his heart!
When I catch up with you,
    I will take your place—,
        The only fitting and proper thing for me to do!"

After Mulian was done weeping, he continued on his way. He then saw a mountain, and on that mountain there were no end of steel swords, sharper than anything in this world! All around there were souls of pigs and goats and buffaloes and horses who were urging the minor ghosts and yakshas to force the sinners up this mountain of swords. The cries of suffering were too terrible to bear. So he immediately asked: "What are the sins for which they were condemned to this Sword Mountain?" The answer was: "When these sinners were in the World of Light, they made and sold fake medicines and, in so doing, killed people; they also made other fake articles in order to cheat people out of their money. There are also people who incited others to get involved in lawsuits, seduced others to go whoring and gambling, created dissension among relatives, broke up the marriages of others, or had affairs with the wives of others, in this way ruining these women's reputations. After they died, they were condemned to the suffering of having to climb Sword Mountain. There is a gatha that describes this:

"The sufferings of the hell of Sword Mountain are indescribable.
All cheats and crooks from the World of Light are executed here:
Those who sell fake medicine and thereby deceive simple folks
And those who use devious schemes to ruin a woman's honor.
    Their thousands of scheming tricks result in many bankruptcies;
In a myriad of evil ways they prey on widows and on the poor.
When sinning souls of this type arrive in the World of Darkness,
They're bound to suffer this torment here on Sword Mountain."

Upon hearing this, Mulian asked: "Has a certain Madame Liu been here?" The answer was: "Indeed! But she has been led away."

Mulian continued on his way, looking for his mother. He then saw a village with not a single human being in it. It was filled with vicious dogs that were barking and howling and snapping at the sinners. Some dogs were dragging the people by their calves; others were biting their hands or their heads or their backs. He saw these souls weeping and crying, crying and weeping. Demon-soldiers stood alongside serving as guards, and Mulian immediately asked them: "What kind of sinners are these being bitten by these vicious dogs?" The demon-soldiers answered: "These male and female sinners conducted affairs in secret chambers, discussed the bedroom affairs of others, despised and hated Heaven and Earth, did not worship the gods, and did not treasure paper upon which there were written characters.[82] After they die, they come here, where they are attacked by these vicious dogs. There is a gatha that describes this, so please listen:

"From the day they are born, these evil dogs look more like tigers
As they rush at you, baring their fangs and spreading their claws.
When you were alive, your outrageous acts frightened Heaven and Earth;
All you wanted was to have affairs and have sex with married women.
    Since you broke up the marriages of others, your karma is heavy—
You didn't bother to preserve the written traces of ancient Sages.
When your soul happens to pass by this place on its journey,
These evil dogs will devour you—with just a snap of their jaws."

Upon hearing this, Mulian asked: "Has a certain Madame Liu been here?" The answer was: "Indeed. But she has been led away."

Mulian continued on his way, looking for his mother. He had not gone very far when he again saw some little demons who were putting sinners into a mortar and pounding them till their skin split and their flesh was pulverized into something like rice powder. He immediately asked: "What kind of sin did these sinners commit in the World of Light?" The answer was: "These people in the World of Light dug up graves and used the bones to make objects for use, which they then sold to other people. Some of them made medicinal mixtures that caused people to lose consciousness. On top of that, they used tampered balances and altered measures, were unfilial to their fathers and mothers, interfered with people making donations and slandered people who recited the name of the Buddha, kept the fast, and cultivated their minds. They didn't believe in the operation of karma or in the practice of goodness. That's why they are condemned to be tortured here. There is a gatha that describes this, so please listen:

"The hell of mortar and pestle is determined by prior karma;
Retribution is clear and bright—it certainly is the truth!
They dig up graves and steal the bones or mix medicine;
They don't care for their parents, treat them as strangers!
　　On top of that, they slander those who make donations;
They don't believe in cultivating the mind, purifying the body.
When these kinds of souls arrive in the earth prison,
They are pounded like rice, until they become new!"[83]

When Mulian heard this, he immediately asked: "Has a certain Madame Liu been here?" The demon-soldiers replied: "Indeed. But she has been led away."

Mulian continued on his way, looking for his mother. As he was walking, he caught sight of a house from which smoke was rising, and heat was spreading all around. But when he looked inside, there was not a single stove. Instead, there were several hollow bronze pillars, each as wide as two arm spans. These pillars were filled with burning charcoal, the flames of which made the pillars red-hot. The demon-soldiers would tie the sinners to these pillars to be roasted, and in an instant skin and flesh would drop off, leaving nothing but charred bones. When Mulian saw this, he was truly terrified. He immediately asked: "What are the sins these souls have committed?" The answer was: "In the World of Light because they liked to eat exquisite dishes, they would place living animals over a roaring fire and roast them till they were well done. Later they would add spices and eat them, with no regard for sentient beings. They didn't believe words that exhorted people to do good and secretly thought of ways to get people to break the fast. After they die, they suffer the punishment of being roasted. There is a gatha that describes this, so please listen:

"This punishment of the roasting pillars is extremely gruesome:
Your living body tied to a pillar—your bones charred and yellow.
When alive you roasted animals because you liked the good taste;

Now that you're dead, it's your turn to be roasted and then eaten.
    You increased your evil karma by getting people to break the fast;
You didn't believe the words of goodness, an unforgivable crime.
If you want to avoid the punishment of being roasted after you die,
You must treasure all sentient beings and also enter Buddha's hall."

When Mulian heard this, he immediately asked: "Has a certain Madame Liu been here?" The demon-soldiers replied: "Indeed. But she has been led away."

    Mulian continued on his way, looking for his mother. As he was walking, he reached a place where he saw demon-soldiers feeding sinful souls upside down into a grinder as little demons turned the wheel. He immediately asked: "What kind of sin did these people commit in the World of Light?" The answer was: "In the World of Light they did not believe in the Buddha and his Dharma, they did not venerate the Three Jewels, and they slandered the true teaching. Abusing their power, they committed evil, bullying and oppressing the good and virtuous. They plotted to get the riches and fields of others and bought the wives and concubines of others. They cheated orphans and maltreated widows, envied the rich and reviled the poor. When they borrowed money, they did not pay it back. They secretly schemed to deceive the weak and did nothing but bad-mouth others. That's why they suffer this retribution. There is a gatha that describes this, so please listen:

"The sufferings of the hell of mills is truly beyond endurance;
As soon as these sinful ghosts arrive, their guts are shattered.
In the World of Light they foolishly committed improper acts,
Of which in the World of Darkness not a single thing stays hidden.
    Their bodies are stuffed upside down into the mouth of the mill;
Their skin and flesh are turned into pulp, their bones into frost.
Want to avoid the sufferings of the mill in the World of Darkness?
Quickly recite the name of the Buddha and be loyal and good!"

When Mulian heard this, he asked: "Has my mother, Madame Liu, been here?" The demon-soldiers said: "She came here a few days ago, but this morning she was led away."

    When Mulian heard these words, he immediately continued on his way, looking for his mother. Very soon he arrived at the teahouse of Granny Meng. When he lifted his eyes and had a look, he saw a great hall with a terrace on either side. On both sides there were stoves, and several hundred side-rooms were situated all around. He saw countless numbers of men and women, some going in, and some coming out. He also saw endless numbers of men and women sitting there, drinking tea. Mulian asked: "What kind of place is this?" The demon-soldiers answered: "This is called Granny Meng's Cottage. She has collected all of the herbs of the whole wide world and combined them to produce a brew that resembles wine but yet is different. That's why it is called the brew that confuses the soul. All the people who have committed evil while in the world are made to drink this, after which they lose knowledge of their former lives. If there are sacred sutras, words of the Buddha, or divine dharanis[84] that people recited assiduously at first but later started to neglect, we immediately record the four characters meaning 'original appearance' and then take these people back to the World of Light—some of these people die after a few days, and some pass away after a few months. Once they have forgotten the true words or Dharma phrases, we summon them again to the World of Darkness and dispatch them to the different hells to be tortured. There is a gatha that describes this, so please listen:

"In the World of Darkness there is Granny Meng's Cottage,
Where this restorative tonic is made that confuses the soul.
If root and practice are solid, then the knowledge remains,
And there's no harm in passing through this special spot.
　　But if you've ruined yourself by not practicing cultivation,
You will probably end up in the earth prison forever.
When orphan souls who committed sins are brought here,
They're made to drink the brew and then see King Yama!"

Upon hearing this, Mulian asked: "Has a certain Madame Liu been here?" The demon-soldiers replied: "Indeed. But she has been led away."

Mulian asked: "What kind of place is this?" The demon-soldiers replied: "This is the bridge across the Alas River. Unparalleled in height, it is eighty-one rods long but only one and three-tenths of an inch wide." He saw the demon-soldiers beating those treacherous, greedy, devilish, deceitful, violent, and cruel souls with iron cudgels till they wept and cried, cried and wept, as they were forced to go up onto the bridge. They took only a few steps before they tumbled down into the waters below to be grabbed and devoured by a frenzy of poisonous snakes and other evil creatures. But he also saw how those people who had been filial, brotherly, loyal, true to their word, decent and righteous, and knowing shame were able to walk firmly and safely, as if borne on a cloud, led across by immortal lads and immortal maidens carrying banners and parasols! Mulian heaved a sigh, saying: "So what has been told is not a lie! There is a gatha that describes this:

"On the bridge across the Alas the divine judgment is clear!
It's all because you hoarded money while you were alive:
Coveting goods and coveting money, not a moment of rest,
Wasting your time for the sake of children and grandsons.
    You created evil karma to be repaid in the World of Darkness;
Because of your heavy karma you drown under the bridge.
Evil creatures and poisonous snakes grab and devour you;
Fish and shrimp, turtles and crabs there block your way.
    Filial sons and loyal men there are guided by immortals;
Because of their merit and virtue, the ghosts respect them.
Some are taken to the Western Paradise to live in glory;
Others who delighted in goodness practice cultivation again.
    In a heart as bright as a mirror no delusion can be detected,
And in a nature firm like a mountain no evil karma is found.
So let me advise you, a future ghost in the World of Light:
Make sure not to be trapped by wrongs when you are here!"

After Mulian had done heaving a sigh, he continued on his way, looking for his mother. Suddenly he came to a large wheel that was endlessly spinning around while some low-rank soldiers were standing guard. Mulian asked: "What kind of place is this?" The demon-soldiers replied: "This is the Revolving Wheel of the Six Paths." Mulian then asked: "What is meant by the 'Wheel of the Six Paths'?" The demon-soldiers said: "The Six Paths are rebirth as a rich and noble person, a poor and lowly person, or an animal born from a womb, born from an egg, born from moisture, or born by magic. The revolving wheel may deposit you as a human being in the world, or it may leave you as a ghost in the World of Darkness. Also, rich and noble may be turned into poor and lowly. At other times animals born from the womb or an egg are turned into animals born from moisture or by magic. 'Revolving' means that you leave and then come back again. That's why it is said: 'You may have a thousand clever tricks, / but you remain caught inside the revolving wheel!'

The first path is the Path of Gold. Those who are deposited here by the wheel become high officials and eminent nobles and serve as rulers and magistrates. This is because in an earlier life their merit was high and their virtue expansive. They had seen through the Red Dust[85] and, knowing that they were caught in the revolving wheel, always practiced good deeds and established all kinds of hidden merits.

The second path is the Path of Silver. Those who are deposited here by the wheel will be dressed in silks and satins and will dwell in water pavilions and shady kiosks.[86] This is because when they were in the world they dared not commit evil, were always on their guard, were circumspect in their actions, and lived a pure and unblemished life.

The third path is the Path of Jade. Those who are deposited here by the wheel become the hunchbacked and handicapped. This is because while in the world their merits were few and their faults were many. Even though they are given a human shape, they will have to beg for food on the streets or, if they are blind, go from house to house, crying for mercy—to have use of your feet and your eyes is the heavenly way!

The fourth path is the Path of Bronze. Those who are deposited here by the wheel will be born without their human shape and be transformed into animals with horns and covered in fur. This is because in an earlier life they cheated people out of their wealth and did not pay back the money they borrowed. They are turned into animals so as to make restitution. Others were haughty and arrogant while in the world and regarded themselves as being above everyone else. This is why they are turned into animals. They would start cursing you as soon as they opened their mouths, and they would threaten to beat you as soon as they raised their arms, but now they do not even dare raise their heads. Their food is foul and dirty, and they sleep in foul and dirty places.

The fifth path is the Path of Stone. Those who are deposited here by the wheel will be born from eggs, and their bodies will be covered in moist feathers. At the sight of a human being they will be filled with fear and fright and fly up high to make their escape. Their lives and their fates are in the hand of others. This is because while in the world they relied on their wealth and power to act arbitrarily—with just one hand they blocked out Heaven![87] And in their eyes, not a single person in the whole wide world counted for anything. Others transgressed status distinctions in committing adultery or ignored generational distinctions and engaged in lewd acts. Therefore they are transformed into birds so as to make restitution.

The sixth path is the Path of Water. Those who are deposited here by the wheel will be creatures born from moisture. This is because when they were living in the world the total number of their sins reached a maximum. Others made a meal out of fish and shrimp or else made a living from them. For this reason they themselves are transformed into fish and shrimp so as to make restitution by being roasted or deep-fried. This is why *The Great Learning* says: "Any wealth obtained by improper means will be lost in the same way."[88] Retribution in the World of Darkness does not make even the slightest mistake. Here is a passage in ten-syllable lines, so please listen to me."

These demon-soldiers
     Replied as follows:
          "Dear reverend Mulian, please listen:
Once you have crossed over
     The bridge that spans the Alas,
          The six paths take different directions.
Those who practiced goodness
     Will, because of retribution,
          Live in blessed peace and prosperity;
Those who committed evil
     Will find out once here
          That not the slightest mistake is made!

Those of the first class
     Will walk the Path of Gold,
          To be turned into people rich and noble;
They will be high officials,
     Achieve highest rank,
          And enjoy many myriads of emoluments.

On their heads they will wear
> The raven-black hat,
>> Inspiring awe and fear in the population;
Their bodies will be clad
> In the ritual court gown;
>> Wide jade belts will circle their waists.
When they assume their offices,
> They'll have a thousand rooms
>> In houses with large courts and high halls—
And all of which will have been,
> By command of the emperor,
>> Constructed for them by the common people.
When they travel outside,
> They will be carried by eight men,
>> Surrounded by a cortege in front and behind.
They will seem to be just like
> Living gods and immortals,
>> Truly enjoying "free and easy roaming"!
Do you want to know
> From where their blessings
>> Originate and from what causes they arise?
It's all because
> In an earlier life they
>> Accumulated merits and cultivated this karma.
Some aided the poor
> And gave to the needy—
>> The civic-minded work of helping the people;
Others donated tea
> And distributed medicines
>> To poor people wandering through the streets.
Some of them restored
> For hundreds of years
>> The dangerous roads through the mountains;
Others again constructed
> For the benefit of millions
>> Bridges on the most traveled and essential roads.

Some of them established
　　Homes for the elderly—
　　　　Their chaste filiality was officially recognized;
Others made brick ovens
　　For burning paper with writing—
　　　　An expression of reverence toward the Sages.
Some of them had Buddha-statues
　　Gilded with gold foil,
　　　　Increasing the visitors' respect and veneration;
Others restored temples
　　And Buddhist monasteries,
　　　　Ensuring the survival of famous establishments.
Some of them became physicians,
　　Studied the extension of life,
　　　　And distributed ginseng and other medicines;
Others printed books
　　And gave them away freely
　　　　So they would circulate throughout the world;
By inspiring and awakening
　　Ignorant and deluded people,
　　　　They practiced the Way on behalf of Heaven—
Having perfected
　　The karma of millions,
　　　　They enjoy Great Peace without any disturbance!

The second path
　　Is the Path of Silver:
　　　　This kind of men and this kind of women
Will wear either silks
　　Or the roughest linen—
　　　　The quality of their clothes is different for each.
This is because
　　In an earlier life they
　　　　Planted a root of goodness that was very large,
And that is the reason why
　　They don't have to worry

Whether or not they will have clothes to wear.
Some of them behaved
As loyal and solid persons,
Always honest and reliable in each little detail;
Others smoked little
And also spent little,
Living a simple live without being corrupted.
Some of them were in their contacts
With friends and relatives
Pure and unblemished in their ritual relations;
Others kept to the fast,
Recited the name of the Buddha,
And showed the Tathagata all due reverence.
Some of them managed their households
Just as was done in the old days
And did not change any established patterns:
Glorious in the past,
Well-to-do in the present,
Bringing glory and renown to their ancestors.
Some treasured grain
As they would costly pearls,
Not allowing a single kernel to go to waste;
Others treasured firewood
As they would precious cinnamon,
Not willing to burn it without a good reason.
Some served their parents
Just as did Old Laizi,[89]
The very perfection of goodness and love;
Others were in their marriages
Just like Liang Hong [and Meng Guang]—
She lifted the tray just as high as her eyebrows.[90]
Some of them were as brothers
Just like the Jiang family—
These brothers at night shared a single blanket;[91]
Others were as business partners
To be compared with

Guan Zhong and Bao Shuya dividing the gold.[92]
Some of them would in speaking
    Never in the slightest
        Deceive or bamboozle other people;
Others would when working
    Take on the extra load
        When other people were just taking it easy.
Some would all their lives
    Cede to others in plowing
        And cede as well in determining boundaries;[93]
Others would when meeting people
    Make sure to guide and convert them,
        Unwilling to lose even a single person to the world.

The third level
    Arrive at the Path of Jade,
        Deposited there by the working of the whirling wheel;
They are the handicapped:
    These are the people
        Whose so-called six roots are neither complete nor whole.[94]
If you should ask me
    The causes or the reasons for
        Their six roots being damaged and suffering diseases,
It is all because
    They have reaped what they sowed:
        They did not protect their Heaven-given true nature.
People with healthy eyes
    Should read only
        Books about the Way of Confucius and Mencius,
But they loved to read
    About heterodox ideas,
        And they ignored the proper rites and norms.
People with healthy ears
    Should listen only to
        The local notables expounding the community pact,[95]
And they should not listen

To strings and pipes,
> Which turn their thoughts to affairs of married folks.
People with healthy noses
> Should desire only to smell
>> Plum and orchid, bamboo and chrysanthemum,
And they should not desire to smell
> Girls who steal the perfume,[96]
>> Who use rouge and powder and dot their cherry lips.
People with discerning tongues
> Should desire only to discuss
>> Loyalty and filial piety, chastity and righteousness,
And they should not discuss
> Tales that scare people
>> With miracles, feats of strength, scandals, and gods.[97]
People with sound bodies
> Have the obligation to exert themselves
>> To repay the dynasty for its favors with pure loyalty,
And on no account should they,
> Just like a flying moth,
>> Singe their bodies by rushing into the flame.
People who keep their wits
> And have no foolish thoughts
>> Will be placid and bland and without desires,
But those who lose their wits
> In a flash of rage
>> Will forget both themselves and their relatives.
And then you have those
> Foolish and ignorant people
>> Who obey their wives and disobey their mothers,
Without giving a thought
> To how their mothers raised them
>> And the many kinds of bitter pain this entailed.
Because of this,
> They are lacking
>> One or two of the six roots,
So they will ponder

The prior fruit and later causes
    In their own earlier existences.

Those in the fourth track
    Arrive at the Path of Bronze,
        Where they manifest as donkeys and mules.
This is all because
    In an earlier existence
        They cheated people out of money and goods.
While serving as officials,
    They were greedy for bribes and kickbacks
        And engaged in all kinds of corruption and deceit;
Once they had your money,
    You would win your court case,
        Because they would then lean in your favor.
Being yamen officers,
    They were all intent on money
        And would happily beat you to death,
But once they got their money,
    They would stop their beating
        And allow you to do as you pleased.
And if they were students,
    They would not even know how
        To correctly punctuate the Four Books[98]
And would even say things like
    'It won't bring in much money.'
        How can that type of person ever face Heaven?
And if they were laborers,
    They'd come to their employer's house
        And would show no signs of being lackadaisical,
But once you gave them their money,
    They would show a different face
        And refuse to budge or put out any more effort.
And if they were pawnshop owners,
    They would be all smiles
        When you went to visit their establishments,

But if you wanted some money,
>
> You would not get even a penny—
>
>> They just stood by with hands in their sleeves.

Then you also will have

> Those down-and-out people
>
>> Who are always complaining and arguing—

Right becomes wrong,

> Wrong turns to right,
>
>> As they turn everything upside down and awry.

Then you also will have

> Those dog butchers,
>
>> Who kill and slaughter all kinds of animals,

And then you have those

> Professional hunters,
>
>> Who are accustomed to enjoying fowl and venison.

When these kinds of souls

> Arrive in the World of Darkness,
>
>> King Yama will make inquiries into their cases,

And he will order the assistant judges

> To check the registers of sins,
>
>> And they will be punished for all their evil deeds.

Demons will be ordered to take them

> Up to Karmascope Terrace,
>
>> Where they will be told to review their own acts,

And then they will be taken up to

> Hometown-Gazing Terrace
>
>> To have one last look at their homes and relatives.

Then their heads are changed,

> And their faces replaced:
>
>> Now they sport horns and are covered with fur!

And only when they have fully

> Repaid their old debts,
>
>> Will they have cleared away their evil karma.

The fifth path

> Is the Path of Stone,

Where you'll be deposited by the revolving wheel:
There you will find
    Evil and violent souls
        Being transformed into flying birds.
In their earlier lives,
    When they were humans,
        They did not cultivate goodness at all—
All those birds
    That are born from eggs,
        They'd capture and catch them while fully alive!
Some of them would
    Kill with a bullet
        One of a loving couple of mandarin ducks—
The surviving bird
    Would cry piteously
        Now it was bereft of its lifelong companion![99]
Others would fire guns,
    And in this way kill
        Mother birds in the third month of spring—
The chicks in their nest
    Would be unaware
        That their mother had left for the World of Darkness.
There would also be the man
    Who caught a single goose
        And put it in a cage at the back of his boat—
He would see up in the sky
    A single goose
        That followed the boat and tearfully cried.
And the goose in the cage
    Would stretch out its neck
        And cry out loudly at the top of its lungs,
And that goose in the sky
    Would then fly down to the boat,
        And they'd cry out together, their necks intertwined.
And then you have those
    Naughty and willful boys

Who climbed up the trees to steal the eggs,
And when the parents returned to the nest,
Only to find the eggs no longer there,
They'd die of grief, weeping at the foot of the tree.
In Suzhou there was once
A certain Wang Dalin,
Who, upon seeing boys catch insects to play with,
Would give them some money
To buy and release them,
Fostering and nurturing a compassionate mind.
Near Lake Tai there was once
A certain Shen Wenbao,
Also a man who loved to practice goodness:
He bought oh so many
Creatures to be released,
And later he was spared during an epidemic.
If you do not believe me,
Just consider the case
Of a certain Mr. Wei, a peasant from Yixing:
While he was lying on his bed,
Birds without number
Came and pecked at his chest until it bled.[100]

Then you have the sixth tier:
That is the Path of Water,
Where you may be deposited by the turning wheel.
Now in the water
All kinds of creatures
Are without exception born from the moisture.
Some people use
The tubes of Lord Thunder,[101]
Fill them with powder, and scour out the river,
But the blasting brings death
To all kinds of water creatures,
Sons and grandsons of many generations.
Some people stand on the bank

And using an iron trident
    Spear the fish and kill them this way,
While others wade in the river
    And using nets of all kinds
        Frighten the fish into frantic and frenzied flight.
Others fish for eels
    And angle for frogs, and
        Trap turtles and catch tortoises,
In all cases using bait
    That entices these creatures to nibble
        Till the hook protrudes from their lips.
If these people
    Don't do these things for money,
        Then they do it just to satisfy their own palates.
How can they be so cruel
    As to create this enmity
        Between themselves and these kinds of creatures?
You have to understand
    That each class of animals
        Also has its own ruler and its own head—
Those born from a womb
    Call the lion their king,
        Those born from an egg call the phoenix most high,
Those born from moisture
    Call the Dragon King
        Of the four oceans their master—
So if you hurt any of them,
    The king of their species
        Will lodge a complaint with King Yama.
Master Kong's
    Heart was filled with humanity,
        And he would not kill without a valid reason;[102]
Zheng Zichan
    Made no distinctions between animals
        And so also displayed the root of understanding.[103]
Su Dongpo

Kept to a long fast,
>All because of the precept against killing,[104] and
Bai Letian
>Released captured creatures,
>>In this way making an effort to keep them alive.[105]
Of these four gentlemen,
>One dwells in heaven,
>>While three of them dwell in the World of Darkness.[106]
The retribution of good and evil
>Has since ancient times
>>Clearly been recorded in written documents.
These kinds of people
>Are deposited by the wheel
>>On the Path of Water, there to be reborn,
And only then
>Will they wake up
>>From the heavy slumber of their spring dream!"[107]

When Mulian heard this, he then asked a question as follows:
"I've visited each of the hells but still not found Madame Liu."
Observing the sufferings of these souls in all of these hells,
He was moved to deliver a sermon that we all should study:

"It depends on you yourself whether you go to heaven or hell;
For good and for evil clearly seek into your heart and nature.
I have traveled through all the prisons of the Ten Courts of Hell,[108]
And as I think of the cruel punishments, my tears gush down.

If you practice goodness, gods and ghosts will wait upon you,
But in the World of Darkness evil people are locked up in jail!
If riches and rank have been accumulated in an earlier life,
You will enjoy unexcelled prosperity and glory in the present.

Use this opportunity to cleanse away any remaining pollution;
Seek out an enlightened teacher to show you the Cinnabar Hill.[109]
The wide gate is open to the Great Way of a Single Thread[110]—
The myriads of dharmas in the end all depend on cultivation![111]

As to the world of the Way: make sure to observe the One;
Make sure to study the classical texts of the Three Teachings.[112]

And on no account can you create the pollution of evil karma—
The beautiful sights of the Red Dust are but a bubble of water!

Don't worry about gold and silver piled as high as the Dipper:[113]
Once Impermanence arrives, no storehouses will be of any use.
The only things you can take with you are merits and vices—
In front of the karmascope you will see and rue your sins.

All of your virtues and sins will there be manifested clearly;
King Yama has a face of iron and will show you no mercy.
Then it will be too late to practice cultivation, even if you wanted,
And you will greatly regret that you refused to practice at first.

Don't say the poor and needy are unable to accumulate merit;
The gate of goodness is large and wide: it depends on practice!
Those who come across aggressive men involved in a fight,
Make every effort to urge them to stop and solve their issues.

Those who encounter people going in the wrong direction,
Point out the road to them clearly so that they will not get lost.
Those who run into travelers who are whoring and gambling,
Counsel them against these flashy pursuits that demean them.

Those who encounter people who release captured creatures,
Remember this, accumulate virtue and leave a fine reputation.
Encountering people who practice virtue, they support their efforts;
Finding pleasure in helping others, they sponsor virtuous projects.

It is up to you to accomplish all such kinds of good deeds—
When your merit is accomplished, you will rise above others.
By doing good deeds in secret, you benefit sons and grandsons,
And you yourself in your next rebirth also will be free of worry.

When you go to the World of Darkness, you'll not be anxious:
You will be allowed to roam freely through all of those prisons,
With no need at all to fear the demons Oxhead and Horseface,
For they will most politely fold their arms and lower their heads.

The Wheel of the Six Paths assigns each his place as it turns;
It determines the pains and the pleasures in your next rebirth.
The womb, an egg, or moisture—it all depends on your actions;
Change and rebirth, rebirth and change—revolving without end!

People of this world, I urge you to see through its semblance:
Keep the fast, recite the name of the Buddha, and honor the gods.

Then one day, when all of your merit has been fully achieved,
You'll leap out of the cycle of rebirth—don't worry about that!"

When Mulian heard this, he quickly left to find his mother. In a blink of an eye he found that he had arrived at a city surrounded by iron walls. He immediately asked: "What kind of place is this?" The demon-soldiers replied: "Inside is the Avici Hell." "May I ask why these souls weep and cry?" "Listen to me:

"The eighteenth layer
    In the World of Darkness
        Is the Avici Hell, which is reserved for
Those who in the World of Light
    Committed acts of violence
        And were evil and vicious people.
The first kind of
    Such evildoers
        Resented Heaven and also hated Earth;
They beat up good people,
    Cursed the friends of the Way,
        And showed no respect to the gods.
The second kind of
    Such evildoers
        Were unfilial toward both their parents;
They beat up their fathers and mothers,
    Cursed their superiors,
        And were rebellious, quarrelsome people.
The third kind of
    Such evildoers
        Killed people and also committed arson;
Stealing other people's
    Riches and treasures,
        They committed manslaughter and murder.
The fourth kind of
    Such evildoers
        Had sex with others' wives and daughters;

They spread about scandals,
> Instigated lawsuits,
>> And ruined the happy marriages of others.
The fifth kind of
> Such evildoers
>> Broke the fast and violated the precepts,
Which is why they've been thrown
> Into the Avici Hell,
>> Never for all eternity to be reborn in any form!"

Mulian asked: "Is Madame Liu also there inside?" The demon-soldiers said: "Yes, she is there."

When Mulian heard that she was there inside, he raised the meditation staff in his hand and pounded on the gate of this prison with all his force! It was as if the sky had collapsed and the earth had been rent: with a tremendous crash the gate of this earth prison was opened up wide. The orphan souls inside had only one thought, that they had all been pardoned by an act of grace, and they came pouring out like a flight of geese! Mulian was concerned only about finding his mother and did not worry about these souls escaping. Although the soldiers guarding the gate refused to allow Mulian to go inside, they could not keep the souls from streaming out. When they saw that the situation was untenable, there was nothing they could do but flee as well to the World of Light, where they were reborn![114] Mulian then caught sight of his mother, wearing a cangue and shackled in chains, as she walked out through the gate of her prison. When mother and son met each other, they shouted and screamed and wept most piteously. There is a gatha that describes this:

The reverend Mulian then saw his own dear mother:
In hemp robes, her iron chains clanging without end.
Her body was as skinny as firewood—a bag of bones—
Her hair a mess, her feet unshod, and she was awash in tears.
> Wearing a cangue, shackled in chains as a punishment,
She crawled through dirt and dust and walked on foot.
Seeing this, he raised his staff that showed no mercy
And shattered open all these instruments of torture.

Flinging down his begging bowl and meditation staff,
He grasped his mother tightly, and he wept and wailed.
When Madame Liu saw her son, she also wept in pain—
"Only now am I filled with regret at not having practiced!

I thought only humans were meant to eat pigs and goats—
I didn't know there would be redress in the World of Darkness!
Had I known early on that I would undergo such suffering,
I would not have broken the precept against eating meat!"

Let's talk no more of how mother and son wept and wailed, but let's tell how the Teaching Lord of Darkness[115] in his Dark Clouds Palace and King Yama in his Senluo Hall quickly heard about the gate of hell being opened with a loud bang. The former did not know who had stealthily opened the gate of hell, so he ordered King Yama to go there, the demons Oxhead and Horseface behind him. When King Yama arrived at the gate of the Avici Hell, he saw that the prison gate had been opened wide and that all the souls had escaped and that Mulian and Madame Liu were weeping and wailing. King Yama shouted: "What kind of wild monk are you?" Mulian replied: "I am no wild monk!" King Yama said: "On whose authority did you enter the earth prison and open this gate yourself? You've allowed all these orphan souls to escape, and you still say you are not wild? If you want to be still wilder, the Teaching Lord of Darkness of the Senluo Hall will give you the opportunity to act even wilder!" He then ordered Oxhead and Horseface to arrest the monk. Upon hearing this, Mulian recited words of truth, and Oxhead and Horseface did not dare go near him. The Kings of Yama's Ten Courts became even more enraged and ordered Madame Liu locked up in the earth prison. She was dragged by some and hauled by others back into the earth prison to undergo suffering. Mulian then composed the following gatha:

The Kings of Yama's Ten Courts are filled with rage and anger,
And together they rush forward to arrest me, the reverend Mulian!
Those who drag me, drag me, and those who haul me, haul me,
Those who push me, push me, and those who pull me, pull me!
  Qingti has once again been taken to the Avici Hell, and the gate
Has been tightly shut and locked by the minor demons and yakshas.

My meditation staff and begging bowl have been taken away—
And in the Senluo Hall of King Yama I will be sentenced!

The Kings of the Ten Courts brought Mulian to the Dark Clouds Palace.
When his father, Fu Xiang, saw him, he ran down the steps, crying: "My
son, why did you take it upon yourself to open the gate of hell?" Mulian
kowtowed and said: "My dear father, here you enjoy your free and easy
pleasures without a thought for my mother undergoing sufferings in the
earth prison!" Fu Xiang replied: "Your mother's case was decided by the
Kings of Yama's Ten Courts. How can I do anything for her? The Yama
Kings told me: 'You cultivated your own blessings, and she created her own
punishment.'" Having said this, together they entered the palace. The Yama
Kings reported to the bodhisattva [Teaching Lord of Darkness]: "It turned
out to be the son of Fu Xiang who on his own authority opened the gate
of hell and allowed the orphan souls to escape." The bodhisattva shouted:
"Mulian, without permission you entered the Underworld, and on your own
authority you opened the prison gate, releasing the orphaned souls. What is
your justification?" Mulian then addressed the bodhisattva, saying:

Mulian knelt down on the ground, in the dust and the grime,
And piteously begged the bodhisattva to show some mercy:
"It is a constant rule that if one son enters the Buddha's Way,
Then nine generations of his ancestors will be reborn in heaven.
     It was only because my mother's love and favors were so great
That, carrying the sutras, I went to visit the World-Honored One.
Considering that my merits were complete, the Buddha then
Taught me how to find my mother in the World of Darkness.
     He gave me a cassock and bowl, and a meditation staff
With which to open up this joyless land and save my mother.
Dear Bodhisattva, if you still are not willing to believe me,
Just have a look at these objects—they are my evidence!"

The bodhisattva King Ksitigarbha said: "The meditation staff the Buddha
gave you can open the thirty-three heavens up above and the seventy-two
courts here below. The Buddha gave it to you to save your mother. He told
you to place the meditation staff on the gate and lightly tap it once! Then,

once the prison gate was open, you were to go and stand next to the gate and call for your mother to come out. But you opened wide the prison gate, allowing all orphan ghosts to run off to the World of Light. They all have escaped with their lives—what are we going to do about that? Now the assistant judges must immediately check to see how many orphan souls have escaped." The assistant judges checked and then reported to the bodhisattva: "In total more than eight million!" When the bodhisattva heard this, he immediately ordered Mulian to go and round them up. There is a gatha that describes this:

Mulian was not sufficiently careful in saving his mother:
He broke open the gate of hell with his meditation staff.
He allowed eight million orphan souls to escape, and
They all came back to this world to be reborn once again.
    When the Teaching Lord of Darkness learned about this,
He immediately ordered Mulian to arrest those orphan souls:
    "Your cassock, bowl, and bright pearl will stay here below,
But I will dress you up in a costume of yellow robes.
A pale-faced good person suddenly turned evil-looking:
Your face will be covered by gold—a frightening sight!"
    He ordered the demon-soldiers to close and lock the gate
And take Mulian to the Chao mansion in the World of Light.
Having received this order, the demon-soldiers took him along
And left him there at Red Wall Village in the World of Light.
    They dumped him in the Chao family's Bird Nest Grove;
He recognized the mother, chose her womb, was reborn.
I'll not say how these souls returned to the earth prison—
Listen again to the next chapter, about the monk Mulian!

PART 2

The story goes that in Red Wall Village of Zhangju County of Chaozhou in the World of Light, there lived a salt merchant by the name of Huang Zongdan.[116] His wife was Madame Tian, who had not yet borne him any child. Because the couple had no children, Zongdan had promised banners and parasols to every temple, provided monks with vegetarian meals and given them donations, and created good karma all around. One day as husband and wife were on their way back from offering incense, they passed by Bird Nest Grove. There, sitting on the ground, they saw a little baby boy dressed in yellow clothes. When Zongdan and his wife rushed toward him, the baby suddenly turned into a puff of fresh air and disappeared. Husband and wife were flabbergasted, but Zongdan said to his wife: "Don't be afraid! It must be the Bodhisattva's response to our sincerity in seeking a son.[117] Heaven has sent this baby boy down to your womb!" There is a gatha that describes this:

When the couple were on their way back after prayer,
She turned out to be pregnant, to be heavy with child.
Having carried the baby for a full twenty-five months,
The child in her belly was finally ready to be born.

One day Madame Tian started to have contractions, but it took three days before she gave birth.[118] When the baby was born, Zongdan came to have a look and saw that he was two feet long with skin like gold paper. On his cheek there was a golden coin, and his brown eyebrows were one straight line; two of his teeth were crooked, and his nose had three holes; on his back were etched the eight trigrams, the seven stars appeared on his chest,[119] and his shoulders were covered in hair. Zongdan was frightened when he saw the child's evil-looking features—his wife had given birth to a monster! He suggested to his wife that they take the child and leave it somewhere, but Madame Tian refused to let go of her baby. However, Zongdan insisted, and took the child away and left him in a ditch. Frightened, the local god of the soil was stirred to action; he went out to protect the baby, which he placed in a bird's nest. That night at midnight the god of the soil went to Zongdan's home and appeared to him in a dream, ordering him to bring the baby home and raise him. After delivering his message, he left. The next day Zongdan returned to the ditch, and sure enough, he found the child and carried him home. Madame Tian was filled with joy; she nursed the baby at her breast and cradled and stroked him. The name they chose for him was Huang Chao,[120] with a style name of Tianzhu. He devoted himself to his books and went to school, where he stuffed his belly with fine writing. When he had grown up and become a man, he served his parents most filially. He also practiced the military arts. When Zongdan saw how accomplished his son was in both civil and martial arts, he was greatly pleased in his heart. There is a gatha that describes this:

Light and shadow, fast as an arrow, urge people on to age;
The sun and moon, moving like a shuttle, never once stop.
When he had grown up and become a man, at age sixteen,
He was accomplished in all hundred kinds of military arts.
  He obediently served his father and mother, now both aged,
Accomplished in civil and martial arts: famous everywhere!
He waited for the examination for the selection of students[121]
So he could sit for the test and leap across the Dragon Gate.[122]

Our story goes on to relate how Emperor Xizong[123] was enthroned in the city of Chang'an. His interior ministers reported to him: "Armed rebels have risen in all four corners, and in all eight directions the dust of war rises. The empire is in the grip of a great turmoil. You should pronounce an edict and send out announcements that you will be holding examinations in order to select students from all over the world."

When Huang Chao heard that the examinations were to be held, he told his parents that he wanted to go to Chang'an to take the test. He selected a good hour and a happy day, prepared his luggage and a horse, and took leave of his parents. He traveled by day and rested at night, and when he arrived in Chang'an, he lodged at an inn for travelers. The day the examinations were held was truly an auspicious day of the Yellow Way.[124] At the fifth watch the cannons were fired, and each and every student from all over the world dressed himself in military garb and went to the place where they were to ride horses and shoot bows. Each and every one hoped to come out number one, the head of the list! We'll not talk about the other recommended students[125] — we'll speak only of Huang Chao, who, while riding a galloping horse, hit the target with his arrow three times in a row. The chief examiner gave the order that he be selected to ascend the Golden Hall to present himself before Emperor Xizong, who, when he saw Huang Chao's violent and evil features, was so scared that his soul fled his body! Hastily the emperor pronounced an edict ordering him to descend from the Golden Hall, and Huang Chao had no choice but to retire and go away. There is a gatha that describes this:

Seeing how things were, Huang Chao's rage turned to anger:
"How I hate that stupid ruler — he cannot be called a man!
With his deluded eyes he cannot see a jade encased in gold,
And mistakenly he takes one who is loyal for a sycophant.
    Even though my appearance has from birth been vicious,
How would I even think of doing evil and becoming a rebel?
It's not true that I've harbored devious intentions from the start;
It's this stupid ruler who has forced me to usurp the dragon throne.
    If only I had three leading generals at my side to accompany me,
I'd fight my way into the palace and become the emperor myself!"
Pondering the matter from all angles, he could reach no conclusion,
And so he left Chang'an so as to turn the matter over in his mind.

Our story goes that outside the city of Chang'an there was a monastery, which was called the Hidden Plum Monastery. A resident monk of that monastery had the religious name of Liaokong.[126] One evening he went to the main hall to burn incense. He set down a glass lamp and was about to light it when he noticed that there was no oil in it. He immediately scolded his disciple, saying: "Why didn't you fill it with oil?" This acolyte replied: "But I fill it with oil every day! I have no idea who might be stealing the oil."

That night the monk hid himself in the main hall so as to watch over the lamp. At the hour of midnight he saw two demon-soldiers enter the hall carrying an earthenware jug into which they poured the oil from the lamp. The monk stepped forward and gave a loud shout, saying: "What kind of monsters are you that you dare to steal our oil?" The demon-soldiers said: "We are no monsters! We belong to the courts of the World of Darkness. Following the orders of our king, we collect oil from each temple for the assistant judges to use to make their registers." The monk asked: "What kind of registers do they have to make?" The demons said: "The World of Light will descend into chaos. Eight million people are fated to die, and blood will flow over three thousand miles. Those who will die are listed in the registers of the dead, and those who will survive are listed in the registers of those who will remain." Liaokong then asked: "In what year will the killing begin? Where will the killing begin? And when will the sword get its first taste of blood?" The demons replied: "The fighting will begin this year, outside the city of Chang'an, and the first victim will be Liaokong." The monk asked: "How many Liaokongs are there?" "Only one," the demons replied. When the monk heard this, [he cried:] "Dear Demon Sirs, please save my life! I am that monk Liaokong!" The demons said: "How could we be capable of saving you? All you can do is hide yourself very well." When the monk heard this—please listen:

When Liaokong heard this, the tears ran down his cheeks;
Afraid of being killed, he knelt down and begged most piteously:
"Ever since my youth when I became a monk and shaved my head,
I have been reading the sutras and reciting the Buddha's name.
    I strictly observe the Three Refuges without any transgression;
I strictly observe the Five Precepts and never once break them.
I beg you, dear Demon Sirs, show some compassion and mercy
And spare my miserable life from this impending disaster!"

The monk said: "I am this monk Liaokong! Demons Sirs, please save my life!" The demons said: "How can we save you?" Liaokong said: "Dear Demons Sirs, please put in a word on my behalf to King Yama; then you will be able to save me!" The ghosts said: "King Yama has a face of iron, without mercy. How could we bring him around? But all right, we will tell you how you can escape. The man who will begin this rebellion is named Huang Chao. If you beg him to spare you, he may be able to save you." The monk then asked: "How will I recognize that Huang Chao as the one destined to rule?" The demons said: "His face is a golden color, and two of his teeth protrude from his mouth. You don't have to go out and look for him; he will come here himself. Wait for him here at the monastery and treat him very well. If you bow to him very politely, he will come up with a plan to save you. That's the way to stay out of trouble!" Hearing this, Liaokong thanked them profusely: "Excellent! Amituofo!"[127] There is a gatha that describes this:

When Liaokong heard the ghosts pronounce this prediction,
He was so terrified that he lost two of his three souls.
He hurried off as fast as he could to the room of the abbot;
Shivering and shaking from fright, he told the whole story.
    When the monks heard the story, they were dumbfounded,
And indeed their entire bodies started to pour with sweat.
Each and every one feared to die by the sword of steel:
Little did they know how friendly Huang Chao could be!

The next day Liaokong ordered his disciple to prepare a vegetarian meal in anticipation, but enough about that.

Let's talk about Huang Chao, who, filled with indignation, was on his way home after having failed the examinations. When he came to the outskirts of the city, he looked around as he rode and saw a monastery just ahead, the halls and pavilions of which were tall and beautiful. As night was falling, he decided to ask for lodging at the monastery and then travel on again the next day. Suddenly he was overcome by poetic inspiration and composed a poem. The poem read:

How grand is this mountain monastery here by the rocks—
Rising up so high that it seems to be linked to the Dipper!
Halls and pavilions, lofty and tall, invade the blue heavens;
Towers and terraces wind their way right to a clear spring.
    The golden bell distantly echoes the clap of the thunder;
The precious pagodas redouble the moon's round reflection.
Listen in silence to the Lotus Sutra—a pure Sanskrit hymn.
Little did I expect to find the Western Paradise right here!

After Huang Chao had composed his poem, he dismounted from his horse and walked to the hall. As soon as the abbot and the other monks saw him, they noticed that his face had a golden color and that his two eyes were perfectly round. This must be Huang Chao! Together they all fell to their knees and said: "Master Huang Chao, please show compassion and spare our lives—we are monks—and you will rule for a myriad of generations!" When Huang Chao heard them talking like this, he had no idea what it was all about. Liaokong then told him the whole story of what had taken place the previous night. "General, when you rise up in rebellion, I, Liaokong, am fated to be the first victim of your sword. So I beg you, general, to show your great compassion and spare my life. The merit will be measureless." When Huang Chao heard this, he said: "How could this be true? The rest of you, please leave the two of us alone." Huang Chao then said: "Since this is fated to happen, I will guarantee your safety. I will not behead you or any other of the monks." The monks then retired, greatly relieved.

That evening Huang Chao saw that the moon was very bright, and strolling about, he came to the flower garden. When he lifted his eyes, in the clouds above he suddenly saw an immortal maiden holding in her hands a precious sword, which she presented to him, saying: "This sword will slay eight million people, and blood will flow for three thousand miles." After she finished speaking, she left, and only then did Huang Chao wake up.

The next day he said to the monk: "On the fifteenth of the Fifth Month I will rise in rebellion and try out my sword. You must all be sure to hide. Don't block the way in front of my horse. Once my sword gets its first taste of blood, everything will be fine. But he who engages in battle must advance, for then it will be impossible for him to retreat." The monks replied: "We will all go off to the village behind to beg for alms, but we will leave the abbot here to guard the monastery. Since he will be all by himself, he should have no trouble hiding himself." They then left.

Although there was no place inside the monastery for Liaokong to hide, outside the temple there was an old hollow tree that was a perfect place for him to conceal himself. Assuming that everything was fine, he sat there in the tree, without a worry in the world. Listen, there is a gatha that describes this:

Liaokong was devising a plan to escape from Huang Chao:
He thought this way and that way but had nowhere to flee.
By chance he saw a hollow tree: "That's the place to hide!
There no one will be able to spot the slightest trace of me!

Not only a mortal man will have trouble locating me there,
But even divine immortals will not be able to figure it out.

Let him go ahead and try out his sword this very moment—
Today I will show off my brilliant intelligence right here!"

The story goes that Huang Chao had selected the hour of noon to engage in battle. He sat astride his horse dressed in full armor and carrying his precious sword. Inside the monastery there was not a single soul in sight, not even a chicken or a dog! He looked all around him but could not see a single creature. All he saw was a hollow tree. "Let me try out my sword on that tree then! Once I have tried out my sword, I will not have killed any monk or broken any taboo."[128] So saying, he gave one stroke of his sword, and out tumbled the head of a monk, which turned out to be that of Liaokong! For in the end his predetermined fate from an earlier life was that he should lose his life at the hands of Huang Chao in this cataclysmic disaster—to be the first of the eight million! Filled with sadness, Huang Chao wrote a poem:

He left the household and exerted great effort at cultivation—
Little did we know that Liaokong was fated to lose his life.
He hid himself in a hollow tree where nobody could see him,
Little expecting that the precious sword would not hesitate.
　　Even before Huang Chao, rising in rebellion, tried his sword,
The other monks of the monastery had already fled far away.
It is not that this Liaokong had not carefully hidden himself:
It's just that he couldn't escape his predetermined karmic fate.

Huang Chao heaved a sigh. Then, spurring his horse on, he stormed toward Chang'an. He had not yet gone very far when from the opposite direction there appeared a few thousand men on horseback, with swords and lances in their hands. Chao gave a loud shout and said: "Who are you and what are you doing?" These student-soldiers replied: "We are students who have failed the examinations and are now on our way home." Chao said: "I am one of you. When that stupid king saw how ugly I was, he did not pass me. Now I have risen up in rebellion and am on my way to Chang'an. Why don't you give me a hand so that we can succeed? You all will receive office and rank!" The warriors said: "We are eager to serve Your Majesty!" They then stormed Chang'an. The corpses piled up like mountains, and blood flowed like oceans. Xizong could offer no resistance and fled with his troops.

Once Huang Chao had conquered Chang'an, his troops elevated him and made him their king. He ordered a man called Zhu Wen to clean out the Inner Palace. There Zhu Wen saw a palace lady, and upon making inquiries, he found out that she was a younger sister of the emperor. Zhu Wen secretly married that palace lady and then devised a plan: disguising himself as a common soldier, he escaped to Xizong's camp together with the emperor's sister. After Zhu Wen had surrendered himself to the Tang, he hired troops and bought horses. One of his men, Li Cunxiao, engaged Huang Chao in a fierce battle, in which the eight million wronged ghosts were avenged and Huang Chao suffered a major defeat.[129]

Following his defeat, Huang Chao went to Raven Valley Mountain, where there was a man who blocked his way. Chao shouted loudly: "Who are you that you dare block Our way?" The man said: "I have come here for the purpose of retrieving your sword." Greatly enraged, Huang Chao lifted his sword and smote him with all his force. But the man just took his sword and then changed into a whiff of clear breeze and disappeared. Chao had no option but to continue on to the foot of the mountain, where he found a stele inscribed with a poem. Let me recite it to you:

Suddenly rising in rebellion, you fought so many battles;
By right it was your destiny to rule for these four years.
After Zhu Wen defected and fled to the camp of the Tang,
Li Cunxiao joined the fray, and the dynasty was restored.
    In the World of Light you slaughtered eight million people;
The World of Darkness received double or triple that number.
Oh General, if you understand the meaning of this poem,
Then come to the World of Darkness and meet the Buddha!

Once Huang Chao had expounded this poem, his heart felt clear: "When in times long ago the Hegemòn-King slit his throat at Raven River, that was the action of a hero, a real man.[130] I'm afraid that I, Huang Chao, am fated to die right here!" Filled with emotion, he composed a poem:

Do not pride yourself as a human being on valor and strength:
The myriad miles of mountains and streams are only a dream.
Riches and glory, merit and fame—a candle flame in the wind;

A heroic cunning that covers the world is but frost on the grass.

Some years ago that monk died while hiding in a hollow tree;
This year it is Huang Chao who will die at the foot of this hill.
Scheming for profit and fighting for fame—nothing but emptiness;
It would be better by far to report as fast as I can to King Yama.

As soon Huang Chao had recited this poem, he killed himself, and his numinous true nature went off to the World of Darkness. After he had formally greeted the Ten Kings, they presented themselves together before the Teaching Lord. Huang Chao, now Mulian again, begged the bodhisattva most piteously: "May you in your compassion allow my mother to leave her prison, so that she may be reborn in the Land of Bliss." The Teaching Lord said: "By virtue of your merit in rounding up these ghosts and returning them to prison, you have compensated for your crime, and so your mother may be released from prison and be reborn, together with you, in the Western Paradise." Just when Mulian was about to express his gratitude for this grace, Lord Yama quickly stepped forward from the side and said: "My Lord, please wait a moment. There is still one matter I must report. He is still required to personally round up the lives of those pigs and goats." The Teaching Lord followed his advice and dispatched demon-soldiers to take the true nature of Mulian back to the World of Light, to be reborn in a family of butchers, where he would kill and slaughter pigs and goats. Only after he had rounded up all of these orphan souls as well would he be able to take rebirth on a higher level. In conformity with this order the demon-soldiers took him to the city of Chang'an to be reborn in the family of the butcher He Xiang and later reported on their mission, but enough of that. A gatha goes:

Huang Chao's true nature entered the World of Darkness;
In his precious hall King Yama greeted him as an equal.
No one escapes the net of earth, your debt of evil deeds;
Nothing can elude Heaven's web, a norm for the people.

The Lord of Teaching followed the advice he was given;
The reverend Mulian was so to be reborn one more time.
If you want to know how the case of Qingti was concluded,
Listen again to the final chapter, which will explain it all.

In his second life Mulian went
On the Wheel of the Six Paths
To the World of Light to be reborn
As a member of the Huang family.

He was given the name Huang Chao,
Caught ghosts, returned them to prison.
Through transmigration, in his third life
He will be reborn in a butcher's family.

By slaughtering pigs and goats,
He will repay his karmic debts.
Mulian will become a buddha,
And Qingti will go to paradise.

PART 3

Giving rise to desires will surely be a source of hindrance;
Maintaining feelings is certainly bound to invite disasters.
When will numinous brightness rise to the Three Terraces?[131]
Once practice is complete, take refuge with your own nature.
    Whether you become an immortal or become a buddha,
You have to start your arrangements from this one point.
Then, perfectly pure, perfectly clean, you'll escape the Dust,
And, in the fruition of truth, soar up to the highest realms.

Original nature is perfect and bright and is one with the Way—
Just make that turn, and you'll leap out of the Five Elements.[132]
It is not easy to achieve transformation through cultivation;
It's far from simple to find life eternal through sublimation.
    Pure and turbid often change places as cycles come around;
Spring and source move east and west according to the kalpas.[133]
Roaming free and easy millions of years, you don't remember:
One speck of divine brilliance fills emptiness for all eternity!

The story goes that in the city of Chang'an,[134] by the East Gate, there was a He Family Lane. Mr. He's personal name was Xiang, and his wife was Madame Xiao. Having no other skill or craft, He Xiang made his living as a butcher. His wife was pregnant, and after having been heavy with child for nine months, she gave birth to a boy. Husband and wife were filled with joy and burned incense to thank Heaven and Earth. They gave the child the name of He Yin. From the day the boy was born, their business at once became profitable and prosperous. The days and nights passed by as quickly as a weaver's shuttle, and before long He Yin had grown up and become a man. Let's recite some lines of verse! The gatha goes:

Sun and moon, passing like a shuttle, are busy from early till late;
On the Yangzi the wave in front is pushed on by the wave behind.
Before long He Yin had reached the age of six or seven years, so
His parents sent him to school, and the boy entered the classroom.
    Little did they know that even after three or four years at his books

Not even half a sentence had managed to fix itself in his brain.
It became very clear that the boy excelled at just one single thing:
He was extremely good at killing pigs and slaughtering goats!

When He Xiang saw that his son had grown up and become a man,
He contacted a matchmaker to find a beautiful maiden for the boy.
When she had found a fine girl, they sent the six engagement gifts;
Within a few days they took her into the home as a daughter-in-law.

But within a year after He Xiang had brought in a wife for his son,
He fell ill and had to lie down, never again to rise from his ivory bed.
And then, after he had passed away, before even a week had gone by,
His wife, old Madame Xiao, found that she was no longer feeling well:

After half a month of being plagued by illness, she turned into a crane.[135]
Sad and in pain, the young couple called to Heaven, stamped the Earth;
They invited monks to conduct the rituals for the rebirth of their parents,
And then husband and wife ran the business and so passed their days,

From the day they inherited the shop from the generation before them,
Their livelihood flourished and prospered and really kept them busy!

Let's not talk about the prosperity of He Yin's business. Let's talk rather about a certain Wang Shan who lived right across the way and ran a small shop that sold incense, candles, and religious prints. Because ever since early youth he had adhered to a vegetarian diet, read the sutras, and recited the name of the Buddha, people all called him Man of the Way Wang. Each day he would rise at the fourth watch of the night to recite the sutras, and then at break of dawn he would open his shop and mind his business, and in this way he passed his days. Every night, as soon as He Yin heard Man of the Way's wooden fish,[136] he would get up to heat water and butcher a pig. After he had completely cleaned the butchered animal, at break of dawn he would put the meat out for sale. Each and every day was like this, never earlier, never later! He Yin then thought in his heart: "I am very much indebted to Man of the Way Wang, but I don't have anything with which to repay him."

One day, having had his meal and with nothing to do, he was sitting outside drinking his tea. Seeing that Man of the Way was also unoccupied, he wanted to have a chat with him, so, taking his tea with him, he went over to Wang's shop and said to Man of the Way: "Please have a cup of tea!" The latter replied: "That is very kind of you. But because I follow a vegetarian diet, I do not share other people's food and drink." He Yin said: "As we have nothing else to do, let's chat for a while." Man of the Way said: "Do you want to hear the wonderful principle of self-cultivation?" He Yin replied: "Of course!" "Then listen to me and I will tell you. There's a gatha I would like to recite to you:

"By keeping the fast and practicing goodness, one goes to heaven;
By creating evil karma, you eventually end up in the prison of hell.
Alas, the time we will last in this bustling world is only so long;
It may be compared to the brilliant sun at noon, so high in heaven.

Merit and fame, riches and glory are only a dream at spring's end;
The fierce hero who conquers the world is like the frost of late fall.
Upon consideration our myriad deeds turn out to be insubstantial—
One can escape from Impermanence only by practice and recitation.

If you practice self-cultivation, your determination must be firm;
You have to lay waste to your former house of loving attachments.[137]
Outside the mind you have no need of any disputes, any quarrels;
Inside the Way you will find your own advantageous yin and yang.

When your merit is complete and fully perfected, you go to heaven;
Escaping from this mortal body, you enter the realm of the divinities.
But if as a human being in this world you crave bloody meat to eat,
You'll have to pay when your case comes up in the Courts of Hell."

After Man of the Way had recited this, He Yin said: "The practice of self-cultivation sure is a fine thing, but how am I going to manage if I don't have a livelihood?" Man of the Way said: "You can practice any of the hundred crafts! I urge you to find another business—you'll make money just the same! Why do you insist on butchering sentient beings? You are creating mountains of karma, and when your end comes after a hundred years, you will not be able to escape retribution for your sins." He Yin replied: "Of course I know that I accumulate sins, but with me it is such that as soon as I see an animal, I want to kill it—I don't know why! It must be that I am predestined to do this. And yet I want to make the effort to practice goodness. I have some lines of verse, so please listen:

Every day I kill and slaughter these pigs and goats—
How many sentient beings have been done in by me?
I know quite well that this killing brings retribution,
But I rely on it to make a profit and get through life.

I may want to stop being a butcher from now on,
But there is no other business in which I am skilled.
Oh how I hate that King Yama—what was his reason
For ordering that I be a butcher in this present life?"

He Yin thought that after a few more years had gone by, he might want to change his business, keep the fast and practice goodness. He then took leave Man of the Way. "When I wanted to thank him, he didn't even bother me for a cup of tea!" So he came up with a plan: "I will secretly give him some money as an expression of my gratitude." And so each day he placed some money inside his door, and from then on, Man of the Way found there an envelope with money. He had no idea where it came from and thought: "It must be that the bodhisattva [Guanyin] has noticed that I keep the fast and practice goodness, but hardly make any money in my business, and for this reason gives me this so I can support myself." But let's not talk about the happiness of Man of the Way.

Let me tell you how it was that from afar the bodhisattva Guanyin had with her eye of wisdom observed that Mulian's negative karma had been exhausted and that Man of the Way Wang too had now been practicing self-cultivation for a long time. "It would be a good idea if I went there and ferried the two of them across, transforming them." So, instructing Dharma Protector Weituo, Good-in-Talent, and Dragon Maiden to follow her,[138] she rode an auspicious cloud until she came to Chang'an, where she stepped down mortal dust and transformed herself into a monk. She then went into the shop of Man of the Way Wang, who said to the monk: "Please take a seat. What is it you wish to buy?" The monk answered: "I am here for incense and paper." Man of the Way said: "Amituofo! Ever since I opened this shop, I have never seen a monk who came for incense. This must mean that you are a good monk! May I ask you, reverend, on which famous mountain is your monastery to be found? From how far have you come?" The monk replied: "I have come from the Western Hills." Man of the Way then asked:

"What business brings you here?" The monk replied: "I have come here in search of the Way. The reason is that in this world there are good men and devout women who keep the fast and recite the name of the Buddha, but because they do not know the Right Dharma, how do they know how to strictly uphold the Tathagata's Threefold Refuge and strictly observe the Five Precepts? And if they don't know how to do that, it will be impossible for them to achieve the Right Fruit. So I have come for the purpose of converting them." Man of the Way Wang said: "From my earliest youth I have adhered to a vegetarian diet and recited the name of the Buddha. All I needed was to find a teacher to instruct me. You have come at the right moment! It is already growing late, but there's no need to go to a big monastery to ask for lodging—why not just stay here for the night?" The monk said: "As this is the house of a good man, that would be fine! But first I have some lines of a gatha, so please listen:

"In vain you've fasted without interruption for many tens of years:
When did you ever penetrate the root and cause of the Buddha?
Don't talk of the Way without first removing foolish thoughts;
When not yet freed of greed and anger, what do you strive for?
    In a face-to-face meeting you'll become a buddha in an instant;
If your heart is deluded, you're forever caught in transmigration.
As long as the key is lost, it's impossible to unlock your chains—
Which buddha will take you into his paradise upon your death?"

When Man of the Way Wang heard this gatha, his heart was filled with joy. Hurriedly he hastened to light a lamp and close up his shop. He prepared a late vegetarian meal, and after they had both eaten, the monk said to Man of the Way: "When you keep the fast, you have to take refuge in the Three Jewels. If you cultivate the Fruit of Truth while you are alive, you will enjoy free and easy roaming after you die, and you will not have to undergo the sufferings of transmigration." Man of the Way said: "If that is the case, I beg you, reverend, to show compassion and enlighten this disciple. I will take refuge tonight and tomorrow follow you to the mountains to practice the Way. My only wish is to serve you as my teacher and practice cultivation together." The monk then said: "As this is your sincere intention, I will lay my hand on top of your hand and give you the prediction of future buddhahood." Man of the Way then asked the monk to sit down and he himself knelt down in the dust. Burning incense, he bowed in veneration and asked the monk to enlighten him. The monk said: "Listen, there is a gatha that describes this:

"The true sutras are the original sutras left to us by the Buddha;
Those who listen to them are many, those who follow them few.
Leave the family while still at home—we can all study their truth,
And it doesn't matter whether one is old or young, high or lowly.
    The single numinous true nature is capable of achieving the Way;
The Three Teachings all share one source—have no doubt of this.
Humbly I urge the people of this world to seek the Right Dharma;
There is no need at all for bickering and mutual recrimination."

Let's not talk about how the monk and Man of the Way discussed the Dharma. Our story tells how He Yin, because he did not hear the sound of the wooden fish that night, overslept for a few hours. At the break of dawn a villager by the name of Wu Dougui came to the city to buy some meat. When he saw that the door of the shop was not yet open, he started to beat on it, shouting madly. When He Yin heard that someone wanted to buy meat, he suddenly awoke with a start. When he opened the door to have a look, he saw the sun had already risen to a height of three rods! That Dougui shouted: "Some day ago I left you a down payment and told you that I wanted the meat today first thing in the morning. So why are you wasting my time, you lazybones?" He was so agitated that he was jumping up and down and screaming at the top of his voice: "I have here some lines of verse, so please listen:

"I live in a certain village some miles east of the city;
I have no one to help me at home, so I am really busy!
I got up at dawn to come to the market to buy some meat
Because back at home we want to celebrate Double-Fifth![139]
    All the other butcher shops in the city are all sold out,
But you have not even started to slaughter your pig!
As a butcher you should get up early, before dawn,
So why did you stay sleeping till the sky was bright?"

Dougui screamed: "Give me back my down payment immediately so I can go to the other shops and buy some meat!" He Yin lowered his head and did not say a word. Filled with gloom, he returned the down payment. When he raised his head and looked, he saw that the door of Man of the Way's house was still closed—why would that be? He pushed open the door and walked in and then asked Man of the Way: "Why didn't you recite your sutras today?" Man of the Way replied: "There was no way you could have known, but last night a monk came, and I discussed the Dharma of the Buddha with him, which is why I have not yet had the opportunity to recite the sutras." Then the monk asked Man of the Way: "Do you recite the sutras on that man's behalf?" When Man of the Way replied in the negative, the monk asked: "If you do not recite the sutras on his behalf, then why is he so angry?" When Man of the Way said that he didn't know why, He Yin said: "You will not understand unless I explain the matter. I have a few lines of verse, so please listen:

"Man of the Way Wang rises in the fifth watch to recite the sutras;
As he beats his wooden fish, the sound reverberates far and wide.
I awake with a start and only then set out to slaughter pig or goat;
I wash them, I clean them, and when all is ready, I wait for dawn.
    The money I make by selling the meat provides me with a living,
Yet when I offered you a bowl of tea, you thought it reeked of flesh.
So the only thing left for me to do was to secretly leave you money,
Just a little bit of money as a token of my thanks and my gratitude.
    This day now happens to be the day of the festival of Heaven's Middle;
Now today each and every shop in this town is as busy as busy can be.
But because you two were discussing the sutras, I missed the moment—
But how could I blame Man of the Way? It's myself I must blame!"

When He Yin had explained this, the monk looked down and, sure enough, saw the envelope with money. Picking it up, Man of the Way immediately said "Amituofo!" a number of times. "So it is flesh-money after all! How can I make use of it?" The monk said: "Since it is a gift, there is no harm in it. Judging from his words, he must blame me for making him lose track of the time. As you have not yet been able to butcher a pig, let me go over and slaughter some for you." He Yin said: "I don't believe it! You are a monk who has left the household, how could you be capable of butchering pigs? If you can kill them, then I will assist you." The monk replied: "I do not need any help when I slaughter pigs. I just call the pigs to come to me: I don't have to tie them up to kill them." Not believing a word he said, He Yin invited the monk to come over to his establishment right then and there. When Man of the Way heard all this, he was flabbergasted: "When sweeping the floor, I am fearful of even taking the life of an insect. And here my teacher is going to kill pigs on behalf of someone else! I'll go along to have a look. If my teacher really butchers a pig, I will not be able to believe in him anymore."

When the three of them came to the pig-killing area, Man of the Way thought: "Let me see how my teacher is going to kill them!" The monk walked up to the pigpen and said: "He Xiang, come here to be killed!" And sure enough, that pig—its eyes filled with tears—went up to the monk and then crumpled to the ground all by itself, where it remained without moving, apart from the heavy sigh it heaved. When the monk raised the knife to kill it, He Yin was so terrified that his souls left his body, and he loudly shouted: "Reverend, just wait a moment! That one is still too small! Just call for another!" The monk then said: "Madame Xiao, come here to be killed!" and he pretended to be ready to kill the animal. He Yin felt as if his heart were being sliced with a knife, and he fell down on both knees. With his left arm he protected the pigs, and with his right hand he blocked the knife, screaming loudly as he did so: "Reverend, please do not strike! I have some lines of verse, so please listen!

"As soon as he saw these two pigs, he felt much pain;
Tears gushed down from his eyes and fell on his breast.
Piteously he beseeched the monk: "Please do not strike;
Please spare the miserable lives of these two animals.

He Xiang is my father, the man I must thank for my life;
Madame Xiao is my mother, the woman who raised me.
One's parents' favor and love are as heavy as mountains.
How could I dare raise my hand and kill my own parents?"

When the monk heard him say this, he put down the knife,
And the filial son embraced the pigs with heartrending sobs.
"After my father and mother died, I hired a number of monks
To perform all the rituals needed to ensure a superior rebirth.

I simply thought they had gone off to a nice place in heaven.
Little did I know that they would be transformed into pigs.
So I urge you never to say there is no Heavenly Principle—
The retribution for these kinds of actions is clear as can be."

The monk said: "Please get back on your feet! I simply won't kill them—
I'll tell these two pigs to go back to their pen." He Yin expressed his
gratitude with a bow and then asked both the monk and Man of the Way
to come inside and take a seat. "Only today have I come to understand
retribution!"

Man of the Way said: "Day in and day out I urged you to keep the fast and
practice goodness, and told you not to kill sentient beings, but you didn't
believe in the Law of the Buddha." He Yin said: "People are always saying:
'If you follow the Law of the Buddha, you will die of starvation, and if you
follow the law of the courts, you will be beaten to death!'" The monk said:
"These are all words said by people who slander the Law of the Buddha. If
it is easy to abide by the law of the courts, it should also be easy to abide by
the Law of the Buddha. All you have to do is keep the fast, recite the name
of the Buddha, and respect and revere the Three Jewels. The father should
be kind, and the son should be filial; the older brother should be loving, and
the younger brother should be respectful; you must live in harmony with
your neighbors, and you must be trustworthy in your contacts with friends;
and you should not commit treachery, robbery, perversity, or adultery
or any other kind of evil and fraud. Of course that means you will 'die of
starvation'?! Listen to me and I will first explain the law of the courts to you.
There is a gatha that describes this:

"Don't violate the courts' codes and your blessings will be vast;
People of insight understand their fate and live in contented joy.
If you maintain at least three-tenths of the Rites of the Master,[140]
You won't come into conflict with the six articles of Xiao He's Law.[141]
Those who are listed on the Golden Placard are all good men;[142]
Those who are depicted in Lingyan Tower are all great heroes.[143]
A day will come when you will again await the imperial gift,
And your name will appear at the head of the Jade Hall list.

This is the royal law. If as a human being you abide by it, all will be fine. But if you abide by the Law of the Buddha, all your evil karma will spontaneously dissolve because you are satisfied with your lot and watch over yourself. People with a heart of faith will be free from evil karma, and step by step they will ascend to a higher plane. Listen to me, and I will explain the Law of the Buddha to you. There is a gatha that describes this:

"If you convert to the Law of the Buddha, take up the Three Jewels,
Practice goodness, observe the fast, and are of superior morality,
Then after your death you will not be sentenced by that guy Yama,
Since your name will be listed on the placard of the Western Paradise.

You'll enjoy Ultimate Bliss among the ranks of immortals and buddhas,
And you'll enjoy free and easy roaming at the Dragon-Flower Assembly.[144]
You will feast on the fruits of immortality, your cup filled with ambrosia:
Summoned by the Queen Mother, you'll live forever and never grow old."[145]

When the monk had finished his exposition, he said to He Yin: "If you practice goodness and keep the fast, you will save your parents and ensure their rebirth on a higher plane. I will conduct a repentance ritual for you, which with one stroke will wipe out all your previous karma of killing sentient beings." When He Yin heard this, his heart was filled with joy. "Since that is the case, I will entrust my business to my wife so she will have something to live on, but I will entrust myself to you, teacher, as your disciple, and go up into the mountains to cultivate the Way." That very moment He Yin lit a candle and burned incense, bowed in veneration before the Buddha, and made the ritual bows to his teacher. The monk touched the top of He Yin's head with his hand, gave him the prediction of future buddhahood, and enlightened him. He Yin thanked the monk with a bow for his compassion. He also bowed to Man of the Way Wang, who responded by extending his congratulations. He Yin then asked him: "Did you also take refuge in the Three Jewels?" The monk told him: "He took refuge last night, so from now on you must call him 'elder brother.'" "If that is the case, I will bow to him again! We will address each other as 'elder brother' and 'younger brother.'"

As the teacher and his two disciples were talking with great animation, they suddenly heard a clerk shouting again and again outside the shop. "If you want to avoid any further trouble, quickly tell that monk to leave. Thanks to his saving grace your pig-father and your pig-mother have both died!" "Why are you so upset?" He Yin said to him. Then he asked his teacher: "Why did they die?" The monk replied: "Your father and mother have been liberated from their animal forms and will be reborn in human form. When they are later reborn, they will go to the Western Paradise." He Yin, who was extremely pleased, recited the name of the Buddha Amitabha and thanked his teacher with a bow. "Please, teacher, stay here for one more day so that your disciple can take care of various matters. Then, when I have put everything in order, I will follow you into the mountains to cultivate the Way."

After he had buried all the tools of his trade, he summoned his wife and instructed her as follows: "I now will follow this teacher into the mountains to cultivate the Way." I have some lines of verse, so please listen:

"He Yin had decided to leave his old home once and for all;
Severing all bonds of love and favor, he was full of sadness.
His mind was set on practicing goodness and keeping the fast,
Sutra reading and Buddha recitation, to avoid Impermanence.
  Repeatedly he instructed his dear darling son and daughter:
"Your mother will now be in charge of the house and fields.
For your three daily meals limit yourselves to pure, bland rice;
Throughout the four seasons of the year wear only old clothes.
  From this day onward switch to a different money-making trade;
From now on you must by no means be butchers anymore.
As for the Buddha-fruit—gathas on cause and fruit circulate;
Heaven-heart's established norm determines every rise and fall."
  After he had instructed them with these heartrending words,
He could not stop tears from pouring down in an endless flow.
His wife, Madame He, was a wise and most capable woman,
But she also wept and found it difficult to let her husband go:
  "If you want to cultivate your heart, I cannot blame you,
But stay at home and devote your days to Buddha-recitation!"
But He Yin did not listen to the urgent pleadings of his wife,
As he was determined to practice cultivation in a monastery.

Then the day arrived when husband and wife had to part;
All were weeping most piteously, and then both went their way.
But let's describe not the painful parting of people once married
But rather the master and his disciples on their way to the hills.

Leaving at dawn, they rested at night under the stars and moon,
Drinking when thirsty, eating when hungry, exposed to the elements.
The bitter pain of their long journey went on for many a day:
As they didn't know where the Western Ridge was to be found.[146]

He Yin followed his teacher, faithfully walking behind him,
But Man of the Way Wang often asked: "Where are we going?"
The two of them had set out together to both cultivate the Way;
Their commitment's sincerity was demonstrated by their deeds."

When the bodhisattva[147] noticed that Man of the Way was constantly asking as to their whereabouts, she realized that his determination was not unwavering. Secretly she instructed Dharma Protector Weituo to transform himself into a mother, and Good-in-Talent and Dragon Maiden into her two daughters, and to manifest themselves in a mountain grotto in order to test the sincerity of her two disciples' devotion to the Way. The three of them, teacher and disciples, were traveling along when night began to fall. He Yin just walked on without saying a word, but Man of the Way said: "Let's find someplace to stay for the night." The monk pointed with his finger and said: "I see a light there ahead of us—there must be somebody living there. Let's hurry and go there and inquire about lodging for the night. Then tomorrow we can continue on." Man of the Way said: "That's good!"

When the teacher and his two disciples arrived at the gate of the house, they heard sounds of grief coming from inside. "That spells trouble! We should not meddle in other people's affairs, so let's go on!" However, the people inside had heard his knock on the door and asked: "Who is knocking on the gate?" The monk replied: "We would like permission to spend the night at your mansion." An elderly woman opened the door: "Ah, so it is a monk and his disciples! Please come in and sit down." When the three of them entered, they noticed a Buddha-hall, so the three paid their respects to the Buddha. They also paid their respects to their hostess, after which the elderly woman said to the three reverends: "Please take a seat." She then ordered her daughters to serve them tea and to prepare some evening food. "May I ask, Reverend, from which precious mountain you come? And what is the business that has brought you here? And what is your relation to these two acolytes?" The monk replied: "I hail from the Western Numinosity Mountain, and I've come here to spread the precepts and deliver people. These two men are disciples I recently accepted in the city of Chang'an. May I ask you, Milady, for your name? How many relatives do you have living here with you? And why were you weeping?" The elderly woman replied: "My family name is Jia.[148] My husband passed away early, before leaving a son. We had only these two daughters, who are not yet engaged to marry. Why were we weeping? Please allow me to inform the three of you at length. Please listen:

"My husband died early on and departed for the World of Darkness
Before an heir was born to us who could continue the sacrifices.
We had only this pair of daughters in hairpins and skirts to raise;
They were both over sixteen and in the spring of their youth.
    But now that they've grown up and reached the age of marriage,
We are unable to find suitable marriage partners of equal status.
Matchmakers have come quite often with suggested matches
With men whose status was either too high for us or too lowly.
    Moreover this family has been vegetarians for generations,
So I refuse to marry them out to a family that feeds on meat.
On top of that, elder and younger sister are truly inseparable,
So now I am at my wits' end—on whom will I be able to rely?
    I hope to bring in sons-in-law as insurance against old age,
Two of those beggars who can serve as fake sons or grandsons.
It doesn't matter whether they are rich and noble or dirt poor:
We have plenty of good fields that will keep them well fed.
    I do not care about age, how old they are or how young—
If they accumulate goodness, they can easily extend their years;
I don't go in for literary talent or for a handsome physique—
They must just be loyal and true and most of all be devout!
    I hope for men of our faith, who keep the fast and precepts,
To be happy sons-in-law and become this household's support.
Each and every day we are filled with sufferings and sorrow;
That's the reason why my daughters lifted their sad voices."

The monk said: "So it's all because your two daughters have not yet found husbands!" The elderly woman said: "That's right." Her daughters said: "Mommy, you must be going mad in your old age! How can you tell such things to other people?" The elderly woman said: "My children, this reverend is a man who has left the household. If we tell it to him, we can ask him to serve as matchmaker for you and find us two husbands! Ah well, my children, it is already late! Get a lamp and take the three monks to their sleeping quarters." The monk said: "My disciples can light the lamp. May you have a good night's sleep." The elderly woman excused herself, and the three of them went to the room in the western wing to take their rest.

Man of the Way Wang said: "They are indeed two very nice girls!" The monk said: "And they are intelligent too! Tomorrow I will serve as matchmaker for the two of you, so you can move in here as sons-in-law. Perhaps the mother will agree to that. Tomorrow morning I will discuss this with her, and we will see what she has to say. If she is agreeable, I will go on into the mountains and cultivate the Way, and the two of you will become sons-in-law and enjoy glory and riches, wealth and status as before. Moreover you won't have to undergo the sufferings of the road." Little did Man of the Way realize that the bodhisattva was testing him. Please listen:

"The bodhisattva Guanyin had come down from her mountain grove,
And she now gave instructions to her personal Guardian of the Law.
She ordered Weituo to transform himself into an elderly woman and
Dragon Maiden and Good-in-Talent to act the part of her daughters.
    In a mountain grotto they miraculously manifested a fine mansion,
Because she wanted to test the commitment of these two disciples.
How ridiculous is mortal man when he fails to recognize the secret:
That Man of the Way was only too eager to tie the marriage knot!
    The monk fooled them by saying he wanted to act as a matchmaker:
"My disciples, you should stay here and marry these nice young girls!
It's not necessary to endure the sufferings of wind and frost on the road,
Drinking when thirsty, eating when hungry, and you won't have to beg!
    If you are willing to respectfully serve the elderly mother of theirs,
The daughters will surely be willing to give you their love and devotion.

And once you have united in harmony, like those intertwined branches,
At some time in the future, they are bound to bear you nice baby boys!"

When Man of the Way heard this, his heart was filled with joy, and he swallowed the bait. He immediately said: "Reverend, allow me to speak. Please listen:

"I've cultivated my mind for tens of years, since earliest youth;
Now today we come to this place, they start talking of marriage.
If you, reverend, act as matchmaker and arrange this wedding,
I'd be a most rebellious fellow if I were to refuse to get hitched."

The monk said: "Wonderful! So you, my elder disciple, will marry one of the daughters. But what does my second disciple think about this? Why don't you marry the other daughter?" When He Yin was confronted with this question, he was not at all pleased. "Reverend, please show some compassion and allow me to explain myself. Please listen:

"I was condemned to be reborn into the family of a butcher,
Knowing quite well the killing of sentient beings is wrong.
Fortunately you have led me on the road of mind-cultivation
And have saved my parents, ensuring their higher rebirth.
   If I now, halfway on our journey, decided to get married,
Everything once again would fall down into that pit of fire.
Much better that this mortal body remain without offspring—
I am only too happy not to have to marry for a second time!"

After the two disciples had their say, their teacher said: "Tonight it is already late. Let's get some sleep. Tomorrow we can discuss this again."

The next morning, after everyone had gotten up, they washed their hands and their faces, burned incense, and venerated the Buddha. Then, after the elderly woman had offered them tea, the teacher and his two students sat down. The reverend then said: "Because yesterday you said that you wanted me to serve as matchmaker for your lovely daughters, I suggest that you have my two disciples marry them. What would you think of that?" The lady said: "I've already told you that I won't reject anyone because of his poverty or low station. I am happy to see them married!" Upon hearing this, He Yin suddenly changed color and said to his teacher: "I left my wife and children to go into the mountains and cultivate the Way. So why do you again talk of marriage?" The elderly woman said: "Our family has kept to a vegetarian diet for generations, reciting the name of the Buddha and reading the sutras. You can practice cultivation here as well. What's the problem? Please do not reject this proposal! Listen to me:

"As human beings in this world we all long for offspring;
The relationship of husband and wife is the human norm.
Once you are united in wedlock, like flower and candle,
You'll enjoy a hundred springtimes of glory and riches!"

He Yin then cried out: "Lady bodhisattva,[149] if I had been craving wine and sex, riches and honor, I would never have been willing to submit myself to a teacher and leave the household. Now you please listen to me:

"Leaving village and hearth for good, my two feet keep walking on;
Abandoning wife and children, I cut through the bonds of affection.
I haven't the slightest craving for wine and sex, for money and honor;
And I am no longer attached to wealth and status, to wealth and glory.
    My one mind is true and sincere, without obstruction or hindrance;
I'm determined to follow my teacher despite thousands of hardships.
As of now I have shattered to bits those stupid and foolish longings;
One leap and I left the Red Dust to return to the path of the Buddha!"

Hearing He Yin's words, the elderly woman realized that he was unwilling to get married and resigned herself to the situation. However, the two girls now also came forward and said: "Sir, please listen to us:

"We urge you, sir, do not go to those mountains and crags;
To be a monk with shaved head is such bitter suffering!
Who cares for you on the road in winter and in summer?
When thirsty or hungry, you must take care of yourself.
    And who is there to succor you and offer you some soup

When your body is struck by some disaster, like sickness?
Far better to be like mating phoenix birds in our house,
Spending your days very nicely as husband and wife!"

He Yin replied: "Dear girls, don't try to persuade me. I also have a few lines.
Now don't get annoyed, and please listen to me:

"When all around me I have nice mountains with new scenery,
I care nothing for the pink of peaches or the green of willows.
A heart that is pure and free of desire will make me an arhat;[150]
Powdered cheeks and oiled hairdos are bewitching monsters.
　　Forgetting both riches and sex, I communicate with the Way;
As soon as anger and greed arise, then true sincerity is gone.
At full force, headfirst, I rammed Heaven's web and broke it;
I've leapt out of that pit that ensnares all men, and I'm free!"

When these girls heard this, they threw away all shame and, blushing all
over, ran up to him and said: "Lover, we also have some lines we would like
to recite. Please listen to us:

"Young man, we beg you, now don't spurn our love;
We are filled with desire, and we want to get married.
Our family happens to follow a strict vegetarian diet.
What need is there to go and suffer someplace else?
　　Three meals throughout the day will fill your belly,
And at night one of us will accompany you to bed.
If you go into the hills, you'll have none to rely on—
Who there will be your understanding companion?"

When He Yin heard these words, his heart filled with rage, and he shouted
at the girls: "Don't talk such nonsense! I have here some lines of verse, so
please listen:

"When your beautiful faces grow old, you'll be like demons—
How are you going to force me to marry against my will?
A century's light and shadow are just like a spring dream;

A hundred years as husband and wife are like autumn frost.

No marvelous medicine can give the mighty a longer life;
No amount of money can buy the absence of Impermanence.
The true mind practices goodness, keeps the fast and precepts—
Who gets attached to such romantic and charming wenches?"

Once the bodhisattva had ascertained that He Yin was utterly devout and sincere in his intention, he said to the oldest disciple: "Then that leaves you to be the one to get married here. If my other disciple doesn't want to marry, I can still use him to carry my luggage." The elderly woman said: "That's fine too. We'll now prepare a vegetarian meal, and as soon as you are done eating, you can be on your way." The monk and He Yin then set out on their way. Man of the Way Wang saw his teacher off and stayed there to get married—but enough of that!

After walking a short distance, the reverend and He Yin came to a bridge. The bodhisattva walked over to the bridge and sat down. He then said: "My disciple, I had a rosary, but in all the haste this morning, I left it at the house of your elder brother. Quickly go back now and get it for me." When He Yin heard this, he hurried off to fetch it. Before long he caught sight of his elder brother's place, but suddenly a whiff of clear breeze blew the house away! Then a fierce tiger jumped out with bared fangs and outstretched claws, seized Man of the Way, and swallowed him up! He Yin was so scared that his souls left his body! He turned around and fled, but when he looked back, he saw that the tiger was chasing him. "I'm dead!" he cried out, but at that very moment, the tiger knelt down and bowed its head. He Yin thought to himself: "There must be something divine about this tiger, since it is permitting me to escape from death." He then walked up to the tiger, who dropped the rosary in front of him and then disappeared. He Yin picked it up and, filled with joy, went back to his teacher. Falling on his knees, he related in complete detail the story of how Man of the Way had been killed by a tiger! But the bodhisattva already knew all about it. "Listen to what I have to tell you. There is a gatha that describes this.

"My original intention was to take you to the Western Paradise,
But I did not yet know which of you would be a good disciple.
I devised a scheme to investigate his heart, test it for its Way—

Little did I know that he would attach himself to those girls!

If one's heart is evil, one can't become a buddha or immortal;
If one's intentions are wrong, one cannot enter the Dharma-hall.
Since time immemorial, lust has been the worst of all the vices—
That is why I had a fierce tiger kill Man of the Way Wang!"

The bodhisattva then said: "You are a most filial person. You do not crave wine and sex, riches and honor, and your practice of the Way is persistent. It is just your body that has not yet been cleansed. Only if you jump down from this bridge and wash your body completely clean will you be able to go into the mountains." When He Yin heard this, he grasped the hidden message and leapt into the river to rid himself of his mortal body. Only when his numinous true nature appeared did he realize that he was actually Mulian, who had taken rebirth as He Yin because he had not yet rounded up all souls. Only now that he had compensated for the number of wronged souls by slaughtering pigs and goats would he be able to save his mother! Then he raised his head and seeing that the bodhisattva Guanyin had manifested her golden body, he hastily kowtowed to her. There is a gatha that describes this.

"The bodhisattva Guanyin descended from the cloud-filled skies;
She came down to the mortal world of dust to save all from suffering.
She found and then guided two disciples in the city of Chang'an:
The butcher turned out to be true, Man of the Way to be wicked.
    The single son of the He family devoutly converted to the Way;
He was saved from the Yellow Springs,[151] his karma melted away.
If one does not cultivate the mind, taking refuge in the Buddha,
How will Lord Yama ever be willing to spare you in his court?
    That fake devotee recited the sutras—but a tiger devoured him,
All because of his lust and desire for the charms of these beauties.
Slaughtering pigs all his life, a butcher achieved the Fruit of Truth,[152]
Whereas Man of the Way lost his life in the jaws of a tiger!"

After speaking these words, the bodhisattva rode away on an auspicious cloud. Mulian expressed his gratitude with a bow, and when he got to his feet, he saw two young lads clad in black who approached him, saying:

"Sagely monk, we've come here by order of the Ten Kings to welcome you."
When Mulian heard this, he followed them to the Senluo Hall. After he had
greeted the ruler Yama and the other kings, they took Mulian along to the
Green Clouds Palace. After he had greeted the Teaching Lord of Darkness,
Mulian pressed the palms of his hands together and begged the Teaching
Lord to show his compassion: "Please pardon my mother and allow her to
be reborn on a higher level." When Ksitigarbha heard this, he was filled with
joy: "You are a filial person, you have persisted in the practice of the Way,
and you have established merit by rounding up those souls. Now listen to
me." The gatha says:

"The Ksitigarbha Bodhisattva, king of the Underworld, smiled for joy
As he said to the sagely monk: 'Dear Radish, now hurry and rise!
The first time, wanting to save your mother, your filiality was great;
This second time, your merit in rounding up those souls was major.
    The orphan souls that transgressed the laws numbered eight million;
Each and every one was registered by surname and personal name.
Because your merit offsets your sins, we will pardon your mother,
So get your meditation staff and tap on the gate of these prisons!'"

The Teaching Lord ordered the cassock, the bowl, and the meditation staff
to be brought in, and he gave them to Mulian together with his precious
rosary made of luminous pearls. When Mulian received them, he expressed
his gratitude with a bow. Overcome with joy, he arrived at the gate of the
iron-clad city, where the demon-soldiers bowed down before him. Grasping
his staff, Mulian ever so lightly tapped three times on the gate. The gate of
the prison screeched open, and Mulian called out to his mother: "Come
quickly!" When Madame Liu heard him calling, she quickly ran out of
the prison, and the prison lord once again closed and locked the gate.
Displaying his marvelous Dharma, Mulian freed her of her shackles and
quelled his mother's hunger with the sweet-dew water from his bowl. Once
his mother was feeling hearty and hale, he helped her along, and together
they went to the Dark Clouds Palace to pay their respects to the Teaching
Lord Ksitigarbha.
    Right then and there Fu Xiang was reunited with his wife and his son, and
sadness and joy intermingled. After weeping loudly for a while, the three of

them together ascended the halls of heaven. Father and son stood to the left and the right of Ksitigarbha and protected the Dharma, while Madame Liu enjoyed her free and easy roaming, and never again did the three take rebirth as humans in the Eastern Land.[153]

Let me now sing the praises of the *Tale of Cause and Fruition in the Three Lives of Mulian*. My dear audience, please listen attentively and practice cultivation in the same way—the blessings and profit will be without limit! The gatha goes:

"The whole family reunited, they rose to the Dark Clouds;[154]
Father and son and mother—all three—loudly cried:
'Teaching Lord of Darkness, please, show some pity!'
He appointed them as guardians of the Law at his side.
    The person who is standing to his left is Fu Xiang;
The one who is standing to the right is the monk Mulian.
And Madame Liu Qingti was housed in the Inner Palace,
Where she roams free and easy through the Buddha-land
    The scroll that I have proclaimed is the *Mulian Scroll*;
Please practice cultivation at the Dragon-Flower Assembly.
I urge you, people of this world, to observe the fast, and
Do not kill any sentient beings because you want to eat them!
    'Having heard their cries, to eat their meat is unbearable!'
How can the flesh of others ever benefit my own body?
Keeping the fast for one day and not eating spiced meats
Are as good as buying captive creatures and setting them free.
    You will not only transcend the three worlds[155] after you die;
You will also lead a happy and contented life in the present.
Just eat some pure and bland plants that bloom into flowers;
Never eat any horsemeat or beef, flesh still reeking of blood.
    No matter if they are your friends or they are your relatives,
Urge people to be satisfied with their lot and recite the sutras.
August Heaven will never refuse to assist those who are good;
It's the ordinary people who call forth their own punishment.[156]
    Gentlemen and farmers, craftsmen and merchants at work,
Getting a wife, having children, doing what they should do:
Above they ensure their parents are reborn in Ultimate Bliss;

Here below their hidden merits bring blessings to offspring.
After a hundred years, you'll then go to the Pure Land,
Leaving behind you a good reputation, praised in the world.
The fierce demons of darkness will politely bend in a bow;
And even the Judges of Darkness will rise from their seats.
Free and easy you'll pass through all eighteen layers of hell;
The demons Horseface and Oxhead will greet you from afar.
Stripped of your mortal name, you'll join the ranks of immortals;
Registered in the Western Paradise—no longer registered on earth.
After roaming beyond the thirty-three heavens, you'll join
The World-Honored One at the Dragon-Flower Assembly.
I have now finished proclaiming this scroll about Mulian,
And I wish everyone in the audience peace and prosperity.
I'm afraid there may have been mistaken words and sections,
So supplement this with Rebirth Tales and the Heart Sutra."[157]

Of the orphan souls who understand the One,[158]
None abides now in the Land of the Springs.[159]
Take the opportunity to grasp the true norm—
Each is fully responsible for his own actions.
If the full light of the inward vision appears,
Each and every place will be heaven itself.

The Precious Scroll of the Three Lives of Mulian:
After all bad karma had borne fruit and been repaid,
He saved his mother, and she was reborn in heaven—
Father, mother, and son all enjoy an eternal spring!

Namo Jile du Pusa Mohasa

Woman Huang
Recites the Diamond Sutra

When Woman Huang recites the Diamond Sutra,
The sound of her wooden fish rattles the hells.
An admiring Lord of Darkness invites Woman Huang
To the hells, where she laments the fate of the multitudes.
Reciting the Diamond Sutra, the buddhas offer protection;
She is transformed into a man, reborn to become an official.
She submits a memorial, quits her office, and seeks refuge in
    the Three Jewels;
Then, escaping from their mortal bodies, her entire family
    achieves Transcendence.

WOMAN HUANG TOURS THE UNDERWORLD
AND RECITES THE DIAMOND SUTRA

From the time that Pangu split heaven and earth into two,[1]
And the Three Emperors and Five Thearchs formed the world,[2]
The generations have endlessly risen and then receded again:
One morning the Son of Heaven—the next morning a slave!

    How many born behind vermilion gates have gone hungry?
How many born in huts of thatch have become men of rank?
The Roads of Good and Evil are both laid down by humans,
And what is recorded in the ledgers of merit is unmistaken:[3]

    Those in the world who always do good will surely prosper,
While those who do evil will be forced to suffer great pain.
The sutras were transmitted to China from India in the west[4]—
Designed to bring salvation to all the good people of the world.

    Even the eighteen arhats[5] were once thieves and robbers,
But by repenting of their sins and cultivating spiritual discipline,
Later they too were able to travel the road leading to heaven
And leave their golden images in the temples of earth below.

    Once there was a market town that had the name of Hanyang,
Which had a reputation for being a place of many good deeds.
Those who lived there took pleasure in the true and the good—
When have those who do evil ever enjoyed a happy life?

    But rather than speak to you any of those many tales,
Listen, and I'll speak of a certain Huang from Caozhou.

In this Caozhou there was a certain Woman Huang
Who was truly one of the woman sages of the world.
Her family lived in the Nanhua district of Caozhou;
Their home was located in the village of Qingping.

    Her father was generous, always doing good works,
And her mother read the sutras each and every day.
Woman Huang was her mother's own daughter,
And of her sisters, she was the fifth one.

    She would not drink the water from the fish-raising pond,
And she would not eat the five forbidden or pungent foods.[6]
At the age of nineteen she was married off to the Zhaos,

And for thirteen years she served as a hardworking wife.

 She gave birth to a son and two daughters:
Her son was given the name of Changshou;
Already by the time he was just three years of age,
He was bright, and he was clever beyond compare.

 Woman Huang and her children were always good,
But she feared that her husband was doing evil
By running a slaughterhouse and butcher shop—
His name was Lianfang, the master of the house.

 Every day he would slaughter two or three pigs,
And he would order Woman Huang to boil the water.[7]
Woman Huang boiled the water, her tears rolling down,
And she cried out: "Listen, husband, and I will explain:

 Today you slaughter the pigs and I boil the water:
The retribution of this lifetime will be hard to bear!
A white blade goes in, and a red one comes out—
It is a frightening thing, no matter what you say.

 The water bubbles, and it boils with a hissing sound;
Then the bristles are removed, the skin white as frost.
These pigs are then sold to other people to eat,
But the retribution must be endured by you and me.

 There are seventy-two good occupations,[8]
Why must you insist on being a butcher?
In the nineteen years that I lived at home,
I did not touch any of the forbidden foods,

 And every day I did nothing but read the sutras.
I am afraid that we will have to pay for our sins!
I urge you not to engage in this manner of work;
Close this butcher's shop and do something else!"

When Lianfang heard this, his heart filled with rage;
He cursed at Woman Huang and called her unwise.
"So, those who butcher pigs and sheep are evil men,
And when they die, they will become pigs and sheep?

 Who's ever seen a good man on the road to immortality?
And yet how many monks have died before their time!

The six domestic animals were originally meant to be eaten,
And it was King Yama who ordered them to be born as pigs.
    If everyone practiced spiritual discipline and non-killing,
There'd be no place to house the world's pigs and sheep!
You can read your sutras and accumulate your merit,
But I'll butcher my pigs and take my own punishment.
    Running a butcher shop may make me prime minister!
Master Li read the sutras, but he did not live very long;
He Jin slaughtered pigs but became a prime minister![9]
Why is there not a King Yama among the living?
    Your Diamond Sutra cannot be exchanged for money and rice,
But slaughtered hogs and butchered sheep can buy a plot of land!"

When Woman Huang heard this, tears ran down her cheeks.
She cried out: "My husband, listen to a few different views.
    You may say that He Jin became a prime minister,
But later he was the only one to perish by the sword!
The Diamond Sutra may not be worth money or rice,
But it will protect your entire family from calamity.
    As a butcher you are committing sins without end,
And the sufferings of hell will be difficult to bear.
Your body will be cut into tiny bits and pieces,
And you will weep endless tears, endless tears.
    Oxhead and Horseface will come and flog you,[10]
And the vats of boiling oil will be impossible to bear.
Beneath the Alas Bridge, your innards will be torn out;
And on Sword Mountain, your guts will be split open.[11]
    If you do not begin to read the sutras right now,
You definitely won't escape from Sword Mountain!
I urge you, Husband, to change your ways right now;
Learn from your wife how to read the Diamond Sutra."

When Lianfang heard these words, he got very mad:
"You're just a woman and don't know anything at all.
Day and night you simply ignore household affairs;
Dawn to dusk you urge me to read the Diamond Sutra.

What is more, you have a son and two daughters,
And in the future they will follow your example!
My family has run a butcher shop for generations,
And we have yet to see that King Yama in the flesh.

Now you say that you have not committed any sins,
But your sins will also be most difficult to absolve!
In winter you wear out so many padded brocade coats,
And in summer you wear out so many light silk gowns.[12]

In every year there are three hundred and sixty days!
How many pairs of embroidered shoes do you wear out?
Rubbing oils and body powders are also sinful objects—
How many thousands of rouge pots have you used up?

Plucking flowers to put in your hair is also a sin,
And it is a sin to waste and scatter the five grains.[13]
And yet even these sorts of sins are not the worst;
There are other kinds even more difficult to redeem.

In the morning you use the basin of water to wash your face;
In the evening you use the basin of water to wash your feet.
When you gave birth to your children, you also committed a sin:
How many bowls of bloody water, how many bowls of fluids?

For every child there were three basins of fluids;
So with three children, then, nine basins of fluids.
The bloodied waters were dumped into the gutters
And in so doing polluted the Sprite of the Eaves.

Three days and you were already back in the kitchen[14]
And by so doing polluted the Kitchen God.[15]
And before ten days were up, you went into the front hall
And by so doing polluted the family gods and ancestors.

And before a month was up, you went out of doors
And by so doing polluted the sun, moon, and stars.
You washed the bloodstained clothing in the river,
And the tainted waters polluted the dragon king.[16]

You also spilled these waters onto the ground,
Which left the spirits of hell with nowhere to hide.
After washing the clothes, you laid them on the bank to dry
And by so doing polluted the Great Yin and Great Yang.[17]

In vain you rely on your reading of the Diamond Sutra,
For your sins of a lifetime won't be so easily redeemed!"

When Woman Huang heard this, she began to weep;
She wept and wailed, and she cried so very piteously.
She took off the red silk robes that she was wearing;
She removed the golden combs that were in her hair.
    And then she dressed herself in brown monk's robes;
Brushing her hair, she used only water to make it shine.
She hung a single strand of white beads around her neck,[18]
Lit incense, and, palms together, recited the Diamond Sutra.
    After she had done all this, she called to her husband:
"My dear husband, listen and I will explain it all:
In bearing children, I have also committed sins—
We should've long ago lived in separate rooms.
    So from this day forward, you and I will sleep apart
And never again have any more sons or daughters.
You take our son and go with him to the east wing;
I'll take our daughters and return to the west wing.
    From now on, do not come again into my room;
Nor will I ever go into your room again either.
If some household matter arises, I'll just ignore it:
Mother and daughters will recite the Diamond Sutra.
    And in the future, whether the problem be large or small,
I shall not go to the east wing in search of Master Zhao."

When Lianfang heard her speak in this fashion,
He cursed Woman Huang and called her a fool.
"Read sutras, recite Buddha's name, that's your affair,
But how can you order me to live in a separate room?
    I took you to wife with three cups of tea and six gifts,[19]
Expecting to grow old together in peace and harmony.
In this world it is only brothers who are separated—
Who has ever heard of a husband and wife living apart?
    If you didn't want to have sons and daughters,
Then you should not have taken a husband!

You and I agreed to share one and the same bed,
Man and woman, talent and beauty in marriage."[20]

When Woman Huang heard him speak in this way,
With tears in her eyes, she most carefully explained.
And she fell to her knees right there in the dust,
Bowed to her husband and poured out her heart.
    "Our time on this earth has always been limited,
And the love of husband and wife is not forever.
You say there is no retribution for good and evil,
But I say there is a King Yama who exists for real!
    I watch how you take those pigs and butcher them,
Uselessly saving silver and gold to buy some land.
One of these days a demon will come to fetch you,
And then no gold and no silver will buy you time.
    And when your corpse is buried somewhere in the wilds,
And your soul tablet stands beside those of your ancestors,
Even if all kinds of offering are laid out on the altar,
How will you be able to come and partake of them?
    Your soul will be taken down into the Underworld,
Where you will suffer all the punishments of hell.
King Yama will pass judgment—he'll be in a rage,
And you will tremble in fear with no place to hide.
    Then you will repent, but it will be much too late,
And you will find yourself suffering terrible pain.
Don't say that you've got a long life ahead of you—
In the blink of an eye, your hair will turn white!
    Every life, every death, is like a spring dream;
All that is good and all that is evil is separately judged.
And all your family's triumphs will vanish into thin air,
And you will weep as everything begins to collapse.
    My husband, think carefully about the life you have led.
Why not change your ways and read the Diamond Sutra?
Right here at home I have the simple robes of a monk;
Let's go to the sutra hall and recite the Buddha's name.

Even if your life were to last a hundred thousand years,
It would still be better to do good and not go astray.
Whether you enjoy riches or fame is all up to Heaven,
So we must heed Heaven's will in living out our days.

Death can't be bought off with cash or gold and silver,
So why then suffer so, dashing frantically to and fro?"

As soon as Lianfang heard his wife's exhortations,
The thoughts in his head turned mournful and sad.

"Our marriage was determined in a previous life—
Why would I wish to live apart in the present one?
But now that you want to sleep in separate rooms,
You are leaving your husband without any choice."

He held his wife's and children's hands in his own,
And tears came to his eyes as he spoke his mind:

"I'd hoped to share the same bed-netting with you,
But I fear it would mean more sons and daughters
Who would pollute the spirits and cause you to sin,
Cause you to commit sins that are hard to redeem.

From this day forward, let's sleep in separate rooms,
So as to avoid having your lifetime cut short.
The three-year-old boy will go along with me,
Severed as with a knife from his mother's milk.

From now on, we'll never again share a bed
Nor think of ourselves as husband and wife."

When Woman Huang heard her husband's words,
With palms together, she bowed to Master Zhao.

"This first bow is for the deep love of my husband;
This second bow is for agreeing to run the household;
This third bow is for having agreed to care for our son;
This fourth bow is for having been so kind to his wife;

This fifth bow is for having had a change of heart;
This sixth bow is for having agreed that we sleep apart;
This seventh bow is for having done a charitable deed;

This eighth bow is so that he will not worry too much;
    This ninth bow is so that all will go smoothly for him;
This tenth bow is for letting me recite the Diamond Sutra."

Woman Huang then rose, having done with her bows,
And husband and wife wept and went their own ways.
Lianfang took his son to sleeping quarters elsewhere,
While Woman Huang took the girls to the west wing.
    She swept the sutra altar until it was sparkling clean;
Then she lit a stick of incense as tall as high heaven.
No talk of worldly affairs ever again reached her ears;
Head bowed, palms joined, she read the Diamond Sutra.
    All the day and into the middle of the night she chanted;
From the fifth watch she chanted until the break of day.
And day and night she did nothing but chant the sutras.
Her chanting was such that all of the gods grew uneasy,
    And then the Senluo Hall began to rock and to shake,
As from the eighteen hells there shone a bright light.[21]
In front of the Maitreya Buddha a golden light appeared;[22]
From Purple Bamboo Grove an auspicious vapor rose.[23]
    King Yama, who was seated there in the Senluo Hall,
Then turned to ask the officials who flanked his throne:
"Could it be that a truly enlightened ruler has been born?
Could it be the Jade Emperor coming down from heaven?[24]
    The Buddha of the Western Regions descending to earth?
Or is it Master Li on his way now to the Western Regions?[25]
Otherwise why would the heavens be shaking like this,
Reverberating with such a noise above the Senluo Hall?"
    The officials in attendance hastened to speak
And carefully explain it from beginning to end:
    "It isn't that a truly enlightened ruler has been born;
It isn't the Jade Emperor coming down from heaven
Nor the Buddha of the Western Regions descending to earth,
And it isn't Master Li on his way to the Western Regions.
    In Caozhou there is a district that is called Nanhua
And, in the area of Qingping, a Zhao Family Village.

In that Zhao family there is a certain Woman Huang,
Who, having fasted and bathed, recites the Diamond Sutra.
　She has already read it through sixteen times,
Startling the Eight Immortals flanking the hall.[26]
All the gods under heaven are now thronging around her;
There is a great rush on the road to the Western Regions."

The officials, having investigated all sides of the matter,
Then presented their findings to the Great Enlightened Ruler.
King Yama wanted to send the demon Horseface to fetch her
So that she might answer his questions on the Diamond Sutra,
　But his civil and military officials hastily advised him:
"Your Royal Highness, please listen to our explanation,
A good person must be summoned by another good person;
Only with an evil person should one use such brute force."
　And so King Yama again called for his messengers:
"Golden Lad and Jade Maiden, listen most carefully,[27]
Go now to the Nanhua district of Caozhou,
To Qingping and Zhao Family Village.
　In the Zhao family there is a certain Woman Huang—
Request that she come and recite the Diamond Sutra."[28]

Golden Lad and Jade Maiden acknowledged the command
And with focused minds set out for Zhao Family Village.
They traveled countless miles through the Underworld,
Passing by countless places where sinners suffered.
　They traveled until they reached a fork in the road,
Where a tablet marked the border of Yin and Yang.[29]
Golden Lad and Jade Maiden asked the god of the soil,[30]
And the god of the soil hastened to carefully explain:
　"Now if you were planning to invite Woman Huang,
Woman Huang is just now reading the Diamond Sutra.
But I must tell you, Golden Lad and Jade Maiden,
That a good person like her is not found every day!
　When you meet her, you must be very polite,
For the Eight Immortals are there on the altar."

Golden Lad then addressed him and said:
"Earth god, listen and I will carefully explain.
You must travel together with us;
Go with us to invite Woman Huang."
    The earth god then answered them and said:
"Golden Lad, listen and I will explain it to you.

    Woman Huang has always been a good woman.
From morning till night reciting the Diamond Sutra.
She keeps the Three Obediences and Four Virtues:[31]
Such virtue and wisdom is not an everyday thing!

    Now if you want to invite her, then go invite her,
But we would not dare set foot in the sutra hall.
But I will now make sure to register your entry,
So the two of you may go your way without fear."

When Golden Lad arrived at the Zhao family gates,
He found the door gods to be very fierce indeed.[32]
Golden Lad and Jade Maiden then spoke and said:
"You two honorable generals, listen to what we say:

    Yama, the great king, has dispatched us to this place;
He has commanded us to come fetch Fifth Daughter
And accompany her down into the Underworld
To recite the Diamond Sutra in King Yama's court."

    When the door gods heard this, they became angry,
And they cursed that young fellow, Golden Lad:
"Now, you had better get out of this place very fast;
There's no point in staying and trying to explain.

    Why should a good woman have her life cut short?
By rights her life should be as long as Heaven itself!
We gods will not allow you to enter this place,
So hurry back to the King of the Underworld."

    Golden Lad and Jade Maiden again pleaded with them:
"Generals, please listen to what it is we have to say.
Since time immemorial we have invited good people
To the world here below to recite the Diamond Sutra.

    If the generals do not allow us to enter,

How can we return to face King Yama?
If the generals will kindly allow us to enter,
After she recites the sutra, we will escort her back.

   Then mother and children will be together again,
And their time on earth will be as long as Heaven."
When the door gods heard this, their rage subsided,
And they let the two enter and fetch Fifth Daughter.

   When Golden Lad arrived inside the kitchen,
He bowed with respect to the God of the Stove.
Again he went through the story of why he had come,
But the God of the Stove was unwilling to decide.

   Golden Lad and Jade Maiden once again pleaded:
"We do beg of you, God of the Stove!"
The God of the Stove then said to them:
"Young Ones, now you listen to me and I will explain.

   Woman Huang's life span should be seventy-two years.
Why then should she die when she is only thirty-two?
You want my seal of approval, which I don't dare give,
So just go back and report to King Yama."

   Golden Lad then answered him and said:
"Most exalted Stove God, listen to what I say.
It was all because the royal throne was shaken
And a bright light shone through the gates of hell.

   The officials reported that it was due to Woman Huang
Reading the Diamond Sutra in this Zhao Family Village.
And so King Yama especially dispatched us to invite her,
Invite her to the Underworld to recite the Diamond Sutra.

   Since Woman Huang's allotted life span hasn't yet been filled,
After reciting the sutra, she will be escorted back to the world.
Colored banners and jeweled dishes will be prepared for her,
And the Underworld will be arranged so it gleams with light.

   Only if we take this good woman to the Underworld
Will we be able to return and report to King Yama.
If the God of the Stove won't accept our request,
How will we then be able to face King Yama?"

   The God of the Stove then answered them and said:

"Once she goes to the Underworld, how will she return?
If this good person's life were to be nipped in the bud,
Later no one will want to recite the Diamond Sutra!

    Although it is King Yama who has asked to see her,
People in the world see it as a matter of life and death.
If today I agree to this request that you have made,
I'm afraid I will have betrayed good Woman Huang.

    But if today I refuse this request that you have made,
It then will make it hard for you to face King Yama.
So I'd best agree to this request that you have made.
Golden Boy and Jade Maiden, listen and I will explain.

    You may take Woman Huang back to the Underworld,
But after she recites the Diamond Sutra, bring her back!
You must be sure to keep the promise you have made.
Do not be a young man who doesn't keep his word."

When Golden Lad heard this, he quickly bowed farewell
And, leaving the God of the Stove, went to the sutra hall.
The God of the Stove had already registered their entry,
And so he arrived at the ancestral hall of the Zhao family.

    As soon as the ancestors saw him, they became angry,
And Golden Lad cried out, in trembling and fear.
Though they were following the orders of King Yama,
They still had to make a plan and talk the matter over.

    So they thought for quite a while before they went in;
Slowly, slowly, they approached the ancestral altar
And asked the ancestors to please register their entry,
So as to get Woman Huang to recite the Diamond Sutra.

    Turning his head, he spoke to the ancestors and said,
"We are Underworld officials come for Fifth Daughter Huang.
If she recites the Diamond Sutra without any error,
Then even you will be allowed to ascend to heaven!"

    The ancestors thought about it for quite a while;
Then they lowered their heads and silently wept.
So Golden Lad and Jade Maiden had no choice
But to beg the ancestors to make up their minds.

"Woman Huang's recitation has moved Heaven and Earth,
And it has also moved the Kings of the Ten Courts of Hell.
We have come here today to present her with an invitation,
How can the ancestors refuse this request we have made?"

The ancestors closed their eyes and just sat in their niches;
The Young Ones begged but could not get their permission,
So they turned and respectfully bowed to the Three Officials.[33]
They begged the Three Officials to give them a written permit.

But when the Three Officials did not respond to their request,
The Young Ones became anxious, and the tears began to flow;
They took three steps forward and went down on their knees
And, addressing the Three Officials, explained the reasons why.

"Since ancient times every saint who has attained the Way
Had to first request a pass to ascend into the heavens.
Now when it comes to Fengdu[34] and the Underworld,
It is also up to the Great King to make the decision.

Woman Huang's chanting of the sutras is very fine.
How could the great Emperor not comment on it?"

The Three Officials slowly, slowly, began to speak, and
They cried out: "Young Ones, listen and we will explain.
Woman Huang's life span has been set at seventy-two,
And when it is fulfilled, we will escort her to heaven."

When the Young Ones heard them speak in this way,
They then begged the city god to make a decision.[35]
When they saw the city god, they hastened to pay respect:
"City God Most High, listen and we will carefully explain.

Yama, King of the Underworld, has dispatched us here,
Dispatched us here so as to fetch Fifth Daughter."
The city god was helpful and said these words:
"Young Ones, listen to what I have to say.

If I do not make a decision in your favor,
You'll not likely gain entrance to the sutra hall.
There are so many gods sitting in the sutra hall,
Who would dare enter to fetch Fifth Daughter?

You must make a deal with the ancestors;

Make it clear that you must go to the sutra hall."
The Young Ones then spoke with the ancestors.
"Ancestors Most High, listen and we'll fully explain.

    The Kings of the Ten Courts have dispatched us here;
Give us your stamp of approval to fetch Fifth Daughter."
Silent thoughts went through the ancestors' minds:
"We must not offend the Kings of the Ten Courts.

    Besides, the God of the Stove has agreed to this.
And the door gods let them come to the sutra hall.
Neither door gods nor earth gods can block them;
It seems she must go and recite the Diamond Sutra!"

    So all they could do was to rise up from their seats
And, with four bows, apologize to the King of Darkness.
After completing their bows, they registered their entry,
After which they were allowed to go into the sutra hall.

    When the Young Ones arrived outside the sutra hall,
They observed there inside a great multitude of gods:
    The Four Patriarchs sat in the middle of the hall;[36]
The Eight Immortals flanked them on either side.
The Heavenly Guardians halted them at the door, [37]
And above the Maitreya Buddha laughed out loud.[38]

    When the Young Ones saw this, they panicked!
"Tell us how we can get inside the sutra hall!
If we try to force our way into the sutra hall,
We fear the Patriarchs will make things hard!"

They thought, but they couldn't come up with a plan.
Then suddenly they got a flash of inspiration:
Quickly they took their banners and held them aloft,
And these banners shone with bright shining light.

    As soon as the Heavenly Kings saw this, they asked:
"Golden Lad and Jade Maiden, where are you going?"
Golden Lad and Jade Maiden answered them, saying:
"Heavenly Kings High Above, listen and we'll explain.

    Today we have come here at the command of King Yama,

Who requests that the good woman recite the Diamond Sutra.
If it were not for this summons issued by King Yama himself,
How would we have dared come here to fetch Fifth Daughter?"

When the Heavenly Kings heard this, they were most angry,
And they gnashed their silver teeth with a terrible noise.

"There are so many evil people in the World of Light,
And yet you must come and take away good Fifth Daughter!
Today we refuse to consent to the request you have made,
And we want you to go back from whence you came!"

Golden Lad and Jade Maiden had nothing to say in reply;
In fear and trembling, how terribly anxious they were!
Although they could see Woman Huang at a distance,
They did not dare go inside and fetch Fifth Daughter

But could only bow with great respect and wait outside.
When the Maitreya Buddha saw them, he had to speak,
And so the Living Buddha opened his golden mouth
And cried out: "All of you gods and Heavenly Kings,

An early birth, an early death, an early enlightenment:
That's the way one avoids having to suffer in this world.
To chant sutras is only to worship the meditation cushion;
It is better to be saved and worship the King of Darkness.

You all must let Golden Lad go inside now;
Let him go inside and fetch Fifth Daughter."
The Heavenly Kings obeyed the Buddha's command,
And they told Golden Lad to enter the Buddha hall.

When Golden Lad heard this, he quickly bowed,
Bowed to all the gods, as happy as he could be.
He lightly, lightly, went inside the sutra hall
And cried out: "Good woman, do stay calm!"

Woman Huang then addressed him and asked:
"To what family do you belong, young scholar?
And what is that you are holding in your hand,
Shimmering and glimmering, shining so bright?

Just say what young woman you are seeking,

And why it is you've come into my sutra hall.
I no longer concern myself with worldly affairs
But instead single-mindedly chant the Diamond Sutra.

 If today you come with a matter that must be seen to,
Then go to the east wing and speak with Master Zhao."

Golden Lad then answered her, and he said:
"Good woman, listen to the long and short of it.

 We are not visitors from the World of Light;
We are a pair of messengers from the Underworld.
Having heard how the good woman reads the sutras,
King Yama wants you to recite the Diamond Sutra."

 When Woman Huang heard this, her blood ran cold,
And the tears from her eyes rolled down her chest.

 "But reading the sutras should lengthen one's life!
Who'd have known that chanting would cut it short!
If you want me to give up my life, I don't mind at all,
But to leave behind my children would break my heart.

 These children of mine—who will care for them?
I have separated from my husband and sleep alone.
How can I bear it, for Jiaogu is still so very young,
And at three, how can Changshou be without his ma?[39]

 Wait three more years, and then you may fetch me.
Why must I go to the King of the Underworld today?
Wait until my son and daughters have grown up—
Until the lantern in one room has lit up the next.

 After my son is wed and my daughters are married,
Then you may come for me, and I will not complain.
Since time immemorial there has been life and death:
In a lifetime, it's hard to avoid the messenger of death.

 If I was taken away today, I would not really mind,
But I pity my son and daughters, who will suffer so.
I will give to you cash of gold and of silver
If you'll return to the Kings of the Ten Courts.

 Wait three more years and then you may fetch me,
And I'll not be anxious at heart or troubled in mind."

At this point Golden Lad spoke as follows:
"We Underworld officials are not like those here above.
Only in the World of Light is value placed on wealth;
We Underworld officials value filial piety, value wisdom.

If King Yama decides you must die at the third watch,
Then we cannot let you wait until the break of day.
You must not be attached to your son and daughters;
You must not be attached to the man you've married.

King Yama makes no distinction between young and old;
Even a one-year-old child must also sometimes die!
Now we must urge you to make haste and go;
There is no need to weep and wail and carry on.

Originally the demon Oxhead was to fetch you,
But an assistant judge quickly stopped King Yama,
And the King of the Underworld sent me instead,
Sent me to this place to fetch Fifth Daughter.

Fifth Daughter, you should not weep too much,
But rather happily go to meet with the King of Hell.
The love between husband and wife will end one day,
And in the future sons and daughters will also leave.

If you go with us and recite the Diamond Sutra,
We will escort you back to the World of Light."

Woman Huang wept and thought to herself:
"It would seem that this is the decree of fate.
I have thought and thought but to no avail;
I might as well abandon life and go along."

She bid the young messengers to sit in the hall:
"Wait until I say farewell to my husband, Zhao."
She bid farewell to Master Zhao and to all the family;
She bid farewell to the family gods and the Stove God.

Brokenhearted, she then bid farewell to her children,
But she could not keep the tears from pouring down.
She bid farewell to her brother-in-law and sister-in-law:
"Do not say that Woman Huang died before her time!

I have to bid farewell to everything and everyone:

Now I will entrust the children to my husband's care."
Woman Huang then went weeping into the west wing.
She cried out: "My husband, listen and I will explain!

　You and I have shared a bed for thirteen years,
And I have borne only two daughters and a son.
It is said that a couple should grow old together—
Who would have known that my days were numbered?

　I thought that chanting sutras would ensure long life—
Who would have known that it would cut my life short?
I have come to bid you farewell, my husband,
Because in the future, I will not see you again."

As she spoke these words, in her heart she thought:
"This is worse than a knife slicing my innards apart!
It isn't that your foolish wife is abandoning you;
It's just that I hate that heartless old King Yama.

　But husband and wife are like birds in the same forest;
When Death comes, each goes off in a different direction."
When Lianfang heard her speak in this way,
He quickly came forward with his complaint.

　"Is it that you have met up with a wandering ghost?
Is it that you have offended some Diamond King?
A long time ago I warned you, but you paid no heed,
So you must travel death's road and join King Yama."

When Woman Huang heard her husband's words,
Weeping, she beat her breast and stamped her feet.
"I was over in the sutra hall chanting the sutra,
When all of a sudden a Jade Maiden came in.

　She said that King Yama had issued the order;
I'm to be taken away to recite the Diamond Sutra.
This is why I have come to bid you farewell;
Husband, please do not continue as before."

　She fell down in the dust on both her knees:
"Husband, please listen to what I have to say.
If you go out the gate, you may return one day,

But if you die, you will never again come home.
I think of our children, who are still very young;
They are entirely dependent on you, my husband.
The boy must study and be respectful of his teachers;
When the girls grow up, they must be suitably married.
After we part today, we will probably not meet again.
How it breaks my heart to leave my children behind!"

When Lianfang heard this, he spoke to her, saying:
"My wife, listen and I will explain to you in full.
I sell meat from early morning until evening falls,
And at night I keep the books until the break of day.
Who'll be there to make sure the boy isn't hungry?
Who'll be there to look over the girls' needlework?
A husband without a wife, a home without a master—
With whom now will I discuss problems that arise?"
Woman Huang wept and answered him, saying:
"Husband, there is no need to feel so sad.
It is Heaven's will that I leave you now.
I will leave you, my husband, to sleep alone.
It's I who have needlessly caused you grief,
But for now try to bear with it for a while,
And after the eighteen months of mourning
Take a good and wise woman to be your wife.
She must keep to the Three Obediences and Four Virtues
And discuss with you the management of your household.
When choosing a wife, make sure she has no children—
If she has her own children, then both of you will suffer.
For after a while she will treat her stepchildren badly,
And it is not likely that she will love them as her own.
And when you go out on the road to do business,
You must remember your children and come home;
When the rice is ready, share it with them,
And do not on any account push them aside.
If their stepmother mistreats my children,
They will of course cry for their own mother.

Children and stepchildren must be treated alike,
So do not listen to a stepmother's complaints.

Each of these matters is your responsibility,
And you must not be swayed by what you hear.
There are stepmothers who are very good,
But there are also stepmothers who are not.

Selfish, they curse and do not keep accounts,
And then they pick quarrels with their husbands
While meals go uncooked and clothes unwashed,
And their foul language is hard to put up with!

Once I've left you, it will be difficult to return:
I entrust everything to you to manage and decide.
I have much to say, but I cannot talk any longer,
And I must go to the west wing to see my son."

Woman Huang then went into the west wing;
When she saw Changshou, her heart broke.

"My son, there you lie still asleep in your crib,
Unaware that your mother is going to King Yama.
Quickly, quickly, let me hold you to my breast;
This milk is called Leaving-One's-Mother's Milk.

Since giving birth to an eighteen-inch-long babe,
I've never been apart from you more than a moment.
I have held you close to me for three whole years,
Changing you, keeping you dry and comfortable.

I just want to caress you—how big you've grown!
Who'd have known that today we'd be separated?
Today, my son, you nurse at my breast;
Tomorrow, my son, you will be desolate.

My son, from now on think no more of me
But go along with your father on his business.
And you and your sisters must be obedient;
Don't go to the sutra hall crying for your mother.

My son, later you must not weep and wail
When your mother goes to hell, never to return.
But now, how can I bear to leave you behind?

King Yama has picked me, although I'm a mother.
My son, quickly drink of your mother's milk!"
Her tears poured down, and she piteously wept:
"I must put you down, and yet I cannot do it!
My heart is breaking with an unbearable pain.

When you grow up and have a family of your own,
Morning and evening light a stick of incense for me.
On Clear and Bright Festival burn paper money for me,
And on Double-Ninth make offerings for your mother:[40]

Lay out dishes of plain rice and meatless vegetables,
And perhaps your mother will come herself to eat them.
Oh how it breaks my heart to leave you behind!
Now I must bid farewell to Jiaogu and Banjie.

My two daughters, listen to what I have to say:
Your mother must leave you and go to King Yama."

She clasped her daughters' hands in her own
And cried: "Banjie, dear little apple of my eye,
Your mother's heart feels like it is being cut open;
Separation in life and death is the saddest of all!

I have things to say, but I can't seem to say them.
To have to abandon my children causes such pain!
Once, you sat with your mother in the sutra hall,
But tonight mother and children must be parted.

As we are about to part, I bid you do as I say:
Don't copy your mother and recite the Diamond Sutra!
It is said that chanting sutras ensures a long life—
Who'd have known that it actually cuts it short?

Your younger brother is still just a baby,
So you must tell him not to call for his ma.
During the day take him out front to play;
At night sleep with him in the west room.

After I have been dead for a year and a half,
Your father will probably take another wife.
You must be careful how you treat your stepmother
For a stepmother is not the same as your own mother.

On summer days you must boil the water for her,

And on winter days you must take fire to her room.
When you sweep the house, begin with her room
And diligently attend to every troublesome task.

    Your stepmother may be ignorant and thoughtless;
In fact, she very well may not be a good woman at all.
Wait until your stepmother has gone to bed
Before going with your sister to your room.

    If you have complaints, don't take them to your father;
If your father hears them, he will scold your stepmother.
If your father scolds your stepmother, she will scold you
And so you will be the ones to suffer her blows and curses.

    When your mother beats you, she knows when to be severe;
When your stepmother beats you, she'll be unbearably harsh.

    You must quickly learn to sew and do needlework,
Master the art of cutting and making your own clothes.
And when, my children, you have mastered these arts,
You will take all these strengths to your husbands' homes.

    The day will come when you'll grow up and be adults,
And naturally you each will be matched up with a fine man.
If the man is talented, then the lady will be lovely,
And their harmonious union will last forever after.

    My children, learn the ways of the women's quarters,
And the Three Obediences and the Four Virtues.
For if something happens and you do something wrong,
It's not you they'll curse, they'll curse your mother,

    Curse your mother for mistakenly chanting the sutras.
I'll leave behind a bad reputation; it'll spread around.
They will say that this pious, sutra-chanting woman
Alive did no good and dead left no shining example.

    Jiaogu and Banjie, now remember: a good reputation
Is hard to acquire, and a bad reputation is hard to bear.
You must always speak up and defend your mother;
Do not give your mother-in-law reason to curse me.

    Obey all your in-laws and your husbands' sisters;
When you become a wife, you must be a wise one.
If you had me with you here, I could teach you;

So after I am dead and gone, you must be strong.
Do not spend your free time in your mother's room,
And at night make no mention of your own mother.
Changshou is yet small and still doesn't understand,
So don't let him go outside and play in the puddles.
You must also be very respectful of your father;
Father and children must put up with each other.
From this day forward, after your mother has left you,
Do not go with your brother into the sutra hall."
Jiaogu and Banjie clung to her tightly,
Calling: "Mother," and crying: "Mama!
How can you have the heart to abandon us
And leave your three children to suffer so?
Now there is no one to wash our soiled clothes
Or to replace our shoes when they become worn.
Your three children are all still so very young,
It would be best to go with you to King Yama!"

When they looked and saw that their mother was dead,
Jiaogu and Banjie rose up startled and panic-stricken;
Their weeping reached up to heaven and down to earth.
Weeping, they cried: "Mother," weeping they cried: "Ma!
You have left us now and gone to the Underworld,
Leaving behind your children with broken hearts.
You've entrusted your three-year-old to our care,
But it will be hard to caress and to feed and clothe him!"
When Lianfang heard this, he grew terribly distraught
And cried out: "My wife, Fifth Daughter Huang!"
With both hands he clasped those of his wife:
"Wife of mine, hasten back to the World of Light!
The sound of our daughters' weeping breaks my heart,
And the sound of our son's crying goes on and on."
Lianfang again called out: "My dear darling wife!
Wife, come quickly back to the World of Light!"
After a while, Woman Huang came to once again
And cried: "Husband, listen and I will fully explain.

It is not that I am recklessly abandoning my children;
King Yama has decided that my life will not be long."

Woman Liu[41] appeared in the doorway of the room
And cried: "Woman Huang!" and laughed out loud.
"Once I urged you not to have faith in the Buddha,
But you insisted on chanting the Diamond Sutra.

And now look where it has all brought you!
You've left your children to suffer so bitterly,
But now it is too late to repent of your actions.
If you hold on, you won't be able to see King Yama,

So just stop worrying and return to the Underworld.
I will take care of your son and your daughters;
I'll make sure that they have three meals a day,
And I will change their clothes and wash them.

Since I can raise your son and your daughters,
There is no need for you to wail and weep such tears.
Your mistake was to not listen to my advice before;
Today there is no escaping the Messenger of Death."

When Woman Huang heard her say this, she said:
"Dear sister-in-law, many thanks for your kindness.
I have lived here together with you for thirteen years,
And between the two of us, we never had bad words.

Now I suddenly have to go to the World of Darkness;
I hope that you will take good care of my children,
So, if his business will allow my man some leisure,
The whole family, old and young, may live happily."

Woman Huang then bid farewell to her children,
And she bid farewell to Woman Liu and Lianfang.
And then she went straight into the kitchen,
Heated water, bathed, and went to the sutra hall.

She bowed when she came to the ancestral altar.
"You gods and deities, now listen and I will explain:
I now bid you farewell and leave for the Underworld;
Never again will I return to chant the Diamond Sutra."

She then bid farewell to the family gods and ancestors,
And she bid farewell to the gods of the kitchen too.
"You, Controller of Fate,[42] are the main family god;
On the first and the fifteenth you ascend to heaven

To inform the Jade Emperor of all the good things,
But don't tell him about any of the bad things.
Today I am going to return to the Underworld;
I'll no longer come to the kitchen to heat water.

So now I will offer you tea and a change of water,
Burn incense, sweep the floor, bow to the Stove God.
I'll burn incense and heat the bathwater.
I will wear only a simple pair of slippers.

Above, I will put on a blue cotton top;
Below, I will put on a black silk skirt.
With a rosary of white beads about my neck
And holding a fly whisk,[43] I'll enter the sutra hall."

Seated in the lotus position, her palms together,
She cried out: "Golden Lad, where are you now?"
Golden Lad and Jade Maiden quickly came forward
And took her to meet with the King of the Underworld.

At the break of dawn Woman Huang passed away,
And Zhao Lianfang wept pitifully in the sutra hall.
He cried out: "Dear wife, my heart is breaking;
You have abandoned your children and husband.

Now that you have gone off to the Underworld,
How am I going to make it through the days?
You lie there and will not say a single word,
Having left your children behind to suffer!"

We will no longer speak of Lianfang's sorrow
Nor describe the children weeping for their mother
But speak of Woman Huang's trek to the Underworld:
Disoriented and lost, she followed behind as if in a daze.

Straightaway they reached the temple of the earth god;
The earth god received her and offered her some tea.
She then thanked both the city god and the earth god,

And with the youths leading the way, continued on.
	Before she knew it, they arrived at a fork in the road
Where a sign marked the gate dividing Yin and Yang.
The earth gods of the Underworld came to receive her,
Bidding the other earth gods to return to their halls.

🔸 Woman Huang then turned to Golden Lad and asked:
"Where is it that these three broad highways lead to?"
Golden Lad then answered her, and he said:
"Good Woman, listen and I will explain it to you.
	One of these highways passes through the world of the living
And the busy confusion of births and deaths, deaths and births.
One of these highways passes through the world of heaven;
Lit up clearly and shining bright, it goes straight to that place.
	One of these highways passes through the Underworld,
And at the very end of it, you will meet with King Yama.
Good woman, this is the highway that you will take,
But we will guarantee your safety and well-being."
	Ahead they came to a shop that gave away tea;
There the tea water was furiously boiling away.
Woman Huang then realized how thirsty she was,
And she wanted to go inside and have some tea.
	However, the Young Ones continued on and said:
"Good woman, listen and we will explain in full:
When it comes to this tea, we advise you not to drink it,
Or you will not be able to recite the Diamond Sutra.
	This is not like the tea in the World of Light,
Because this tea is called the Broth of Oblivion.
Parents who drink it don't recognize their children;
Children who drink it don't recognize their mothers."
	Woman Huang, hearing this, did not dare drink
But, following the Young Ones, went on her way.
Suddenly she raised her head and looked about:
The entire road had grown most fearfully dark.
	Woman Huang again asked the Young Ones:

"Where will this great highway lead us to?"

The Young Ones then answered her and said:
"Listen, good woman, and we will explain it all.
This is the great highway that you must travel;
Ahead lie dangers that will be hard to endure!

The Wasted Money Mountain is difficult to cross;
The base of Slippery Oil Mountain is something fearful.
Its sufferings and tortures no words can describe:
Atop Sword Mountain are guts that lie exposed.

Mulian the filial monk once passed along this way
On his way to the Underworld in search of his mother.
The Lustrous Emperor on Double-Fifth opened the hells,
His one intention being to find the location of a good man.[44]

That good man passed safely through these places,
So you may go ahead now and you will be protected."

Woman Huang continued on behind the Young Ones.
And then ahead, as they came to Hazel Grouse Village,
They passed a row of evil-looking demon-soldiers,
All with iron whips in their hands, as fierce as tigers.

Woman Huang saw them, her heart filled with fear:
All she could hear was the loud cracking of iron whips.
But the Young Ones sang out: "Hurry and let us pass!
For this is Fifth Daughter Huang from Zhao Family Village."

The demons Oxhead and Horseface then replied:
"We are just on our way to Zhao Family Village,
For in the Zhao family there is a certain Woman Liu;
We are going specifically to bring her to King Yama."

When Woman Huang heard this, the tears rolled down.
"Woman Liu is none other than my elder sister-in-law.
In the past I warned her, but she would not do good,
And now she must also appear before the King of Hell.

Now the demons Oxhead and Horseface have left.
How can I keep from feeling anxious and distraught?"
Golden Lad at this point answered her and said:
"Do not concern yourself with other people's affairs.

On the road to hell there are all kinds of travelers.
Truly, good and bad must go their separate ways.
After a while, when she has arrived at this place,
She will realize that there is a Yin and a Yang."

Woman Huang then slowly, slowly, went on her way,
Until ahead she caught sight of yet another mountain.
Then she asked the Young Ones what place this was,
And the Young Ones came, and they explained it all.
    "That is none other than Slippery Oil Mountain:
Many are the sinners who are kept on its summit.
Once they lose their footing, they can hardly cross,
And so they remain there on the mountain to suffer."
    When Woman Huang went forward to try and see,
Golden Lad and Jade Maiden cried: "Fifth Daughter!
You cannot go on to this Slippery Oil Mountain—
We are afraid the blood will stain your clothes!"

And she went on, the Young Ones leading the way.
But when she saw a mountaintop as white as frost,
Woman Huang again turned to the youths, asking:
"Brother, is this also a place where sinners are kept?"
    The Young Ones then took her there to have a look:
Hanging guts and entrails gave off an unbearable stench.
They then went forward a few steps to yet another place;
It was Sword Mountain, so desolate and so bare.
    Woman Huang wanted to keep going and have a look,
But Golden Lad and Jade Maiden cried: "Fifth Daughter!
Exposed intestines and hanging guts are what's up ahead,
Flogged feet and whipped hands and tears pouring down."
    When Woman Huang saw this, she chanted the sutra,
But the Young Ones ordered her to keep moving on.
They walked until they reached the shade of a tall tree;
Woman Huang sat down, wanting to cool herself off.
    Golden Lad and Jade Maiden stood on either side,
With colorful banners and a luminous canopy of jewels.

We'll not speak of Woman Huang seated under the tree,
But we'll sing of Woman Liu of Zhao Family Village.
Woman Liu was extremely evil in her behavior:
Beating monks, cursing priests, and being abusive,
Tinkering with the truth and ruining human affairs,
Deceiving both herself and others with an evil mind.
Not only did she touch the floor with her hands and feet;
She entered the main hall with messy hair and absent mind.
When she saw people in need, she was unwilling to help,
And she refused anything to do with her own kith and kin.
Scolding her in-laws and tyrannizing her sister-in-law,
She would be up bright and early ready to start a fight.
Here, she'd call her father-in-law a useless bum;
There, she'd call her mother-in-law a stupid fool.
But of herself she had only good things to boast about,
Spending each day comparing herself to everyone else.
Ever since Woman Huang had left for the Underworld,
Woman Liu made fun of Fifth Daughter every day:
"She refused to wear silks, refused to drink wine;
She refused to eat chicken or duck, refused to eat lamb.
That good-for-nothing woman died in such misery
Because she spent her life chanting the Diamond Sutra.
Neither monk nor priest, she recited the Buddha's name;
Morning and night she'd endlessly strike the wooden fish.[45]
At nighttime she made so much noise no one could sleep;
In daytime, she burned incense haphazardly everywhere.
But what about that now, where is she gone to now?
Why doesn't she come and recite the Diamond Sutra?"
Just as Woman Liu was saying these very words,
Then both Oxhead and Horseface walked in —
Flanked by evil spirits and fierce demons,
Iron clubs and whips reverberating loudly.
Unhindered by house gods and Underworld officials,
Then Oxhead and Horseface just laughed.
As soon as Woman Liu saw them, she lost her head,
And she fainted and fell over into the dust.

Crying out: "Husband, come here quickly!"
And her children cried in confused dismay.
"I have seen a ghost in broad daylight;
I think that must mean my end is near."
Then Oxhead and Horseface grabbed her,
And they locked an iron cangue around her neck.
    As soon as Woman Liu saw her husband's face,
She pointed to her breast and opened her mouth.
She wanted to speak but found that she couldn't,
And all he saw were the tears welling in her eyes.
    The demons Oxhead and Horseface had no pity,
And they took Woman Liu away to see King Yama.

They went straightaway to the earth god temple,
And then the earth god sent her on to the city god,
Who threw her down and gave her twenty lashings,
And then sent her to the earth prison to suffer its torments.
    The demon-soldiers picked up Woman Liu and left,
And they walked down the road as fast as they could.
Before they knew it, they came to a fork in the road
And handed their documents to the earth god there.
    Then the earth god scolded Woman Liu and said:
"When you were alive you did not behave well!"
He quickly turned her over to the two messengers,
Who were to take her to the place for evil people.
    Seeing they'd arrived at Slippery Oil Mountain,
They ordered Woman Liu to climb up to the top.
But Woman Liu could barely stand up on her feet;
Her whole body was covered with drops of blood.
    In a while she came to the foot of the mountain;
The demon-soldiers helped her up and then left.
They had been walking along for not very long
When she saw from afar the gleaming pale swords.
    When Woman Liu saw these, she couldn't move,
But they beat her mercilessly with whips of iron.
She regretted not being good when she was alive

And wondered how she would ever get to King Yama.
Woman Liu was just then in an impossible bind,
And demon-soldiers were milling about on all sides.
Suddenly a rosy cloud rose over the mountaintop,
And the mountain itself gave off a brilliant light.
The demon-soldiers said it was Yama's command
That Woman Liu did not have to cross this mountain.
Who would have guessed that Woman Huang, by the tree,
Could not endure the sight of this Sword Mountain,
And without thinking began to recite the Diamond Sutra?
This is why the mountain gave off such a brilliant light.
If Woman Huang had not started reciting the sutra then,
How would Woman Liu have ever crossed this mountain?
The Young Ones then asked the good woman to continue on,
So Woman Huang stood up and quickly went on her way.
But when she looked up, she caught sight of Woman Liu,
And she cried to her relative with tears rolling down:
"In the past I warned you, but you didn't behave;
You cursed me instead and called me a lazy wife.
Please do not grab onto me with your hands;
I fear you will stain my clothes with blood!"
Woman Liu now blamed and rebuked herself;
The sins of her vile self were truly unbearable.
She cried out: "Sister-in-law, come and save me,
And let me accompany you to see King Yama!"
Woman Huang's eyes started to fill with tears,
But the demon-soldiers came and explained to her:
"Good people mustn't worry about bad people's affairs.
The six paths of transmigration are determined by fate;
On the road to the Yellow Springs, all must travel alone.
It is true that good and evil must go their separate ways.
At this time even father and son cannot help each other—
How much less so if someone is just your sister-in-law!"

When they reached the place of the Gate of Ghosts,
Woman Liu was made to suffer terrible punishments,

But as soon as the officials of hell saw Woman Huang,
Their faces shone with joy, and they laughed out loud.
　The demons Oxhead and Horseface respectfully bowed;
Golden Lad and Jade Maiden placed incense in her hands.
After Woman Huang had passed through that gate,
She then turned around to look for her sister-in-law.
　She saw Woman Liu sitting there outside the gate.
Her whole body was flayed and flowing with blood;
Blood dripped from her body and covered the ground.
She cried out over and over again: "Fifth Daughter!"
　Woman Huang followed the Young Ones and went on;
She saw the torn paper money piled up mountain high.
When Woman Huang asked Golden Lad what it was,
The Young Ones turned around and explained it to her:
　"This is the place called Wasted Money Mountain,
And it has its origin in the bad nature of people on earth.
At the beginning of each season and at the eight nodes,
Impatient for the paper money to burn to ashes,
　They break it up with a stick into little bits,
And the wind scatters the ashes all over the ground.
They beat the money, but they do not beat their sins—
The outside is not round; the inside is not square.[46]
　When this is received in hell, it cannot be used;
All of this money will be tossed on this mountain,
Which is why it is called Wasted Money Mountain.
Have a look, good woman, for it will do no harm."
　When Woman Huang raised her head to take a look,
She saw that Woman Liu had arrived at this mountain,
And that Woman Liu was being prodded up the slope:
Blood dripped from her body and covered the ground.

Woman Huang wept as she made her way forward.
She then saw a river that was furiously raging:
In the upper part of the river were strange demons,
On the lower part of the river the king of serpents.
　Although there was a bridge at that place,

It was only seven inches wide and ten inches long.
The winds caused the bridge to pitch and roll;
When someone tried to cross, it pitched and rolled.
    Oxhead and Horseface stood there on either side,
And ferocious spirits and evil demons made a din.
The good woman hastily asked the Young Ones:
"This bridge—what is this bridge here called?"
    The Young Ones then answered her and said:
"Good woman, listen and we will explain it all.
    Speaking of this bridge, it does have a name,
Its name is Alas! Alas!—Alas is this bridge.
It is truly hard to cross over to the Underworld.
Now that you've come here, you see, good woman,
    How those people who on earth did not behave well,
Didn't respect Heaven and Earth, sun, moon, and stars,
Who wasted the five grains and wasted the six kernels
And did not respect their ancestors or their parents,
    Who cursed and scolded both their in-laws and uncles
And mocked their husbands, had affairs with outsiders,
Who could not live peacefully with their family and kin
And could not live in harmony with their sisters-in-law,
    When they get to this place, how they will suffer,
And on the bridge how very anxious they will be!
Bronze serpents and iron dogs will snap at them,
And the waters of the river will be of boiling oil.
    A good person will be able to cross over quickly,
But for an evil person, it will be difficult to bear."

When Woman Huang arrived, she didn't want to cross;
Gazing at the platform, her heart was filled with fear.
    Golden Lad and Jade Maiden came and supported her,
And had Woman Huang stand right in the very center,
While the demons Oxhead and Horseface took the lead,
And all the demon-soldiers held incense in their hands.
    And so Woman Huang lightly, lightly, crossed over,
Unafraid since she was supported in front and behind.

Then Woman Huang saw that Woman Liu had arrived,
And she clung to Woman Liu, and she began to weep.
    We will speak not of Woman Huang's cries and tears
But of the chief of the demon-soldiers on the bridge:
He quickly grabbed Woman Liu and pushed her off,
To endure endless tortures and near unbearable pain.
    When Woman Huang saw this, she could not bear it,
And in a loud voice she recited the Diamond Sutra.
    As soon as she chanted thirty sections and two parts,
Then all the bronze snakes and iron dogs disappeared,
And Woman Liu clambered up and crossed the bridge
Along with countless sinners who were also spared.

Then with Golden Lad leading, the good woman went on;
Before they knew it, they'd reached Vicious Dog Village.
Golden Lad quickly called out to the good woman,
"You now must protect yourself from these vicious dogs."
    So Woman Huang again called out Maitreya's name,[47]
And before very long, she gave off a brilliant light.
And so it is that reciting sutras has real benefits.
How many sinners have experienced it themselves?
    Woman Huang then tried to look for Woman Liu;
She looked around but could not see her anywhere.
The evil woman had gone down to the hall below,
Where she would have to drink the Broth of Oblivion.

They had not yet traveled more than a mile,
When she saw two roads that were most grand,
Between them towered a building like a yamen,[48]
Where the good were separated from the evil.
    At the gate the Great King held up a big scale,
Which, day and night, he used to weigh people's souls.
Those who committed evil weighed a thousand pounds,
While those who had done good weighed four ounces.
    Woman Huang weighed just these four ounces,
And so the Great King laughed aloud with joy!

"Now this is a good and pious woman!
Be so kind as to take her to King Yama.
    As for the good, we lead them along a wide road;
As for the evil, we lead them along a narrow road.
    The narrow road is dark and obscure all around,
All you can see is dim skies and murky ground.
All you can hear around you is the roar of thunder
And the sound of the iron whips cracking loudly.
    Along the wide road all is bright and well lit,
With a thousand oil lamps that light up the way."
Then Woman Huang hurried to the Senluo Hall
And stood at the jeweled gates of the Senluo Hall.
    The youth then called to the good woman, saying:
"You wait for a moment right outside this hall.
Wait until I go inside and present my papers
And report to King Yama and let him know."
    Hearing this, Woman Huang quickly clasped her hands:
"Golden Lad, quickly present my documents to King Yama."
When King Yama heard that the good woman had arrived,
He ordered the good woman to quickly proceed inside.
    Woman Huang quickly followed the Golden Lad inside
And with focused mind went forward to greet King Yama.
She walked into the yamen and then raised her head to look,
But when she saw all the sinners there, then her heart broke.
    There were some whose feet were in shackles by the wall;
There were some who were locked in chains in the yard.
There were some with feet in chains and hands in locks,
And there were some who were lightly bound by iron chains.
    There were those who were beaten till their blood flowed;
These sinners were weeping and crying in piteous tones.

When Woman Huang walked into the Second Court,
There Oxhead and Horseface stood on either side,
And right there in the center stood a general's pillar,[49]
And lashed to that general's pillar were all of the sinners.
    Ferocious gods and evil demons sawed them to pieces;

They dismembered those sinners, now covered in blood.
One pulling here and one pulling there, they were split;
They were split in the middle, two halves of one body.

Then they went on to the Third Court of Hell;
That Third Court of Hell was truly frightening.
There were three cauldrons there of boiling oil;
Iron prongs and large pincers stood on both sides.
    The clear oil had been heated up till it bubbled;
The sinners boiled till they were reduced to pulp.
There were also those waiting to be tossed in,
And they wept and wailed in horror and fear.
    If you wanted to go to heaven, there was no road;
If you wanted to enter the earth, there was no gate.
    Then Woman Huang quickly turned and asked,
She asked the Golden Lad to explain it to her:
"Seeing how these poor sinners suffer so,
What evil did they commit while they lived?"
    Golden Lad quickly answered her and said:
"Listen, good woman, and I will tell you why.
These sinners had hearts that were wicked;
When on earth, they had the evilest of minds.
    Cursing the wind and swearing at the rain are sins;
Cursing Heaven and scolding Earth are no minor crimes.
So the officials of hell brought them here to suffer
By flinging them into these cauldrons of boiling oil."

Hearing this, Woman Huang was awash in tears,
And her tears coursed down as she continued ahead.
Before she knew it, they reached the Fourth Court of Hell,
Which was lined with huge stone mortars most horrific.
    The sinners would be placed inside these mortars,
Their flesh would be crushed into bits and pieces,
Their fresh blood flowing down in long rivulets—
Any person seeing this would be filled with fear.
    She also saw there a pair of iron grindstones.

How the sinners suffered when it came to this!
They were ground into the tiniest bits and pieces,
Their flesh ground until it was nothing but pulp.

When Woman Huang arrived at the Fifth Court of Hell,
The sinners there were weeping with abandon and fear.
    Those who were lashed to the general's pillar
First had their bellies gutted and then their bones crushed.
Then they were flayed into the tiniest bits and pieces,
And their flesh was tossed onto the dirt on the ground.
    Then the bronze snakes and the iron dogs appeared
And went down to the hells to devour those sinners.
When Woman Huang saw this, she began to weep,
And again and then again she called out: "Amituofo!"[50]

Then she went through the gates of the Sixth Court:
From these gates there shone forth a brilliant light
As the Vehicle of Rebirth came to fetch the people
And take them to the World of Light to be reborn.
    Good people would be reincarnated in human form;
Evil people would be turned into beasts and birds.
Insects, bugs, mosquitoes—it was all decided here;
Male or female, good or evil—they were all reborn.
    There were those without noses, eyes, or ears
As well as those who lacked legs or who lacked arms.
There were bright and lively and very smart women,
And there were students and teachers as well.
    There were those who were bowlegged or deformed
As well as those who were born deaf or born mute.
There were those who were officials and ministers
As well as degree candidates and Hanlin scholars.[51]
    There were those who were farmers and artisans,
Those who ate no meat and recited Buddha's name;
There were nuns, and there were Daoist priests;
There were monks and also Buddhist followers.
    And there were thieves, and there were robbers;

There were those who made a living as gamblers.
There were those with scabby heads or dirty teeth,
And there were young men with handsome faces.
     When Woman Huang saw all this, she gave a sigh:
"How grateful we should be to King Yama for his work!
In determining good and evil, not the slightest mistake:
Each and every case of good or bad is made manifest.
     If while you are alive, you do not do any good deeds,
It will be impossible to escape King Yama's judgment"

And then she entered the gate of the Seventh Court,
And the tortures she saw there were truly terrible.
     All the sinners were stripped of all their clothing,
And their bodies were covered with bloody slashes.
Their sinews were pulled out, their stomachs cut open;
Fainting and reviving, they were tortured yet again.
     When Woman Huang saw this, she asked him:
"Golden Lad, please listen to what I have to say.
I see these sinners suffering in such a terrible way:
What sins did they commit when they were alive?"
     Golden Lad then replied to her question, saying,
"Good woman, listen to me and I will explain.
All of these sinners indulged in dining on meat and
Acted brutish when they were in the World of Light;
     Operating butcher shops, they marketed animal flesh,
Making a living by butchering animals and taking life.
How many lives did these butchers harm in this way?
And so they were brought to hell to suffer punishment.
     Here their bodies are strapped to these tall pillars,
Their guts opened, their intestines exposed, as you see.
Once they have served their measure of punishment,
They will be sentenced to hell, never to return to earth!"
     Hearing this, Woman Huang was awash in tears,
And she cried out: "My husband is also a butcher!"
Golden Lad quickly urged the good woman on:
"Let us take you with us as we go on our way!"

Then they entered the gates of the Eighth Court of Hell.
Matters in the Eighth Court were clear for all to see:
On the one hand the good were lodging accusations;
And on the other the evil were undergoing tortures.

Woman Huang slowly passed through this place,
Escorted by the demons Oxhead and Horseface.

They then entered the gate of the Ninth Court of Hell.
Golden Lad and Jade Maiden walked on either side.
Golden Lad brought water for her to wash her hands:
"Brush off the dust and make ready to meet King Yama."

Hearing this, Woman Huang washed her hands and feet
And lightly lifted her lotus feet[52] to enter the court gates.
On her head were arranged clouds of raven-black hair;
Around her neck she wore her string of Buddha beads;

In her hand she held a fly whisk, which she waved a few times,
So she would not be defiled by any dust clinging to her clothes.

When Woman Huang was ready, she went on ahead.
The Golden Lad came again and said: "Good woman,
Ahead of us is the palace called the Senluo Hall;
The Tenth Court is what you now see before you.

There is no need to fear the demon-soldiers on either side;
Be not scared by the martial music of the bells and drums.
Bow down with lowered head and hands pressed together
And do not rise until they tell you to do so by name.

When you recite the Diamond Sutra, do not rush;
Character by character, line by line, recite it very clearly."
Woman Huang nodded her head and said: "I understand."
She thanked the Golden Lad for his careful instructions

And went forward through the gates of the Tenth Court,
Where the burning incense of sandalwood circled about.
When she raised her eyes and lifted her head to have a look,
King Yama of the Tenth Hall was very frightening indeed!

The judicial clerks and military officers were vicious and violent;
The civil and military assistant judges were lined up on both sides.

And the demon-soldiers on the two sides shouted so loudly
That the earth seemed to be rent and the mountains to collapse.
　　Golden Lad said to the good woman:
"Now you can just continue on ahead."
As soon as Woman Huang heard Golden Lad say this,
She lightly lifted her lotus feet and so went on ahead.

　　And when she thereupon arrived at the Senluo Hall,
She greeted King Yama, head bowed and palms together,
And as she recited the name of the Buddha Amitabha,
The attendants ceremoniously formed two files alongside.

　　As soon as King Yama caught sight of Woman Huang,
His heart filled with joy and there was a smile on his face.
It was then that King Yama, seated in the Senluo Hall,
Spoke: "Good woman, listen carefully to my words.

　　Please stand to one side so that I can question you
To see if you recite the Diamond Sutra without error."
Woman Huang then stood up, and she replied, saying:
"When I recite the sutra, I do so with a sincere heart."

The Yama King[53] of the First Court spoke up and asked:
"In the World of Light you inhabited a female body—
How is it you came to learn to recite the Diamond Sutra?
How many years now have you been reciting this sutra?"

　　Woman Huang bowed her head and answered him, saying:
"Your Royal Majesty, please listen and I will explain.

　　I was indeed originally born with the body of a woman,
And I spent my life washing clothes and preparing meals.
My father and mother back home were both pious folk,
And they were the ones who urged me to recite the sutras.

　　At seven I began to chant sutras with my mother,
And now I am over thirty and two years of age,
So I have been chanting sutras for twenty-five years,
And I've never been without sutras for even half an hour.

　　I never did eat meat, and I did not drink wine;
I have kept the precepts ever since I was a girl."

When the Yama King heard this, his heart filled with joy.
"What a very good and pious woman you have been!"

The Yama King of the Second Court spoke up and asked:
"Listen to me, pious person Woman Huang,
Maybe you didn't eat the five spices or six creatures,
But how did you ever manage to raise your children?
    I am afraid you have polluted both Heaven and Earth;
You must have dirtied them with many bowls of blood.
You have polluted the sun, the moon, and also the stars,
And yet you dare say you have done good until now?"
    When Woman Huang heard this, she quickly replied:
"Most exalted Yama King, listen and I will explain.
What is the gravest unfilial behavior in the world?
Despite Heaven's and Earth's nurture to not produce sons!
    If I had cut off the line of the Zhao family, I'd have
Recited the Diamond Sutra in vain for all those years.
If you say that I should not have borne any children,
Then I shouldn't have been married off to a husband!
    Once husband and wife marry, they must have children.
So how can you, Yama King, seriously consider this again?
Since time immemorial, the Underworld's been a bright mirror—
It is we who live in the World of Light who are muddleheaded!"
    The Yama King of the Second Court did not know what to say;
Dumbfounded, he remained speechless, unable to utter a word.

Then the Yama King of the Third Court spoke to her, saying:
"Good Woman Huang, listen carefully to what I say.
Let us not waste any more time with irrelevant matters:
You have been called here to recite the Diamond Sutra.
    You say you began reciting the sutra at seven years
And have been reciting it for more than twenty years.
Can you tell me all about the origins of the sutras,
And which is the one called the Diamond Sutra?"
    Woman Huang, palms together, respectfully replied:

"Your Royal Highness, listen to me and I will tell you.
The Diamond Sutra originated in the country of India,
And it is a sutra spoken by the Tathagata Sakyamuni.
    When the Patriarch Bodhidharma came to the East,[54]
He brought the Diamond Sutra to deliver good people.
And because this sutra is both sagely and important,
That is why it is given the name Diamond Sutra."
    Hearing these words, the Yama King was delighted:
"You indeed have truly studied all about this sutra!"

Then the Yama King of the Fourth Court hastened to speak,
Saying: "I ask you, Woman Huang, in reading the sutra,
    Into how many chapters has this sutra been divided?
How many vegetarian, correct people have recited it?
If you can explain it all the way from the beginning,
We will escort you back to the World of Light."
    Hearing this, Woman Huang quickly replied to him:
"Your Royal Highness, listen to me and I will explain.
The Diamond Sutra consists of thirty-two divisions,[55]
And every character and every line describes the truth.
    The Great Master of Fragrant Mountain read this sutra
And discarded her human body and so became Guanyin.[56]
The Second Patriarch Shenguang also read this sutra[57]
And then left the earth and ascended to the heavens.
    The Third Patriarch Jinshan then also read this sutra;
Abandoning his mortal frame, he became an immortal.
    And then the Patriarch Caodong also read this sutra,
Which led him to practice cultivation on Mount Po'e;
Achieving the Way, he passed it to the Fifth Patriarch,
This very sutra, the one that is called the Diamond Sutra.
    On top of Double Peak Mountain he recited this sutra,
And at the age of seventy-three he ascended to heaven.
Enlightened, the Fifth Patriarch passed it to the Sixth Patriarch,
Who, atop the platform, taught the Dharma, enlightening others.[58]
    But there was no one to whom the Sixth Patriarch could pass it,

And for this reason the text was stored away in the sutra library
Until it came to the Seventh Patriarch, who taught the Way freely,
Master at liberating all those in the world who practice goodness.

    Although the Diamond Sutra can still be found in the world,
One who chants sutras and the Buddha's name is hard to find.
I began reciting the sutra at the tender age of seven years,
So why has King Yama cut my life short to call me here?"

    When the Yama King heard this, he gave a little smile
And said: "Good woman, how little you know!
To die early is actually the much better thing—
You'd rather remain forever in a woman's body?"

Woman Huang clasped her hands and took her leave.
Then the Yama King of the Fifth Court spoke to her.

    Loudly he called out to her: "You, Woman Huang,
You have explained the Diamond Sutra very clearly,
But the words that are written in the Diamond Sutra,
Character by character, line by line, let me hear them."

    Woman Huang then knelt down on the golden steps:
"Your Royal Highness, listen and I will explain.
There is much of which the Diamond Sutra speaks,
But it all comes down to filial piety and reverence.

    One must revere Heaven and all the divine beings;
One must respect one's parents and all living things.
If one doesn't revere Heaven and Earth and the gods
And curses the wind and rain, one commits a great sin.

    Demon eyes and a demon heart—all of this is sinful.
If one breaks sticks of incense, one dishonors the gods.
The gods and sages of heaven have all read this sutra;
After reading the Diamond Sutra, they ascended to heaven."

    Hearing this, the Yama King's heart was filled with joy.
"My good Woman Huang, you have done very well!
Although you have not yet recited the sutra for me,
You have explained each character and each line."

    Then he ordered Golden Lad and Jade Maiden

To flank her with their banners and their parasols,
And he gave her a golden stool to sit by his side
And also gave her fragrant tea and refreshments.

After drinking her tea, she placed her bowl down.
The Yama King of the Sixth Court said, "Good woman!"
And then he insistently requested again: "Woman Huang,
Please explain the Diamond Sutra to me once more.

How many Diamond Sutras can one recite in a full year?
How many seasons does it take to read the Diamond Sutra?
And what is the benefit of reading the Diamond Sutra text?
And how can people in the world learn to recite the sutras?"
Hearing this, Woman Huang replied, saying:
"Your Royal Highness, listen and I will explain.

Fifty-four hundred eight and eight scrolls
Make up the text called the Diamond Sutra.
Each day I recited ten scrolls, and therefore
I recited all of the sutra in only half a year.

Do not say that the Diamond Sutra has no uses:
If one cultivates oneself, one can go to heaven.
If the Son of Heaven recites it, the world will be peaceful:
If a nobleman recites it, he'll be assured of long life.

If a poor person recites it, he may become wealthy;
If a base person recites it, he will obtain prosperity.
If one recites it in a crisis, one will be rescued;
If an ill person recites it, he will become well.

If a lame person recites it, he'll be able to walk,
And if a blind man reads it, he will be able to see.
If a humpback reads it, his back will become straight,
And if a deaf man reads it, he will regain his hearing.

If a man reads it, he will enjoy wealth and blessings;
If a woman reads it, she will obtain the body of a man.[59]
If a religious disciple reads it, he will become a master;
If the Son of Heaven recites it, there will be lots of rain.[60]

There are too many benefits to even mention them all.
And to think that I would die at the age of thirty-two!"

When Woman Huang said this sorrowful thing,
All she could think of was absolving herself of sin.
In the first place she wanted to safeguard her children;
In the second place she wanted to safeguard her long life.

"All I know is that I could not live out my allotted span.
I fear for those in the world who don't cultivate themselves,
When I, for one, made sure to recite the sutra every day!"
One after the other the tears welled up in her eyes.

Then the Yama King of the Sixth Court heartily laughed:
"Good woman, there is no reason for you to be sad!"

As soon as Woman Huang sat down again on her stool,
She saw before her the Yama King of the Seventh Court.
The Yama King of the Seventh Court asked her to sit down,
And with a hearty laugh, he called: "Good woman!"

When Woman Huang heard the king call her name,
She quickly clasped her hands and rose to her feet.
The Yama King then hastened and addressed her, saying:
"Now you listen to me and I will explain to you.

Today you've traveled the road to the Yellow Springs,⁶¹
Can you still remember how to recite the Diamond Sutra?
And why did you not pass it on to your children?
And why did you not pass it on to your husband?"

When Woman Huang heard this, she quickly replied:
"Your Royal Highness, listen and I will explain to you.

You ask if I remember how the Diamond Sutra goes—
Every character, every line, is clear in my mind.
If I should decide to pass it on to someone else,
He may not be as sincere as I about reciting it.

My elder daughter is now nine years of age,
The daughter that follows will be only six this year,
And my son has only completed two years of age—
How could I teach them how to recite the sutra?

Lianfang is indeed my own husband and man,
But he is a butcher and so not a religious person.
There was no one to whom to pass the Diamond Sutra,

So I hid it beneath the kitchen floor in the east wing."
  The king, when he heard this, replied, saying:
"I know all the circumstances about this matter,
  That Lianfang is a butcher, not a religious person,
And that it is true that your children are still young.
But if he doesn't do good, he'll be the one to pay;
It will not have the slightest thing to do with you."
  Woman Huang then clasped her hands to apologize;
Apologizing to the king, she then rose and stood tall.

The Yama King of the Eighth Court asked her a question:
"Woman Huang, now you listen to me carefully.
  Did you merely take the sutra and blindly recite it,
Or did you seek enlightenment, cultivating yourself?
Did you merely pay respects to the Tathagata Buddha,
Or did you recite his name and pursue the religious way?"
  When Woman Huang heard this, she quickly bowed
And said: "Exalted One Above, listen and I will explain:
I did take the sutra and recite it, for the very purpose of
Accumulating merit to save me from danger and need.
  I sold all my golden hairpins to repair the roads,
And I gave all my clothes away to aid the poor.
In the cold winter, when snow covered the ground,
I took out rice and offered it to the fasting monks.
  Every day at the break of dawn I would burn incense—
First I would worship the Holy Tathagata Buddha;
Next I'd worship the Heavenly Kings, the Sun and Moon;
Then I would thank the emperor for all his great graces.
  Next I would worship the divinities of Good Fortune
And then give thanks for the Emperors of Water and Earth.
I would worship the God of Wealth and the Three Generals,
And I would worship the God of the Stove, the Kitchen God.
  Then I would pay respects to the kindness of my parents,
And also I would pay respects to my elderly in-laws.
And every day, after the incense had all burned down,
I would straighten my clothes and recite the sutra."

Hearing this, the King of the Eighth Court was delighted:
"Because you indeed really are a very good woman
    I present you with a bowl with the true samadhi fire[62]
So that you will be able to go through the gates of hell.
And I will also present you with a seven-copper fan,
So fierce demons and evil shades will not touch you."
    Woman Huang quickly thanked him for his kindness,
And quickly and gracefully she continued on her way.

The Yama King of the Ninth Court opened his golden mouth:
"Good woman, now you listen to what I have to say.
    How many bridges and roads have you repaired?
How many people in desperate straits have you saved?
How many chapters of the Diamond Sutra have you read?
And how long has it been since you have not eaten meat?"
    Woman Huang then answered his questions, saying:
"Your Royal Highness, listen to what I have to tell you.
    I've been repairing bridges and roads since the start
By donating my golden hairpins as well as my clothes.
If there were those in desperate straits who sought my aid,
I have given them clothes with which to cover themselves.
    Every single year, every single month, all the time—
If you ask me to explain the situation to you clearly—
Every night I recited ten chapters of the Diamond Sutra,
And I have been reciting the sutra for twenty-five years.
    In a year I'd recite three thousand six hundred chapters,
And the Buddhist canon I have read for fifteen years.
Even while still in the womb, I ate neither fish nor meat,
And ever since I was born, I have kept a vegetarian diet."
    When the king heard this, his heart filled with joy:
"So you really are a good person, Woman Huang."

Then King Yama of the Tenth Court parted his golden lips[63]
And said: "Good woman, listen to what I have to say.
    I want you to light some incense and recite the sutra;
I want you to mount the platform and recite the sutra text.

And if you do so without missing even a single character,
I will not in good conscience be able to send you to hell."
    When Woman Huang heard this, she bowed respectfully.
"Your Royal Majesty, please listen and I will explain.
I remember every single character of the Diamond Sutra,
And I am sure I will not make even the slightest mistake."
    King Yama of the Tenth Court then quickly issued an order,
He ordered that all the ghosts and gods, irrespective of rank,
Should build a high platform one *zhang* and two feet high[64]
And adorn it with festive flowers, incense, and candles.
    Woman Huang went and stood atop this high platform
And straightened her robes, prepared to recite the sutra.
Palms together, lowered head, she bowed four times
And prayed to all the gods passing through the skies.
    "Your humble servant has recited the sutra since childhood,
And now at thirty-two, I have been called to see King Yama.
The Underworld officials want me to recite the Diamond Sutra,
And I beg the gods and the buddhas to watch over me now.
    Greatly dispense the Dharma rain all over the Eastern Land[65]
So I may save all good people here in the Senluo Hall."
    As soon as Woman Huang had finished this prayer,
The terrified earth gods were covered in sweat.
The earth gods and city gods wasted not a moment;
The Golden Lads for reporting deeds did not tarry a second.
    The many gods transmitted the information even to India,
And the news spread to the famous Four Sacred Mountains.[66]
Woman Huang began to recite the sutra there on the platform,
In the presence of all the Kings of the Ten Courts of Hell.
    She recited all thirty-two sections of the sutra:
The smoke of the incense swirled in colors to Heaven,
And from four sides pink-hued clouds surged upward,
Over rings and rings of all the great sages and gods.
    The Four Heavenly Kings all sat on this platform,
The Eight Immortals flanked her on either side,
And the Four Heavenly Patriarchs all showed up too—
King Yama of the Tenth Court welcomed them all.

The Myriad-Dharma Patriarch of Mount Emei came,
As did the bodhisattva Kṣitigarbha of Mount Jiuhua.[67]
From the Western Regions came Śākyamuni Buddha,
And from Heaven came the Immortal Lü Dongbin.[68]
    Then all of the demon-soldiers also came to report
That the Xuandi Patriarch had descended from above.[69]
The Fourth Patriarch and Fifth Patriarch also came,
And from the Southern Sea there came Guanshiyin.[70]
    The King of the Tenth Court hastened to greet them,
And he welcomed Xuandi into the court gate.
Xuandi then came and took a seat in the middle,
And King Yama took his seat there by his side.
    The Patriarchs and Heavenly Masters also sat there,
With the Queen Mother and Wen and Zhao on either side.[71]

Then the Underworld judges came and reported,
Came and reported to King Yama of the Tenth Court
That all of the earth prison had opened up wide,
And millions of hungry ghosts had made their escape.
    Holy clouds had risen over Sword Mountain,
And all the steel blades had suddenly grown dull,
And even the River of Blood had also dried up,
While the Alas Bridge was nowhere to be seen.
    When King Yama heard this, he grew very worried.
"You can come down now and stop chanting the sutra."
Woman Huang, palms together, descended the platform
And proceeded to the jeweled gates of the Senluo Hall.
    Then all of the gods mounted their pink-hued clouds;
King Yama escorted them out of the large main hall.
He then invited the good woman to take a seat;
Offering her some fragrant tea, he spoke with her.
    King Yama then parted his lips and said:
"Good woman, you have recited this Diamond Sutra,
But I did not know that it had such a pedigree
And that its recitation would have such potency!"
    Hearing this, Woman Huang quickly rose, saying:

"That is why I do not dare recite it recklessly!"
King Yama then said: "Good woman, please sit down,
Listen and I will explain it to you from the start.

　If you recite this sutra three times from start to finish,
All the living buddhas of the Western Heavens appear!
And the Thearch on High will open up the Avici Hell,[72]
And the gods of the Underworld will not kill people.

　The North Star will not dare determine life and death;
The South Star will not dare determine one's life span.
The good and the bad will be difficult to distinguish,
And human kings and emperors will also get worried.

　I am now going to return you to the World of Light;
Please continue to be faithful in your sutra recitation."

　Woman Huang quickly thanked him for his kindness,
And taking her leave of the king, she stood up.
But the official judges then came and reported:
"Exalted One Above, please hear what we have to say!

　The good woman's soul came into the Underworld
During the scorching heat of the Sixth Month—no way![73]
It would be better to let her be reborn on a higher plane
And reward her with blessings and the body of a man."

　King Yama agreed with what the judges proposed,
And he ordered that she be given a different body.

In the Eastern Capital lived Landowner Zhang,[74]
And he and his wife lived a very pious life,
But at the age of fifty, she had not yet had a son;
They had only a daughter to keep them company.

　When King Yama heard about this case,
He ordered Woman Huang to be reincarnated there.

　Woman Huang then spoke up and said to them:
"Long-Lived Exalted One, please hear my words,
If you want me to reincarnate, I do not mind,
But it breaks my heart to abandon my children.

　If it is a good family, then I will agree to go,
But if it is an evil family, I will not agree to go.

Let my parents come from a family of literati;
Let my parents have accumulated good karma.

I will not go again into a family of butchers,
Where I would have to bear the sin of taking life.
My husband, Lianfang, did so many bad things—
Slaughtering pigs, butchering lambs, all his life!"

Again he inspected the ledgers of life and death
So as to see how many years each one had been given.

"Lianfang has been allotted only forty years,
And your son Changshou assigned only eighteen.
For your elder daughter there are only thirty-six,
And for your younger daughter a mere fifty years."

When Woman Huang heard this, she began to weep;
She wept and wailed, wailed and wept so piteously.
She got down on both her knees in the dust, saying:
"Long-Lived Exalted One, do hear my words!

Don't look at the Diamond Sutra but look at the Buddha;
You must look at the face of this poor woman here.
Add a few decades to my husband's allotted time;
Add a few more years to the ages of my children."

The king then parted his golden lips and said:
"Woman Huang, what you ask is not very reasonable.
One's life on earth is determined in a previous life—
How can one possibly add even a single minute?"

Weeping, Woman Huang came and begged:
"Long-Lived and Exalted One, please hear my words.

If the book of life and death cannot be changed,
Then why was my own allotted life span cut short?
Your humble servant was given seventy-two years on earth,
But at thirty-two she was called down into the Underworld."

When he heard her question, King Yama could not reply,
Speechless and mute, he could not utter a single word.
The assistant judge then came forward and said:
"Long-Lived One Above, please listen to what I will say.

The ledgers of life and death cannot be altered,
But her recital of the Diamond Sutra was without peer!

Let's make a correction to the ledgers of life and death,
So that we will not cause this good woman to weep."
    And so King Yama agreed to this suggestion
And said: "Good woman, now hear my words.

    If I do not change what is written in the book,
Then you would always be on my conscience,
But if I add on to the allotted number of years,
I am afraid that good and bad will get confused.

    Lianfang's life span is especially hard to change,
But I see the love that you bear for your husband.
Your children are also your own flesh and blood,
So I will order wealth and blessings on their lives."
    He ordered the assistant judge to fetch the ledgers
And to carefully note down all of these changes:

    Lianfang was given forty more years to live on earth;
Thus he would be called down at the age of eighty.
Changshou was allotted eighty-two more years,
Which meant that he would live a full hundred.

    The elder daughter, Jiaogu, was allotted fifteen more years,
Which meant she'd meet with Yama at the age of eighty-two.
Banjie was allotted an additional thirty-three years,
So she'd have to go to the Underworld at eighty-three.[75]

    And on each were bestowed blessings and a long life,
So they might pass their time free of trouble and care.
The assistant judge noted all this down very carefully;
Character by character, line by line, he wrote it clearly.

    Woman Huang knelt down before the golden stairs,
Thanking him for his kindness with twenty-four bows.

Then King Yama parted his golden lips and said:
"Good woman, pay heed to what I have to say.
I have ordered Golden Lad and Jade Maiden
To take you back to the gate of your old home."

    Woman Huang lifted her head to look around
And catching sight of her children felt very sad.
    Jiaogu was holding her little brother and weeping,

There by the ancestral tablet, weeping for her mother;
The three-year-old boy dressed in mourning clothes
Wept at every word for his dearly beloved mother.

Woman Huang wept as if her heart had split in two,
And then she said: "My good little ones, how sad I am!
My little boy Changshou has no one to care for him,
And Jiaogu and Banjie, they both also weep piteously.

I should not have continued the Zhao family line;
I should not have borne a son and two daughters.
The sons and daughters I bore are still so young,
Yet I abandoned them and went to the Underworld."

Then she fainted and fell onto the dusty ground;
Wordless and mute, she could not utter a word.

Golden Lad and Jade Maiden, not wasting a moment,
Helped her get up, saying: "Good woman, be quiet!
In half an hour we will return to the World of Light;
Already the red sun sinks fast behind the Western Hills."

"I am weeping for my orphaned son and daughters;
I'm weeping for my relatives, and especially my husband."

Golden Lad then spoke to her, and he said:
"Listen, good woman, do not be so heartbroken,
For I am going to take you back to your home.
I will lead you back to your home to see them."

Woman Huang thanked them for their kindness;
She thanked both Golden Lad and Jade Maiden:
"After I have visited with my son and daughters,
Then I want to visit with my husband as well."

All along the road to her home she was weeping,
But quickly she reached the gate of the Zhao home.
When she lifted her eyes and raised her head to look,
Her tears welled up and poured from her eyes:

"My son, from now on you must forget me;
Your mother will never again come to see you.
You and your sisters must be filial and obedient,
Always on the way that leads to the Ten Heavens."[76]

Jiaogu woke up and cried out for her mother;

The boy, Changshou, wept for his mother too.
"This makes me feel like I am being cut by knives!"
Clenching her silvery teeth, she walked out the door.

    Hardening her heart, she abandoned her children;
Then she went to her own husband, Lianfang.
Woman Huang then went into the east wing
And, when she saw her husband, began to weep:

    "Way back then, I, your wife, ordered you,
As I was lying on my deathbed, I urged you,
I urged you to take the boy and the two girls
And not to let the boy weep for his mother.

    In the west wing I saw my children's faces;
I wanted to see the love between husband and wife.
Now I regret having moved into separate quarters
Halfway through our marriage; I broke your dear heart.

    And to think we shared a bed for thirteen years
And together had three kids, a son and daughters!
If you can't do it for my sake, do it for their sake:
They keep weeping and crying till daylight!

    At the time that we separated, then I told you
To pass your days together with the children.
You sleep comfortably in the eastern quarters—
The children lie cold and shivering elsewhere.

    After a hundred lives of cultivation, one shares a boat;
After a thousand lives of cultivation, one shares a quilt.

    The words of the ancient sages of the past say it well:
'One night as husband and wife, a hundred years of love.'
Ten nights as husband and wife, heavier than a mountain;
A hundred nights as husband and wife, deeper than the sea.

    Even if you don't do it for the golden-faced Buddha—
These three children are your own flesh and blood!
Even if not for our thirteen years as husband and wife—
Do it for your three kids, your son and daughters!

    A thousand words cannot express all I have to say.
I urge you, husband, to change your ways and repent."

    She then fell on her knees at the foot of the bed.

"My dear husband, please take note of my words.
On this night your wife has come to urge you:
From now on, do not butcher animals for sale.

If this time you decide not to heed my advice,
Then you must be an evil-hearted butcher indeed.
If I would stay and speak with you any longer,
The rooster will crow and I won't be able to go." [77]

She then rose to her feet and gave him a push:
"My dear husband, please remember this well!"

Golden Lad and Jade Maiden addressed her,
Saying: "Good woman, listen to what we will say.

We will now take you to the Zhang family home,
As you will be reborn there in the Eastern Capital. [78]
Luck and riches in that life will be beyond words;
As a fourth-rank official you will govern the people."

At that point Woman Huang simply had no choice
But to follow the Young Ones to the Eastern Capital.

Now we will not speak of Woman Huang's rebirth
But speak again of Woman Liu coming back home.

When evil demons brought her to the front gate,
The two door gods were not cooperative at all.
"Such an evil person cannot be admitted inside;
She will pollute the incense fire of all the gods."

Woman Liu came forward, begging and pleading:
"Door god generals, please hear my words.
When I was alive, I never offended you at all, so
Why do you now refuse to open the gate?

I can return back home only this one time,
So please let me go in and see my husband.
I also have one son and then two daughters;
Leaving the children behind pains me no end.

Before I could even say a single word to them,
I was summoned to go and meet with King Yama.
Now I have been dead for a full six months—

Please have pity on me, you two generals!"
The two door gods did not answer her plea,
So she turned and pleaded with the two guards.
Hearing her words, the guards couldn't bear it,
And so they opened the door for Woman Liu.

They took her and flung her inside the walls.
"Go on inside and there see your children!"
Woman Liu pulled herself up and hurried inside,
Went to the hall, and worshipped the family gods.

When the ancestor saw her, he was furious
And cursed her, saying: "A lot of nerve you have!
When you were alive, you didn't do a bit of good;
Every day you stayed at home just wasting time!

You cursed Heaven, and you also cursed Earth,
Not knowing that in hell there was a King Yama."

Woman Liu bowed down to them and then stood up
And in the kitchen worshipped the God of the Stove.
Her entire body dripping with blood, she knelt down,
And the Stove God also cursed her: "Get up quickly!
Don't stand there in front of me all bloody like that!
Hurry to see your children, so you can return to hell!"

Woman Liu then went to the bedroom
And, weeping, called out to her children.
She also urged her husband to do good:
"Now that I see you, I feel so very sad.

Although ever since that day when I left you,
I have not come to your pillow to speak to you.
Today I come to the foot of your bed to see you,
As I am always thinking of you, my husband.

Together we had one son and two daughters,
And we completely relied on your bitter toil."
Just as Woman Liu was speaking these words,
The guards came in and were pitiless.

The guards grabbed her and held her tight:
"Quickly, make haste and come with us."

Woman Liu then answered them, saying:
"You two generals, please hear my words.
  I have a couple of kids, a son and daughters;
Please let me go and see them personally."
Then the guards grew very angry indeed;
They grabbed her and wanted her to leave.
  She called to Heaven, but Heaven did not reply,
And again she called to the two powerful guards.
Weeping and wailing as she walked along,
Weeping and wailing, she reached the Underworld.

We will no longer speak of Woman Liu's departure,
But we will speak of Woman Liu's own husband.
The husband wept until his heart was broken,
Wept and wailed and made a piteous sound:
  "How could you have gone and died like this?
Who will your abandoned children rely on now?"

Woman Huang's daughter entered, weeping and crying:
"In my dream I caught sight of our beloved mother.
  And when I called out to her, I woke up,
As clearly, so clearly, she walked through the door.
She walked up to the bed and said, 'My daughter!'
She called for her son and called for her daughters.
  She told her daughters to be filial and obedient,
To stay together every day from dawn to dusk,
And, because their brother was still young,
To take him with them wherever they go.
  In my dream I saw the mother who bore us,
But when I woke, she was no more to be seen.
Now, although her words linger on, she is gone,
And our dear old mother is nowhere to be seen.
Quietly, so quietly, I woke my brother and sister,
'Did you see your own mother a moment ago?
For our mother has just come here to see you—
You were not yet awake and didn't understand!

Rise quickly, put some water in the teakettle,
And put some fresh water in the teacup for mother."
They then laid out three bowls of fresh tea.[79]
The two girls then wept with a mournful sound.
They called to their mother: "Come and drink,
Come and fulfill your children's deepest wish.

For now we will never again meet in the flesh,
And we'll not see Mother until the Underworld.
If, Mother, you have some supernatural powers,
Please do take your children along with you!"

The three-year-old Changshou wept and howled,
Calling on Heaven and Earth for his own mother.
Jiaogu and Banjie could not hold back their tears;
They wept until Heaven and Earth were distraught.

The two girls wept in front of the ancestral tablet—
Even hearts of iron or stone would be moved to tears!

Then Lianfang, who was in the east wing, woke up,
And when he heard his children weeping so piteously,
He very quickly made his way to the ancestral hall
And saw his children weeping with such a pitiful sound.

The children clung to the ancestral tablet, and they cried,
They cried for their mother, cried to Heaven and to Earth.
Since ancient times children are the ones who suffer most,
Deeply upset at High Heaven's lack of clear discernment.

The three children were weeping, weeping so bitterly,
Beating their chests, stamping their feet, clothes wet with tears.

Lianfang then went forward and held them tight.
"My dear little darlings," he cried again and again,
"Since time immemorial people have died like lamps put out:
Who has ever heard of the ghosts of the dead still walking about?"

Lianfang then lit a stick of incense,
And he also poured out a cup of tea.
He called out: "My dear wife, may your soul drink;
Listen to your husband, and he will explain why.

Once you wanted to sleep in different rooms;
Now we have been separated for an entire year.

You took the girls into the west wing,
And I took the boy into the east wing.
　　Now I do not mind so much that you have died,
But to have abandoned your daughters is very sad.
Your husband is really suffering great bitterness.
An empty room and an empty bed are to be lamented.
　　The children shout and cry all day and all night;
They weep and wail, and my heart breaks for them.
During the day breakfast must be put off till noon,
And dinner must always wait until the day breaks.
　　Your orphans and I together make four people.
So sorrowful and so lonely and so very alone,
In my heart I've thought about taking another wife,
But I worry that she'll beat and scold the children.
　　My dear wife, you abandoned me in midstream
And left your children behind to bitterly suffer.
My dear wife, where is it you've gone to now?
And tell me, how am I going to pass my days?
　　The children's tears make my heart break,
And I cannot help being filled with sorrow."

We will not say any more now about Lianfang's sorrow
But turn to Woman Huang's arrival at the Eastern Capital.
　　The Three Mothers were then waiting for Woman Huang;[80]
They were waiting for her to arrive at the Eastern Capital.
They commanded the earth god to quickly send out the edict
And quickly inform the ancestors of the Zhang family.
　　"Tell them that because the family has been very pious,
We have bestowed upon the Zhangs a most noble heir.
In the future this child will pass the examinations,
And with high official titles he will govern the people."
　　The earth god, having received this order,
Then went on his way to the Eastern Capital.
　　He hastily entered the gate of the Zhang family home,
Where the ancestors received him, smiles on their faces.
As soon as the ancestors saw him, they couldn't refrain

From falling down on both knees to receive the immortal!
The Three Mothers, who were seated there on the altar,
Then took Woman Huang into their hands and bathed her.
Woman Huang was then transformed into a peach;
As an immortal peach she was then carried inside.

Just then Madame Li of the Zhangs suddenly awoke,
Only to find that, without knowing, she had conceived!
At dawn she rose and went to her husband, saying:
"I dreamt that an immortal peach entered my body."

When Landowner Zhang heard his wife's words,
His whole face lit up with happiness and joy.
And straightaway he went to the main street
And there asked for a certain diviner of dreams.

The master then hastened to interpret this dream,
And he said: "Landowner Zhang, hear what I have to say.
I must congratulate you, I must congratulate you;
She will give birth to a son destined for greatness."

When the man heard this, he was filled with joy,
And thanking the master, he returned to his home,
Returned and told his wife what the diviner had said.
And then he ordered his wife to take very good care,

Since the soothsayer had promised him a noble son,
A son who would be destined for greatness one day.

We will no longer speak of this couple's great joy
But speak of Woman Huang inside her mother's womb.

In the first month the fetus has just taken form;
The red blood and the white mix and combine.
At the start of the first month the mother feels unsure
And doesn't relax until the menstrual flow stops.

In the second month, with the fetus in her womb,
The mother stays in her room, loath to move.
She longs to eat and drink all sorts of things
And feels lethargic and low almost all the time.

In the third month, with the fetus in her womb,
Her hands grow numb—she finds it hard to move.

She can't keep anything down, neither food nor tea,
And finds it very taxing to sit, to stand, or to walk.

In the fourth month the fetus develops four limbs:
Her eyes blurry, her head dizzy—she doesn't feel well.
From early dawn until late at night her mouth is sour;
Now cold, now hot, she's feeling most uncomfortable.

In the fifth month the fetus becomes male or female,
And both the mother and the fetus suffer most bitterly.
In the day it is hard to sit, in the night hard to sleep,
And she feels both upset and anxious and also ill at ease.

In the sixth month the fetus starts to grow hair,
And slowly it begins to expand inside the womb.
During the fifth watch, at midnight, it begins to stir,
And she gets upset and anxious and is worried sick.

In the seventh month, the fetus becomes a person,
And the child tosses and turns inside the womb.
The finest of delicacies now all taste like mud,
And even her eight-gored skirt has split in two.

In the eighth month the child can hardly move,
And the child weighs ten tons inside the womb.
The mother wants to move but finds she cannot,
And she becomes cranky and angry in her speech.

In the ninth month it is all painful beyond words,
And the mother's thoughts start to wander away.
She fears that she will give birth to a monster
Or that she will give birth to a child deformed.

In the tenth month to do anything becomes hard;
The mother carrying the child is choked with fear.
She is so frightened that she cannot even speak,
Overcome by a depression she does not express.

When it comes to the day for her to give birth,
She is trapped, and there is nothing she can do;
She clenches her teeth until they nearly break,
And she shivers, then breaks out in a cold sweat.

Incense is burned three or even five times,
But they must wait for hours for the child to come.

Master Zhang made vows for three days on end,
Made vows to the God of Wealth and the ancestors.

The Child-Bringing Goddess has brought the child,
The Child-Expelling Goddess has expelled the child,
And only when their son finally was born
Could Master Zhang finally feel at ease.

Only when the midwife hastened to offer congratulations,
Then Master Zhang was overjoyed and completely at ease.
When he laid eyes on the child, he was filled with joy;
He lit incense and candles, and he thanked the gods.

And right then and there he chose a name,
And the name that he chose was Shouxiang.
He slaughtered a pig to celebrate the Third Day,[81]
And thanking the Mothers, he sent them back to heaven.

Later with incense and candles they celebrated Full Month;
Two wet nurses accompanied the child everywhere.
And every day relatives came to watch over him;
They watched over that little child Shouxiang.

Guards were also placed at the gate to watch
So as to keep all strangers from entering the room.
The wet nurse came often to nurse the child;
The rich man and his wife were filled with joy.

They watched over the child from morning till night
And then again from evening until the break of day.
The wet nurse nursed him several times each day
And was even more careful to hug and hold him.

The ten-month pregnancy was truly a bitter time,
So they carefully nursed him for three years.
Every day they took him outside to play,
And so in this way Shouxiang slowly grew up

And, before he knew it, had turned six years old.
He went to school to study the *Odes* and the *Documents*.[82]
If someone taught him one thing, he would learn ten;
He was intelligent and bright and without peer.

He was good at memorizing and at composition too,

Clever at poetry, lyrics, songs, and rhapsodies as well.
When the landowner saw this, his heart filled with joy:
"In the future he will most definitely sit for the exams!"

We'll speak now no more of Shouxiang's studies
But speak again of the man named Zhao Lianfang.
Ever since the death of his Woman Huang,
He had spent his days in mournful thoughts.

Jiaogu had been paired off with He Wenxiu,
Who was from a scholar's family in Hongmen.
Banjie was promised in marriage to Li Wenpu,
Who was still in school studying the Classics.

The couple's son, Changshou, had also studied
And filled his head with essays beyond compare.
He then adopted the studio name Zhao Jinbang,
A name he would keep until the day he died.

At the age of nineteen he went to sit for the exams,
And at the age of twenty he passed in the first group.
When he returned to the Zhaos with his good news,
All of his family and all of his kin came to see him.

All his dearest friends also came to congratulate him,
And they also offered their congratulations to Lianfang,
Who killed a pig and slaughtered a sheep for the feast
So that he could entertain all his friends and relatives.

They drank without stopping for three days straight,
And Lianfang was so very happy he laughed out loud.
His son-in-law from the Li family was also a scholar,
He too was a "flourishing talent" from Hongmen.[83]

Lianfang then sat there up on the high dais,
With joy in his heart and a smile on his lips,
Thinking that for three generations the Zhao family
Had never seen such blessings bestowed on them.

"Today my son and son-in-law have succeeded,
And hustling and bustling everyone has come here.
It must be that I'm blessed with fortune and riches,

And that is due to the ancestors' hidden protection."

Jinbang then spoke up: "Most Honored Father,
Please be so kind as to listen to what I have to say.
I've heard the court is holding the big examinations,
And your son has in mind to go to the Eastern Capital.

If I succeed in becoming a 'presented scholar,'[84]
Then I can be appointed a district magistrate.
In that way our family will truly grow prosperous,
And we'll be able to completely renovate this hall,

Which will show the Zhao family's great fortune
And be a memorial to my mother who read the sutras."

When Lianfang heard this, his heart filled with delight,
And he gave these instructions to two of his servants:
"Tomorrow is a day that is very auspicious for travel,
And you'll accompany the young master to the capital."

We'll speak no more of Jinbang's journey to the capital;
We'll speak instead of the one named Zhang Shouxiang.

From the age of seven to the age of fifteen he studied,
And the knowledge he mastered was without compare.
He then chose as his official name Zhang Jinda
And applied himself to studying to pass the exams.

At the age of sixteen he passed the lower exams
And at the age of seventeen the provincial exams.
Then he heard the emperor was going to hold exams
To select the most talented men from all over the land.

As soon as Jinda heard this, his heart filled with joy,
And he bid farewell to his parents to go to the capital.
But when his parents heard this, they began to weep,
And they said: "Dear son, hear what we have to say.

To have passed the provincial exams is very good,
Why then must you insist on going to the capital?
You are the only son that your parents have,
And we will worry if you go to the capital."

When Jinda heard what they said, he sadly wept:
"Most Honorable Parents, hear what I have to say.

If at these exams I can become a 'presented scholar,'
I will be given an official post to govern the people.

　　After thanking the emperor, then I'll return home;
After thanking the ancestors, I will desire no more."
When his parents heard this, they then said:
"If you must go, than please take care of yourself."

　　And so Jinda said farewell to both of his parents,
And gathering up his bags, he set out on his way.
He went straight to the gates of the capital city,
Where all the candidates were assembled in a big hubbub.

　　Inside the Eastern Floriate Gate the scholars all gathered;
Inside the Dragon-Phoenix Gate, the posts were announced.[85]
Beside each person's name was written his official post,
Once the three sessions of essay writing had been done.

　　Jinda's essays had all been very well written,
And he was very satisfied with how he had done:
"I rather think that I may pass the exams this time —
I really expressed myself well and with great force!"

　　As it turned out, he pleased his examiners,
And he obtained the rank of "top of the list."
The emperor himself came out to appoint him
And award him the office of a Hanlin scholar.

　　Then he was appointed the head of Caozhou Prefecture,
A position that would begin the third month of next year.
Jinda thanked the emperor for his grace and went home;
He went home to offer sacrifice at the ancestors' tombs.

The second-place "presented scholar" was Zhao Jinbang;
He was sent to Tongcheng County to be its magistrate —
From the fifteenth of the Eighth Month of the next year,
Taking up his post at Tongcheng, he'd govern the people.

　　He took his leave of the emperor, and he went home,
And he went home to make offerings to the ancestors.
When Lianfang heard this, he was delighted, and so he
Slaughtered a pig and killed a sheep to offer the ancestors.

We'll speak no more of the happiness of the Zhao family
But instead speak again of the prefect of the Zhang family.
When it came to the fifteenth day of the Third Month,
He set out with his parents to take up his official post.

When they reached the yamen of Caozhou Prefecture,
All the people of the prefecture were at peace and content.

Jinda turned out to be a very honest and upright official:
The winds were smooth, the rains on time—all was at peace.
Before they knew it, it was the fifteenth of the Sixth Month,
And in every temple everywhere incense was being lit.[86]

Jinda visited the temples and lit incense for an entire day;
After which, weary and tired, he returned to his home,
But before he knew it, he found it was the third watch,
And so he lay down on his ivory couch to get some rest.

Zhang Jinda then lay on his bed and was about to fall asleep
When the Astral Deity of the Great White suddenly appeared.[87]

Our story goes that the Great White Star had transformed himself into an old man. On his head he wore a black gauze cap, and on his feet he wore white-soled shoes. He came into the room and called out: "Prefect Huang, do you know about your previous life?" When the prefect saw him, he quickly replied: "I don't know anything about my previous life, so I hope that you, elderly sir, will enlighten me. I will be deeply indebted to you." Then the Metal Star said: "In your previous life, you lived in the Qingping area of the Nanhua district of Caozhou Prefecture, the daughter of Huang Baiwan. Your mother ate a vegetarian diet and recited the Buddha's name. She always ministered to the poor and widely did good works. At the age of seven you began to read the sutras with your mother and to recite the Buddha's name. You were given the name Fifth Daughter. When you reached the age of nineteen, you were married to a man from the same area by the name of Zhao Lianfang. You gave birth to one son and two daughters. The elder daughter was called Jiaogu, and the second daughter was named Banjie; the boy's name was Changshou, and his studio name is Zhao Jinbang. Last year he passed the examinations along with you and took second place. This year on the fifteenth of the Eighth Month he went to Tongcheng to take up his post. In your last life you died at the age of thirty-two. Before you died, you took the Diamond Sutra, wrapped it in a white sash, and, after inscribing the cover with your own hand, placed it in a copper chest, which you then buried beneath the east wing. Why don't you go and dig it up and recite it— then go and find a reputable teacher and cultivate the Great Way so you can quickly ascend to heaven!" The Metal Star then shook him awake, and with the command not to forget what he had said, he disappeared. Startled, Jinda woke up only to find that it had all been a dream.

Let's speak no more of the Gold Star's appearance
But return instead to the topic of Prefect Jinda,
Who, the next day, while at leisure in his office,
Remembered the dream he'd had the night before.
    "Clearly it was an immortal come to enlighten me;
I must go to Nanhua and look further into this matter."
So, accompanied by only two of his underlings,
In a blue robe and simple hat, he left the office.
    "I am going to go to that Zhao Family Village,
But I don't want to frighten anyone along the way."
The two men acquiesced to his command,
And so secretly they left the office in haste.
    The three men walked quickly along the road
That stretched long and endless ahead of them.
From the mountaintop the landscape spread out so vast,
But with focused mind they went to Zhao Family Village.
    They walked along the road as fast as they could,
And soon Zhao Family Village lay only a short distance away.
Suddenly, as they walked in the shade of some willow trees,
They noticed a gravestone by the side of the road.
    On this gravestone was inscribed in black letters
"The Pious Woman Huang of the Zhao Family."
When the prefect saw this, his heart filled with joy;
He bowed four times and prostrated himself eight times.
    After paying his respects to the gravestone, he rose up,
And then he ordered his companions to lead the way.
They then came to the gates of the Zhao family home,
Where Lianfang and his son came out to welcome him.

They invited him into the hall and bid him be seated;
The servants brought tea and placed it before him.
After he had drunk the tea, he put the cup down,
And then the prefect said what he had come to say:

"Now I am actually none other than a certain one;
I am none other than the prefect of Caozhou Prefecture.
I have come here to your home especially to see you
Because I have something I greatly wish to clear up."

When Lianfang and his son heard these words,
They scrambled and knelt right there in the dust:
"We didn't expect that Your Excellence would visit
And hope you will forgive our crime of negligence."

But the prefect just went to help them to their feet,
Help to their feet both Lianfang and his son:
"Your wife was surely Woman Huang;
She surely bore one son and two daughters.

The son was given the name Changshou,
And he later took the studio name Jinbang.
The elder daughter was named Jiaogu;
And the second daughter was called Banjie.

Your wife, Woman Huang, was always reciting sutras,
And at the age of thirty-two she left for the Underworld.
The wife that you later married is named Woman Wei,
And all your children have been promised in marriage."

When Lianfang heard the high official speak,
One by one the tears rolled down his cheeks:
"My wife recited the sutra since she was very young
And at thirty-two was summoned to the Underworld.
Just talking about my former wife is truly difficult;
She was none other than the pious Woman Huang.

The elder girl was only nine years of age,
And the three-year-old boy wept for his mother;
The second daughter was only six years old,
And she too wept, and she cried all day long.

Before my wife died, she commanded me,

She commanded me to take another wife.
My wife separated from me and then died,
Leaving behind her three little children.

The elder daughter got married to He Wenxiu,
And she has now provided me with a grandchild.
The second daughter is now engaged to Xu Wenpi,
Who is also a 'flourishing talent' of Hongmen.

And my son, who now has the name Jinbang,
Has been appointed a magistrate by the emperor,
So then on the fifteenth of the Eighth Month,
He will go to Tongcheng to govern the people.

Now that Your Excellency has come to see me,
Word by word, line by line, we've told it clearly."

When the official heard this, he began to weep:
"In my last life, you and I were as one!
For in my last life I was Woman Huang,
The one who shared your bed and pillow!

My father's name was Huang Baiwan,
And I was the fifth of all his daughters.
At the age of nineteen I was married to you,
And then I gave birth to three children in all."

When Lianfang and his son heard these words,
For a full hour they found they could not speak!
Then finally they addressed the prefect and said:
"Your Excellency, please do not make fun of us!"

And then the tears welled up in Jinbang's eyes,
And without realizing it, Lianfang began to shake.

It was then that the prefect spoke up and said:
"Please listen, both of you, to what I have to say.
If you're still unwilling to believe what I've told you,
There is something written that will serve as proof.

In the east wing a Diamond Sutra lies buried;
It is hidden away there inside a copper chest.
On the cover are characters written in my hand;
If you dig up this Diamond Sutra, all will be clear."

Hearing this, Lianfang didn't waste a moment,
And then they dug up the sutra without delay.
When they took out the chest and opened it up,
Each character, each line, was carefully inscribed.

On top was written "Caozhou, Nanhua district,
In the Qingping area, in Zhao Family Village.
I am Woman Huang from the Zhao family,
Who from childhood has recited the sutras.

I gave birth to one son and two daughters, and
At thirty-two I was summoned to the Underworld.
I did not pass the Diamond Sutra to my children,
Because I was afraid that they were not yet sincere.

And so I am burying it here below the east kitchen,
Without my husband and children knowing about it.
Written on the third day of the Sixth Month
And left for future generations as testimony."

Seeing this, the two of them began to weep,
And their weeping moved Heaven and Earth.
The prefect then turned to them, and he said:
"Both of you listen now to what I have to say.
Let us all go to the gravestone by the tomb
And dig up the body to make completely sure."

The two of them went to the memorial stone, and
They dug up the grave to distinguish true from false.
As it turned out, the bones were as white as snow,
And the simple strand of beads shone so bright.

They then replaced the gravestone as it had been,
And the prefect turned around and headed back.
The prefect then commanded Lianfang,
Commanded him to summon his two daughters.

Lianfang then went and issued the order,
Ordered two servants to go fetch the two girls.
"You must hasten now to the He family;
Go and bring the young mistress home."

The two servants acknowledged the order,
And off they raced like arrows and clouds.

When they finally arrived at the He family,
The women invited them into the high hall.
They then bid the two fellows to have a seat,
And the servant girl brought them fragrant tea.
    After they had drunk, they put down their cups,
And then the servants delivered their message.
"The old master has sent us to this place
To fetch the mistress and take her home."
    Wenxiu did not waste a single moment,
And he ordered two palanquin carriers
To quickly take his wife in a sedan chair
And escort the mistress back to her home.
    She and her husband returned together,
And quickly they traveled along the road.
Before long they came to her home,
And then the mistress quickly alighted.
    Lianfang and his son came out to meet them,
And together they all went into the main hall.
Lianfang then spoke and told them the story:
"Prefect Zhang, who sits there in the hall,
In his past life was your beloved mother!"
    When they all heard these words,
With bows and prostrations they paid respects.
All of the children then wept and cried;[88]
The prefect and Lianfang also wept.
    "Although mother and children have met again,
I will never again see the form of my long-lost wife."
Lianfang then set out wine in honor of the reunion,
And then he bowed to Heaven, Earth, and the gods.

It was then that the prefect thought to himself:
"The official life cannot compare to the religious life."

And so he turned to his children and said:
"Listen, my daughters, and hear my words.
When you are in another's home as a daughter-in-law,
You must respect your father-in-law and your husband.

I have here three thousand ounces of silver,
Which I will use to buy some clothes for you."
Hastily Jiaogu and Banjie made their bows
And bid farewell to their mother from a previous life.

It was then that the prefect asked Jinbang:
"Would you rather be an official or do self-cultivation?"
Jinbang did not quite know how to reply,
But Lianfang quickly spoke up and said:
"It's been generations since the Zhao family
Has managed to produce an official.

If you, my son, leave to practice self-cultivation,
Who will then care for me when I am old?
For now, just go and take up your post at Tongcheng,
Serve for a time, and then go pursue the religious life."
When the prefect heard this, he spoke up and said:
"Listen, Jinbang, and hear what I have to say.
If you are an official, you must be honest and upright,
And you must not be greedy and harm the good people.

I happen to have an uncle on my father's side
Who is currently serving as prefect of Anqing.
His name is Zhou Zheng, and he is quite well off,
And his second daughter is still living at home.

This year she is already twenty years old,
And yet she has not found a suitable match.
Tomorrow I will go and visit them at home,
And I will most gladly serve as matchmaker.

So many young nobles, yet none that she desires,
But I'll make sure they'll be willing to accept you!
I urge you to marry when you take up your post
So that you may provide the Zhao family with an heir.

As for me, I no longer wish to serve as an official;

Instead I long to cultivate virtue and read the sutras.
   Come the Seventh Month, I will write a memorial
To recommend your talent and learning to the court.
I will recommend you to be the prefect of Yunnan,[89]
So you'll no longer serve as magistrate of Tongcheng."
   Lianfang and his son bowed and expressed their thanks
For the heartfelt concern of this most generous official.
The prefect then took his leave and returned to his home;
Speedily and with haste, he then returned to his office.

After he had returned to his office, he wrote a letter,
For he was fully determined to serve as go-between.
   In that letter he wrote: "Zhao Jinbang of Nanhua
Is a young and highly talented 'presented scholar.'
He has been appointed magistrate of Tongcheng,
And he would indeed be a fine and fitting match.
   I would be delighted to serve as the go-between—
I wonder what Uncle would have to say about this?"
When he had finished writing this letter,
He gave it to a messenger to take and deliver it.
   When Old Zhou read the letter, he was truly delighted,
And immediately he wrote a letter to accept the offer.
It was decided then that on the fifteenth of the Eighth Month
The Zhao family would be asked to come and fetch the bride.

We will not speak of her marriage into the Zhao family
But return now to our story about His Excellency Zhang,
Who on the fifteenth day of the Seventh Month
Bid farewell to his parents and set out for the capital.
   Before he knew it, he found himself inside the city gates,
Where he waited for the emperor to convene his court.
   First he wrote an official letter of recommendation
In which he praised the talent and ability of Jinbang.
He also composed an official letter of resignation—
Every character and every line was written most truthfully:
   "A hundred times I deserve to die, a thousand times to perish,

But what I wish is to cultivate virtue and study the Way."
After he had done with composing these two letters,
At the fifth watch[90] the following day, court was held.

   He took his petitions and addressed the emperor:
"I hope and beg that Your Royal Highness will show pity,
For if Your Highness does not agree to his subject's request,
Instead of going home, I will die on these golden steps."

   The emperor then opened his golden mouth, saying:
"You are allowed to read the sutras and practice religion."

Jinda then thanked the emperor for his benevolence
And, bidding him farewell, returned to his home.
The journey home went quickly, as fast as could be,
And before he knew it, he had arrived at his office.

   He then went to the hall to pay respect to his parents,
Saying: "My dear parents, listen and I will explain.
Your son has resigned from his post as a prefect;
Please come with him to practice self-cultivation."

   When his parents heard this, their tears began to flow.
"Why have you resigned your post for no reason at all?"

   Jinda said: "To cultivate the religious life is far better,
Better than being an official and governing the masses.
By practicing religion, one can enjoy everlasting purity;
By being an official, one creates a great deal of bad karma."

   When his parents heard this, they were truly delighted
And agreed to practice self-cultivation with their son.

We'll speak no more of the prefect's practice of self-cultivation
But will switch the subject and speak of the one named Zhao.
While Lianfang was sitting in his high hall,
Suddenly a messenger appeared at his door

   With a letter in which it was written that Zhao Jinbang
Had been promoted to the post of prefect of Yunnan,
And on the third day of the Tenth Month of this year,
He should go to his Yunnan post and govern the people.

Time passed more quickly than the weaver's shuttle:
Both the Eighth Month and the Tenth Month drew near.
The Zhao family decorated their home in high style
In order to welcome the young lady of the Zhou family.
Zhao Jinbang rode a sedan chair carried by four fellows
And, accompanied by flutes and drums, fetched his bride.

The Zhou family had prepared everything in advance,
And now the complete dowry glimmered and gleamed.
There were one hundred and twenty caskets and cases
And also forty-eight trunks filled with silver and gold—

It was truly a dowry nearly impossible to describe—
And around her there were also four maids-in-waiting.
Thrice-sounding firecrackers startled Heaven and Earth
When the Zhou family daughter entered the sedan chair.

With four steeds galloping ahead to open up the way,
Banners waving, drums sounding, and a great hullabaloo,
They traveled along the road, and they traveled quickly.
The Zhao family was all gathered outside the front gate.

The bride and groom went up to the hall to pay their respects,
They paid their respects to the ancestors and to the family gods,
They paid respects to the Stove God and to Heaven and Earth,
And then they paid their respects to the bride's elderly in-laws.

The young lady of the Zhou family was a very beautiful girl,
With glossy brows and lovely eyes that were beyond compare,
Her ten fingers long and slender like young shoots,
And her three-inch golden lotus feet stepping down,

Her hair like black clouds, her brow like the moon,
Her eyes like autumn waves, clear and shiny bright.
Bride and groom then bowed, the one to the other,
And so the young talent and the beauty were wed.

After which they met together behind the bed-curtains,
The love between husband and wife deeper than the sea!
The days and months sped as fast as a weaver's shuttle,
And soon the third day of the Tenth Month drew near.

Father and son, husband and wife, together set out

For Yunnan, where Jinbang would govern the people.
Jinbang was an extremely honest and upright official:
The winds and rains were timely, bringing great peace.[91]

We will speak no more of Jinbang's life as an official
But speak again of the one named Zhang, called Jinda.
    All day he recited the sutras, recited them until dusk,
And then at night he recited them again until dawn.
Day after day, night after night, he recited the sutras,
Until it caught the attention of the God of the Metal Star,
    Who came down to the mortal world to teach Jinda;
In the second quarter of the third watch he descended,
When Jinda was just in the middle of a hazy sleep.
The God of the Metal Star stood by his bed and spoke,
    Saying again and then again: "Prefect Zhang,
There is something on my mind I wish to say!
Without seeking an enlightened master and cultivating the Great Way,
It will be a waste of effort to engage in fasts and recite Buddha's name.
    Yin and yang will go together, water and fire will support each other,
Qian and *kun* will then change places, and dragon and tiger will roar.[92]
The precious jewel of Sakyamuni can then be attained,
And you will join the immortals of the highest heavens.
    In the Great Compassion Pavilion, forty miles from the city,
There dwells a famous teacher who is named Master Li.[93]
His Dharma name is Master Enlightened-as-to-the-One:
He's fully mastered the Great Way of Former Heaven."
    After saying these words, the God of the Golden Star left,
And the dreaming man suddenly woke up with a start.
Zhang Jinda then got up but felt uneasy in his mind,
Remembering clearly the words of the Metal Star God.
    He went to the high hall to tell his father and his mother,
And he told his parents, wanting to see what they would say:
"This is how the gods have chosen to come and instruct me;
I must seek an enlightened master, refine the Spirit of Emptiness.[94]
    In the Great Compassion Pavilion forty miles from the city
There lives an enlightened teacher by the name of Master Li.

I hope that my parents will accompany me to pay him a visit;
We will entreat the master to bestow his kindness upon us."

When the two old folks heard this, they were filled with joy,
And they fasted and they bathed so as to purify their minds.
Then they set out in three small sedan chairs along the same road.
They took along with them five hundred ounces of glistening silver.

As they traveled along the road, and they traveled with haste,
Soon the Great Compassion Pavilion stood there before them.
In front of the temple gate they dismounted their sedan chairs
And went inside the gates of the temple to light some incense.

One of the monks who lived there hurried to greet them,
And addressed them as "Good People" over and over again.
When they offered incense, the bells and drums sounded.
Jinda and his father wanted an audience with the famous master,

So they donated two ounces of silver to have the drum sounded,
And the monk took the silver and gave them a big smile.
Then the old man addressed the monk, saying:
"In this temple is there not a certain Master Li?"

The monk immediately replied and said to him:
"Why does the old gentleman ask me this question?"
Jinda then hastened to reply to his query, and he said:
"We have come just to see this countryman of ours."

When the monk heard him explain it in this way,
He went to the Cinnabar Room to call out the master.
As soon as Jinda saw him, his heart filled with joy;
Parents and child, all three of them, knelt in the dust.

The master bowed back and hastened to help them rise;
He bid his guests be seated and passed around cups of tea.
The master then addressed the old gentleman and said:
"I am afraid, my dear sir, I can't place your face too clearly."

Jinda then hastened to respond quickly to his words:
"Our home is located in the Eastern Capital,
And my own humble name is Zhang Jinda.
I came out 'top of the list' in the capital examinations

And was appointed as erudite in the Hanlin Academy;
Then as prefect of Caozhou, I governed over the people,

But having seen through the Red Dust, I cultivated the True Way;
And leaving behind both emperor and post, I retired to the hills.

Last night a deity appeared to me in order to instruct me,
Saying I must come to pay a visit to the venerable master
That he may initiate this disciple into the path of cultivation,
To point out how I should begin to refine the Spirit of Emptiness.

If some day in the future I am able to realize the Way,
I'll testify to your compassion in the Dragon-Flower Assembly."[95]

The master then fell down on both of his knees.
"So you are a great official and also a great man,
While I am nothing but an ignorant country bumpkin!
Why have you taken so much trouble and come so far?"

The old gentleman helped him rise, saying: "Please!
The master is being too humble—we won't accept it!
We entreat you to be compassionate and initiate us,
So that we may clearly see the Great Way of No-Self."

The master then answered them, and he said:
"Great sir, please be so kind as to listen to me.
Since ancient times few have trod the Way of Former Heaven,
Yet as the Sage said, 'Having heard it at dawn, one can die at dusk,'[96]

Offering incense and relying on the Buddha, one must make a vow;
One makes a vow to the Great Way—the only thing to do as proof.
You must strictly keep to the Three Refuges and Five Precepts,[97]
And by fasting and releasing life, embody the Heavenly Mind.

Use your money to nourish virtue and generously give alms
And print morality books that can be used to convert people.
There are certain virtues that will nourish the spiritual root,
So why be worried that the Great Way is not easily realized?"

When Jinda heard this, his heart was filled with joy,
And he vowed to act according to the words of the master.
He took the five hundred ounces of silver he had brought
And handed that amount over to the master to use for merit.

"The printing of books and releasing of life are your work;
I beg of you, Master, to undertake this all on our behalf.
Day and night I will dedicate myself to works of charity;
After weighing out the family treasure, I'll give it away."

When the master heard this, his heart filled with joy.
"You indeed are a man of great and profound wisdom!"
He then hurried to arrange for offerings and vegetarian dishes;
He lit candles, burned incense, and presented a written petition.

"If in front of the censer, you make a single-hearted vow,
I will transmit to you the root of the Master's Great Way.
Through the single Dark Gate, I will transmit the True Way
As the stars bow in the direction of the Northern Dipper,

Stopping only at the place of ultimate joy and realization,
Focusing until all else is forgotten at the Great Way's gates.
The six extremities all turn to spring and return to the Maoyi,[98]
And the subjugated Six Thieves[99] will obey your command.

Below the Crystal Tower you will subdue the divine fire;
Then the Eight Immortals will appear in their golden forms.
Building a base, refining the self, gathering the cloudy herb,
Purity retained, filth washed away, the purple vapor warms.

When Water and Fire change places, and Dragon and Tiger meet,
As the Dharma Wheel endlessly turns, the cinnabar forms of itself.[100]
The Great Way Encompassing Heaven must add to the fire, and
One can transcend the mundane and in an instant become a sage."

Jinda and his father bowed with their hands above their heads.
"We are grateful to the master for showing us his compassion."
Then Jinda and his parents hastened and bid him farewell,
And the master hastened to see them off at the temple gate.

After the formalities of parting were over, they entered the sedans,
And in the three small sedan chairs they made their way home.
Walking they were enlightened, and sitting they were enlightened;
They were enlightened as to the One True Sutra of No Words.[101]

Breathing they touched and moved the Original Primary Ether,
And so Guanshiyin of the Southern Sea appeared to them.
Nature returned to its original *qian*: a pure-yang physique.
They smelted and refined the indestructible Diamond Body.

Leaving the male and entering the female, yin and yang united;
The fire medicine flared up, and the golden cinnabar congealed.
Ten months an embryo in the womb and three years at the breast:

Shedding the embryo and miraculously manifesting the yang spirit.

Nine years of silent meditation, diligently cultivating enlightenment,[102]
Startled and moved the many divinities with their various functions.
Quickly, oh so quickly, these divinities submitted a report
And presented it to the Buddha of the Western Heaven.

The Tathagata Buddha parted his golden lips and spoke:
"Hasten and report to all members of the Zhang family
That together they will ascend to heaven in broad daylight
As five-colored auspicious clouds fill all of the heavens."

Then Jinda together with his father and his mother
Mounted a rose-hued cloud and ascended into the heavens,
And their ancestors, because of his merit, were also saved.
The nine kin and seven ancestors were all reborn in heaven.

Then Golden Lads came two by two to lead the way,
Leading Jinda into the presence of the Most Honored One.

The Tathagata Buddha parted his golden lips and spoke:
"Jinda, my good person, do listen to what I have to say.
Three days from now you will all achieve nirvana,
And the whole family will ascend to be lotus lamps."[103]

Let's say no more of the Zhangs' path to immortality
But rather switch our topic and recount a different tale.

Jinbang of the Zhao family served as a prefect,
And the people of the Yunnan area were pleased.
Husband and wife were both extremely filial,
And the couple was blessed with three children.

The second son was given the name Zongbao,
And he was adopted by the Zhangs as Jinda's heir.
Later, having passed the highest exams, Zongbao
Was given the position of secretary of the Inner Court.

The Zhangs became immortals but also had descendants,
As the five sons of Zongbao all became famous.

Lianfang lived until he was seventy-two years old;
Then he too retired and went to cultivate religion.
He built himself a terrace nearly fourteen feet high,

And, forswearing wine and meat, he recited the sutra texts.
  "All I care about now is ascending to the Immortal Realm
And making up for the life of sin I once led as a butcher."
Lianfang recited the sutras, widely practicing goodness;
He didn't abandon the sutras for even an hour or a minute.
  Later on he also ascended to the position of earth god;
Indeed the earth god of Nanhua was none other than he.

Jinbang was very pure and upright in his official duties,
And the emperor promoted him higher and higher again.
He rose to become the governor of Shandong Province,
And was appointed prime minister in the imperial court.
  In this way he lived out a life span of a full hundred years;
Five generations of sons and grandsons served the emperor.
There were no less than twenty black-gauze hats,
And there were twenty jade belts of high office.
  The emperor awarded them a Dragon and Phoenix Plaque,[104]
And thus five generations of one family won everlasting fame.

This has been the story of just a single good woman
Who in both this life and the next was a good person.
The Zhaos' and Zhangs' enjoyment of wealth and rank
Was all due to the merit earned by this Woman Huang!
  So let me urge the people of the world to behave well,
And Heaven will bless you with good sons and grandsons.
Gold and jade will fill your halls—exams will be passed.
The Hall of Five Generations—who does not respect it?[105]
  Who says that Blue Heaven does not repay and respond,
When the gods are there, just a few feet above your head?
  Although this morality book may not be that profound,
It has been well known for many thousands of autumns.
Thus good men and pious women should read it with care:
It will inspire them to do good deeds and earn great merit!

NOTES

Introduction

1   The word *dui* in the second title, translated here as "recites," has another more common meaning, which is "to respond." In this book's version of the story, Woman Huang is called down to the Underworld to recite the Diamond Sutra and also to respond to questions about its content and significance posed to her by Yama, king of the Underworld. By so doing, she demonstrates that she is not merely mouthing the words of the sutra but fully understands their meaning.

2   Huijiao 1992, 512–13.

3   See Idema 2004.

4   For example, the *Complete Story of Mulian* (Mulian quanzhuan), a play in the Chenhe *gaoqiang* (high-pitched music) style from Luxi county, Hunan, includes the story of Woman Huang (or, as she is referred to in this play, Woman Wang). See He Fang et al. 2008.

5   See Teiser 2006.

6   Translation in Teiser 1988, 49–50.

7   Teiser 1988, 50.

8   There has been much scholarly discussion on the meaning of the term *yulanpen*. The *pen* may simply refer to the bowl into which offerings are placed. A common explanation of *yulan*, which means "hanging upside down," is

that it refers to the sufferings of those poor souls, "hanging upside down" whether literally or metaphorically, in the Underworld.

9 See Teiser 1988. The date of the Yulan Bowl Festival coincides with an important date on the Daoist ritual calendar, and Buddhists most likely appropriated a preexisting festival for their own purposes. The Mulian story also appears to have exerted a significant influence on the development of medieval Japanese Noh drama. See Tian 1983.

10 The title in one of these manuscripts suggests that the text originally was accompanied by one or more illustrations, which, however, have not been preserved.

11 While ballads all in verse (and of epic proportions) are not uncommon in late imperial China, the prosimetric format would appear to have been much more common from the end of the first millennium down to the present day. See Mair 1997; Idema 2010.

12 For an English translation of the transformation text version, see Mair 1983; also reprinted in Mair 1994, 1093–1127. This translation replaced the earlier rendition in Waley 1960. For a translation based on a different manuscript, see Eoyang 1978. Other prosimetric versions from Dunhuang include the Yulan Bowl Recitation Text (Yulanpen jiangjingwen) and a retelling in the format of a "tale of causes and conditions" (yinyuan). For a Dutch translation of all of these versions, see Idema 2004, 231–94.

13 See Kikkawa 1991; Kikkawa 2003.

14 The Mulian plays have inspired a sizable body of scholarship. See, for instance, Dauth 1996; Hou 2002; Johnson 1989; Judd 1994; Judd 1996; Liu 1997; Peng and Seaman 1994; Zhu 1993.

15 See Guo 2005.

16 See He et al. 2008.

17 Scholars have often suggested that precious scrolls are a direct continuation of the prosimetric literature found at Dunhuang. In fact, *The Precious Scroll of Incense Mountain*, probably one of the earliest precious scrolls, refers to itself as a tale of causes and conditions, a well-established genre among Dunhuang texts. See Idema 2008, 11–12. For a listing of precious scrolls on Mulian, see Che 2000, 164–68. Also see Zhu 1993, 92–98.

18 See Nadeau 1993; Overmyer 1999.

19 See Bender 2001; Berezkin 2011. Also see Che 1997, 131–59. The ritual recitation of a Mulian text was intended to assist one's deceased mother to be reborn in heaven.

20 For a description of this manuscript, illustrated by extensive excerpts from its text, see Zheng 1959, 318–27. For a small color reproduction of one of the

pages, see Liu Zhen 1997, and for a discussion of this text, see 241–57. While earlier scholars read the date of the surviving manuscript as 1371, Kikkawa 2005 insists that it actually is 1337. The text may well have been composed up to a century earlier than either date. Kikkawa 2003 provides a complete transcription of the preserved section of the text, which probably continued to circulate well into the fifteenth century. This text is the earliest version of the Mulian legend to mention a Blood Bowl (that is, Blood Pond).

21 Che 2009, 302–8, describes the preserved fragment of *The Precious Scroll of the Divine Maudgalyayana Rescuing His Mother So She May Leave Hell and Be Reborn in Heaven* (Muqianlian zunzhe jiumu chuli diyu shengtian baojuan), a late Ming manuscript of a long rewrite of the Mulian legend by a member of the religious sect known as the Wuwei jiao (Non-action School). This version mostly likely was composed in the final decades of the sixteenth century; it is the first retelling that includes a detailed description of the Blood Pond Hell. A text that originated within a certain sect was not necessarily limited to that sect, especially if the text had been printed and circulated in larger numbers.

22 Although conventionally also translated as "precious scroll," the term used in this title is *baozhuan* (lit. "precious record").

23 See Johnson 1995.

24 The translation in this volume is based on the printed edition of 1885, as reproduced in the published collection of popular literature texts located in the Fu Ssu-nien Library of the Institute of History and Philology of the Academia Sinica on Taiwan, *(Zhongyang yanjiu yuan: Lishi yuyan yanjiusuo) Suwenxue congkan* (Collection of folk literature), (Taipei: Xinwenfeng, 2004), 352:197–362. In the final decades of the twentieth century, this precious scroll was not only recited at Blood Bowl Rituals in Jingjiang, Jiangsu, where it was known as the "Blood Bowl Precious Scroll" (Xuepen baojuan), but also circulated in western Gansu.

25 See Teiser 2006. See also Schmid 2008.

26 On Guanyin, see Yü 2001. Also see Dudbridge 1978; Idema 2008.

27 These temptation scenes are clearly modeled on the attempted seduction of Siddhartha Gautama by the daughters of Mara, just as he is about to attain enlightenment and become the Buddha. As one might imagine, Guanyin's attempted seduction of Mulian was very popular among audiences of the staged versions of the story.

28 See Grant 1989 for a detailed study of all of these various versions.

29 There is a rare edition of this text published in 1592. See Che 2009, 388, citing Sawada 1975, 158.

30 Che 2009, 389. It is worth noting that Luo himself was a native of northern Shandong, which is also the home province of the Woman Huang of the story translated here. For a reconstructed biography of this fascinating figure and a discussion of his basic teachings, see Seiwert 2003, esp. 216–35.

31 Che 2009, 389.

32 Shek 1980, 161.

33 For an English translation of this section of the novel, see Roy 2011, pp. 437–58.

34 Cited in Che 1997, 390–91. For more on the Great Way of Former Heaven, see Topley 1963.

35 Sawada 1975, 157–59.

36 See Zhu 2001.

37 The legend of Woman Huang was one of the inspirations for the novel *The Butcher's Wife*, by Li Ang, a female novelist from Taiwan. In this feminist transformation of the tale, however, the brutalized wife eventually murders her husband. See Li Ang 1986.

38 Quoted in Iovene 2010, 186–87.

39 Idema 2009a, 135–57. The story of Woman Wang clearly was on the mind of Asian American novelist Lisa See when she wrote her best-selling novel *Snow Flower and the Secret Fan* (2005), which describes the women's-script culture.

40 See Wang 1984.

41 It should be mentioned that the text is printed in extremely small characters, so small that at times they are almost illegible. This makes our reading of the text in a few places quite tentative. The same text was also published by the printing house Huaiyin shanfang. This edition, a copy of which is also kept at the Fu Ssu-nian Library, is printed in equally small characters. Both editions contain one full-page lithographic illustration. The illustration in the Chunyin shuzhuang edition shows Woman Huang in front of King Yama; the illustration in the Huaiyin shanfang edition shows Woman Huang on her way through the Underworld, approaching the Senluo Hall of King Yama.

42 For an overview of these diverse views, see Sponberg 1992. For a vivid description of some of the more grisly manifestations of early Buddhist misogyny, see Wilson 1996.

43 For short introductions to women and Chinese religion in general, see Grant 1995; Grant 2008a; Overmyer 1991. For a selected but comprehensive bibliography on the subject, see Grant 2008b.

44 See the discussion in Lhamo 2003.

45 For discussions of the role of filial piety in Indian Buddhism, see Schopen 1984; Strong 1983; Guang 2005.

46   Translated and quoted in Guang 2005, 85.

47   Confucian gender ideology has received considerable attention in recent years. See Bray 1997; Chengyang Li 2000; Mann and Cheng 2001; Ko, Haboush, and Piggott 2003; Rosenlee 2006. The conventional norms for women (filial piety, chastity, obedience to parents-in-law, loyalty to husbands, and self-sacrifice for the sake of their children) were by late imperial times promulgated not only through moral tracts for women and biographies of exemplary daughters, wives, mothers, and widows but also through plays and ballads. See, for instance, Idema 2009a.

48   See Hansen 1995.

49   See Teiser 1994. Also see Sawada 1969; Xiao 1996. Paintings of the Ten Courts of Hell and their punishments often are displayed at funerals. For a study of this type of painting, see Donnelly 1997, which is richly illustrated. Many temples contain three-dimensional displays of the Underworld courts and the tortures of hell. See, for instance, Goodrich 1981. Also see Eberhard 1967; Pas 1989.

50   One of the most famous of such stories tells of an Underworld tour made by no less a figure than the Tang dynasty emperor Taizong (599–649). For an English translation of the early (and fragmentary) Dunhuang version of this story, see Waley 1960, 164–74; reprinted in Minford and Lau 2002, 1081–89.

51   Cole 1998, 177–78, argues that the transformation text adaptation of the legend also clearly implies the sexual nature of the sins of Mulian's mother. His main argument is that Mulian's mother is portrayed as tied to a red-hot iron bed, a punishment that elsewhere in the text is identified as the specific punishment for sexual misconduct. It also should be kept in mind that meat and alcohol were considered sexual stimulants. In other legends of sons saving their mothers from "earth prisons," the sins of the mothers are identified as outright cannibalism and improper sexual desire. See Idema 2009b, xvi–xx.

52   This was especially true of many Buddhist sectarian groups that emerged during this period.

53   For a concise discussion of Chinese traditions of vegetarianism and their interaction with Buddhist vegetarian traditions, see Goossaert 2005, 23–76. For Buddhist vegetarianism and its practice in sectarian religions of the Ming and Qing, see Kieschnik 2005.

54   See Ahern 1975; Cole 1998; Chu 1980.

55   The notion of the Blood Pond Hell also spread outside China to Japan. See Moerman 2005, 211–31. See also Takemi 1983. For a study of the question of female pollution in China, see Lin 2008.

56   A Daoist text, *The True Scripture of the Heavenly Worthy of Primordial*

Beginnings Who Saves [Beings] from the Blood Pond (Yuanshi tianzun jidu xiehu zhengjing), which may date anywhere from the late Tang to the Yuan dynasty, uses very similar language: "Childbirth causes various predicaments. During their monthly flow, when they clean dirty clothes, or when they bear sons and daughters, their blood dirties the earth gods. Dirty fluids pour out into streams, rivers, ponds, and wells. People, without knowledge and awareness, draw water for drink and food and offer it as sacrifice to the spirits. Thus they violently offend the Three Luminaries." Translated in Lee 2003, 22. See also Mugitani 2004, 117–19.

57 See Baptandier 2008, 181.

58 Whereas religious traditions in China considered women's menstrual blood extremely polluting, the tradition of learned gynecology considered regular menses essential to a woman's health. See Furth 1999.

59 This section is a modified version of the translation in Cole 1998, 199.

60 This section is a modified version of the translation in Cole 1998, 202.

61 See Seaman 1975. Also see Che 2002, 171–94, which describes a comparable ritual in Jingjiang, Jiangsu.

62 In China, a pregnancy is said to last ten months, beginning from the month in which a woman becomes pregnant to the month in which she gives birth.

63 For yet another version of "The Ten Months of Pregnancy," which circulated in Jiangyong, Hunan, see Idema and Grant 2004, 558–61. In that text, the description of the pains experienced by the mother during the ten months of pregnancy is followed by a description of her worries and cares as her son grows up.

64 For a concise account of the rather convoluted history of this indigenous text, see Yifa and Romaskiewicz 2008b, esp. 92–146. This text is part of the Woodenfish Project's Sutra Translation Project and can be found online at www.woodenfish.org/sutras.

65 This is a substantially modified version of the translation by Yifa and Romaskiewicz 2008b, 63.

66 This is a slightly modified version of the translation found in Cole 1998, 206.

67 See Cole 1998.

68 Kang 2009, 52.

69 This is a modified version of the translation in Cole 1998, 206.

70 For an excellent study of Dizang, see Zhiru 2007. Ksitigarbha is featured in *The Precious Scroll of the Three Lives of the Buddha* and *Woman Huang Matches the Diamond Sutra* as the supreme divinity of the Underworld, the Teaching Lord of the World of Darkness, but he plays only a minor role, as King Yama is entrusted with administering the Underworld.

71　This translation, slightly modified, is in Mark 2005b, 291.

72　Ibid., 293–94 (translation slightly modified).

73　Ibid., 294 (translation slightly modified).

74　The precepts against eating meat extend to prohibition of strong spices and alcohol.

75　Many religious teachings addressed to women teach that a woman first has to "slay the red," that is, suppress any loss of menstrual blood, before she can make any progress on the path to enlightenment. See Despeux and Kohn 2003, 177–243; Valussi 2003. Woman Huang's failure to convince her husband of the necessity of abandoning his profession may be contrasted with the efforts of Liu Xiang, the title heroine of *The Precious Scroll of Liu Xiang* (Liu Xiang baojuan), first printed in 1774. In this story, when Liu Xiang learns from a nun about the sinful nature of the female condition, she not only becomes determined not to marry at all but also successfully convinces her parents to turn their butcher shop into a teahouse. It is worth noting, however, that while Woman Huang is unable to persuade her husband either to abandon his trade or to join her in the recitation of sutras, he does not forbid Woman Huang from pursuing her religious activities. This may well reflect the relatively greater social tolerance of women's religious activities inside the home during the late imperial period, compared with the negative social attitude toward women's participation in religious activities outside the home. See Zhou 2003.

76　For translations and studies of the Diamond Sutra, see Mu 2000; Red Pine 2001; Wood and Barnard 2010.

77　Teiser 1994, 96–98.

78　In *The Precious Scroll of Incense Mountain*, Guanyin is politely asked to leave the Underworld as soon as her preaching turns it into a blessed realm. See Idema 2008.

79　Seaman 1975, 384.

80　The story of Mulian's rebirth as Huang Chao was already current by the seventeenth century, as it is discussed as a common superstition in ch. 12 of the anonymous mid-seventeenth-century novel *Cu hulu* (Vinegar Calabash). See Anonymous 1999, pp. 1693–95. For a detailed account of the Huang Chao rebellion, see Somers 1979.

81　This story is, for instance, already told in chapters 2–5 of the sixteenth-century historical novel *Historical Romance of the Destruction of the Tang and the Five Dynasties* (Can Tang Wudai shi yanyi zhuan). See Anonymous 1983, 4–13.

The Precious Scroll of the Three Lives of Mulian

1   The term *yuanwai* originally denoted a supernumerary official, but in late imperial China, it was widely used to refer to very wealthy citizens without any official rank and, in that usage, might be translated as "magnate" or "millionaire." The author of this text evidently understands Fu Xiang's personal name Xiang as "Minister."

2   To keep the fast means to maintain a strictly vegetarian diet, not eating any meat or strongly spiced dishes, and abstain from alcohol throughout the year.

3   A popular form of gaining religious merit in Chinese Buddhism was to release live animals who would otherwise be destined for the cooking pot. Special ponds designed to hold released fish are even today found on the grounds of many Buddhist monasteries and temples.

4   A gatha is a Buddhist poem or hymn.

5   Impermanence (Wuchang) is the Buddhist personification of death, represented by two figures, one short and one tall, one white and one black.

6   The term "dhyana-forest" (*chanlin*) refers to a monastery. The Sanskrit word *dhyana* (in Chinese, *chan*; in Japanese, *zen*) means "meditation."

7   If a corpse were found on the doorsteps of a house, its owner would be the first to be suspected of foul play.

8   "The Tathagata" is a term of respect used to refer to Sakyamuni Buddha.

9   The Dharma is the teachings of the Buddha.

10   Here, "flowers" refers to women and sex.

11   King Yama is the highest judge in the Underworld, where the souls of the deceased will be judged according to their deeds, words, and thoughts during their lifetimes (see the introduction to this volume).

12   "The gate" refers to the entrance to enlightenment and eternal bliss.

13   The Three Jewels are the Buddha, the Dharma (the body of his teachings), and the Sangha (community of monks and nuns). The Five Precepts stipulate that Buddhist followers should abstain from killing, stealing, lying, engaging in improper sexual conduct, and indulging in alcohol or other intoxicants.

14   "Earth prison" (*diyu*) is another term for the Underworld.

15   The Three Officials (or Three Offices) of heaven, earth, and water are known from early Daoist texts as deities in charge of observing and recording human actions and posthumous rewards and punishments.

16   "Returning home" is here used as a euphemism for dying.

17   The consumption of wine, meat, and spices (including strong-smelling

vegetables such as onion and garlic) is believed to arouse aggression and sensual desire and thus is to be avoided by the pious.

18 Monks were invited to read sutras for the benefit of the deceased on the seventh, the fourteenth, the twenty-first, the twenty-eighth, the thirty-fifth, the forty-second, and the forty-ninth day following a person's death. Such rituals were commonly referred to as the "Sevens." More rituals would be conducted one hundred days and then one full year after the person's death as well as at the end of the prescribed twenty-seven-month mourning period.

19 *Mencius* 1A.3.4. Mencius lived in the fourth century B.C.E.

20 *Mencius* 1A.7.8. "The Sage" usually refers to Confucius, but Mencius is often designated as "the Second Sage."

21 "God on High" is the translation of "Shangdi," which refers to the supreme heavenly deity in ancient Chinese religion.

22 The Chinese character for "meat" (*rou* 肉) is made up of three different components; one represents an enclosure and the other two are the characters for "human" (*ren* 人).

23 No further information is available on Man of the Way Chen or Man of the Way Ma.

24 That is, her innermost physical nature.

25 According to Buddhism, there are six possible realms of rebirth. The three good realms are those of gods, demigods, and humans. The three bad realms are the animal realm, the realm of the hungry ghosts, and the hells. Sins of lust and greed are usually said to lead to rebirth as hungry ghosts.

26 Yili is Mulian's servant. He has returned ahead of his master to announce Mulian's imminent arrival.

27 Two of the most important prison guards and torturers in hell are Oxhead and Horseface, their names reflecting their depictions.

28 As explained in this book's introduction, the blood shed by women in menstruation and childbirth was believed to be highly polluting. Women who had given birth were supposed to refrain from household duties for one full month so that the gods would not be polluted.

29 According to traditional belief, each brook, river, lake, and sea has its own dragon, who lives in a palace underwater. Thus, by washing blood-stained clothes in a river or lake, women pollute the resident dragon kings.

30 The following songs "to the tune of 'Yinniuxi'" are sung by the women in the Blood Pond. Precious scrolls often include songs that are to be sung to a variety of popular tunes.

31 In premodern China, the night was divided into five watches of equal

length. Songs that describe a sequence of events that takes place over the five watches of the night are quite common in popular literature.

32   To pray for blessings from the gods.

33   In Indian Hindu and Buddhist mythology, yakshas are nature spirits, usually considered benevolent. In the Chinese tradition, yakshas often are described as deformed and evil monsters.

34   The Hall of Transformation probably is to be identified with the Wheel of Rebirth, which determines one's path of rebirth.

35   The Senluo Hall is the official residence of King Yama.

36   The iron plaques are symbols of authority given to these demons when they are ordered to arrest a sinner, in this case, Liu Qingti.

37   What we have translated here as "guts," in the original Chinese is actually "gallbladder," traditionally believed be the seat of courage, as reflected also in the English expression "to have the gall."

38   King Yama is here designated as Son of Heaven because he is the supreme ruler of the World of Darkness.

39   The karmascope is a mirror that shows all the sins of the person who looks in it (that is, his or her karma). It also shows the true nature of demons who have taken on human form.

40   The Avici Hell is the deepest of the various Buddhist hells and the one in which the suffering is the most unremitting and long-lasting.

41   The Yang Terrace is the place where, in a dream, an ancient king of the state of Chu slept with the goddess of Mount Wu.

42   In a famous Tang dynasty tale, a man experiences a happy marriage and a glorious career in a dream. When he wakes up from his drunken stupor, he realizes that the events in his dream had taken place in the kingdom of ants on the southern branch of the acacia tree in his courtyard.

43   This refers to the Western Paradise of the Buddha Amithaba. Any person who has sincerely called on Amithaba will be admitted into his Pure Land upon death (but only in a male body).

44   The eight characters are the two characters each for the hour, day, month, and year of one's birth. They are believed to determine one's future and are essential for marriage negotiations. These pairs of characters derive from a cycle of sixty two-character combinations.

45   Traditionally (and even today in many rural areas of China), babies and toddlers would wear split pants instead of diapers and, especially at night, must have often wet the bed.

46   "Heavenly flowers" is a euphemism for smallpox, which, in the absence of modern medicine, was an often fatal childhood disease.

47   "Spirit Mountain" (or Spirit Vulture Mountain) refers to both an actual place frequented by the historical Buddha (Mount Grdhrakuta) and the mythical location where he preached the famous Lotus Sutra.

48   The most efficient way to bear a carrying pole is on one shoulder. Carrying the pole on both shoulders is inefficient and painful. However, Mulian wants to honor equally both the sutras and his mother, yet another indication of the tension between religious salvation and filial piety reflected in these tales.

49   On Mount Putuo (Putuoshan), a small island off the coast of Ningbo that was identified with Potalaka, the mythical abode of the bodhisattva Guanyin.

50   In popular Chinese Buddhism, Good-in-Talent (Shancai, Sudhana) is the young male acolyte of the bodhisattva Guanyin.

51   In the original, Guanyin asks Mulian if he want to be a "living-in son-in-law"—that is, a husband who lives in the home of his wife. Normally, a woman would go to live in her husband's home, but in premodern China, when a household was lacking a male heir, the family would seek a husband willing to live in his wife's home. While such an arrangement might be economically attractive for the husband, it was also considered somewhat demeaning, as his children would bear his wife's surname.

52   The song is referred to as a *Dao qing* (sentiments of the Way) tune. *Dao qing* is a common form of storytelling in many parts of China, in origin related to Daoist preaching of the Quanzhen sect. This type of storytelling frequently made use of the tune "Shuahai'er," which therefore often was known as the *Dao qing* tune.

53   This line is printed as a line of verse in the Chinese edition on which this translation is based but should be read as a line of prose.

54   This attempted seduction of Mulian is probably inspired by the episode of the daughters of Mara attempting to seduce Siddhartha Gautama, when he is about to achieve enlightenment and become the Buddha.

55   Incense Mountain (Xiangshan) is the place where Princess Miaoshan, the future Guanyin, achieved enlightenment.

56   The term "Heavenly River" usually designates the Milky Way. Here, it refers to the Weak-Water River at the edge of the world, which the dead must cross on the way to heaven. Its water is so weak that it cannot support a regular vessel, which is why it can be traversed only in a bottomless boat. A person who is able to take a leap of faith and plunge into the river will be able to shed his or her mortal body and cross without difficulty.

57   The voice of the Buddha preaching the Law is often compared to a thunderclap.

58   "Teaching Lord" is used to refer to founders of religions and therefore also to the Buddha. Later, the term was more commonly used as one of the many synonyms for the Buddha. In this text, however, "Teaching Lord" is one of the honorific titles of the bodhisattva Ksitigarbha (Dizang).

59   Divine beings travel between heaven and earth on clouds.

60   Ghost-Gate Pass marks the border between the World of Light and the World of Darkness.

61   In the new religions of the Ming and Qing dynasties, human beings are the children of the Eternal Mother. Hoping for her children's return home, the Eternal Mother dispatches teachers to the world of men, but only a few mortals accept these teachings and practice them in order to be reunited with the Eternal Mother in their original home in paradise.

62   The Chan School of Buddhism teaches that the highest teaching is a wordless teaching that can be communicated by a sign, such as a single smile.

63   This probably refers to the three paradoxical questions that are commonly posed to neophytes in the Linji (Rinzai) branch of Chan and which are compared to three passes one has to cross. The term may also have been borrowed from Inner Alchemy mysticism: the three stages of Inner Alchemy practice are often represented as a path that requires the crossing of Three Passes, which are imagined as located along the spinal column.

64   Every sentient being possesses the Buddha nature by birth, and enlightenment follows as soon as one's mind is aware of this truth.

65   Buddhism classifies animals in four categories according to their manner of birth. An example of animals that are produced by miracle are the beautiful birds that adorn Pure Lands.

66   Literally, clothes made of raw linen, which, unlike clothes make of silk and other fine material, were worn by the poor.

67   It was widely believed that the location of the graves of ancestors influenced the fate of descendants.

68   A woman's fourfold virtue is her chastity, correct speech, correct demeanor, and correct work. The threefold obedience means that, as a daughter, a woman was expected to obey her father; as a wife, her husband; and as a widow, her grown-up son.

69   Yidi is the mythical inventor of alcoholic beverages. He is said to have lived during the reign of the mythical emperor Yao. While the common word for alcoholic drinks, *jiu*, is usually translated as "wine," technically it refers to a kind of ale, as *jiu* was brewed from grains.

70   "Opulent Metropole" (Fengdu) is one of the designations of the Underworld.

71   This refers to prescriptions for aphrodisiacs.

72   These lines refer to people who, enraged because they feel slighted, kill the offending party and will have to pay for that crime with their lives.

73   That is, cavorting with prostitutes.

74   According to the Sutra of the Ten Kings, the souls of the deceased pass the First Court on the seventh day after death, the Second Court on the fourteenth day, the Third Court on the twenty-first, and so on, and during this progression, their descendants should invite monks every seventh day to read sutras for the benefit of the deceased. This series of ceremonies is called the "Sevens." The fifth Seven refers to the thirty-fifth day following death.

75   Buddhist homiletic literature often points out that offering meat sacrifices to the ancestors only adds to the sins of the dead and the living.

76   The performance of plays in honor of the gods was a common feature of temple festivals throughout China, and in many temples there was even a stage built directly across form the main hall, so that the deities whose statues were housed in the hall could enjoy the performances.

77   "Red mercury" is another name for cinnabar, which was used in many medicines intended to strengthen yang in order to increase one's life span or bolster one's potency.

78   "Sexual combat" refers to techniques for extracting vital energy from one's partner during sexual intercourse in order to strengthen one's own vital power and extend one's life. Early sexual handbooks described such techniques, and in later imperial times, practitioners of so-called sectarian religions commonly were accused of engaging in such practices. These rumors were fed by misunderstandings of the teachings of "internal alchemy" (*neidan*) that called for the mystical union of opposites in metaphorical language.

79   "Stuffed bellies" is our tentative translation of *fuquan*.

80   In traditional China, a man was supposed to have only one official wife, and only if she proved to be childless could he legitimately take a concubine. A wife's opposition to taking a concubine under such circumstances was considered a valid reason for divorce.

81   Cf. *Mencius* 4A.26, 1. "Mencius said: 'There are three things which are unfilial, and to have no posterity is the greatest of them.'"

82   As written characters may embody the highest truth, they are considered sacred. Paper that carries writing should therefore always be treated with

reverence and never be treated as trash (or used as toilet paper). To this day, many traditional Chinese temples have an oven for the ritual burning of paper with writing on it.

83 That is, cleansed of their sins.

84 A dharani is a string of words (often in Sanskrit) with magical power.

85 "The Red Dust" refers to the mundane world, which obscures people's true spiritual nature with its sensual enticements.

86 They will not have to suffer the worst excess of the heat during the hottest months of summer.

87 A description of their disregard for authority.

88 *Daxue* 10.10. The *Daxue*, or *Great Learning*, is a short text traditionally ascribed to Confucius. Originally part of the collection of classical texts known as the *Rites*, in the twelfth century, the famous Neo-Confucian philosopher Zhuxi (1130–1200) identified it as one of the four texts that he considered to contain the essence of Confucian teaching. In the Ming and Qing dynasties, these texts, known as the Four Books, became the basis of the educational curriculum for all aspiring scholar-officials.

89 Lao Laizi is a famous exemplar of filial piety. When his aged parents had become senile, he dressed up in colorful clothes and pretended to be their little boy in order to amuse them.

90 Liang Hong lived in the first century. When his wife Meng Guang dressed herself in her finest clothes, he did not pay any attention to her, but when she dressed simply and served him deferentially, he treated her with love and affection.

91 Jiang Hong and his brothers lived in such harmony that they often slept together, sharing a single blanket.

92 When Guan Zhong and Bao Shuya engaged in trade together, Guan Zhong often took a larger share of the profit, but Bao Shuya did not complain as he realized that Guan Zhong needed the money.

93 That is, as farmers they would not fight with their neighbors over the exact boundaries of their fields.

94 The six roots are the six sense organs of eye, ear, nose, tongue, body, and mind.

95 The community pact is a list of rules and norms drawn up by local leaders and regularly expounded to the members of their community.

96 That is, girls who conduct premarital affairs. The image is from an anecdote about an unmarried girl who stole the rare perfume her father had received from the court in order to give it to her lover, and when the young man started to use this perfume, their affair was discovered.

97 Cf. *Analects* 7.20. "The subjects on which the Master did not talk were extraordinary things, feats of strength, disorder, and spiritual beings."

98 The Four Books are *The Analects, Mencius, The Great Learning,* and *The Doctrine of the Mean.* See note 90.

99 Mandarin ducks were believed to be monogamous and to mate for life. As such, they were a common symbol for true love and loyal friendship.

100 We have no additional information on the three persons mentioned in these lines.

101 A primitive type of grenade.

102 Cf. *Analects* 7.26. "The Master angled, but did not use a net. He shot, but not at birds perching."

103 This probably refers to the anecdote recounted by Mencius in his dialogue with Wan Zhang in *Mencius* 5B.2, 4. When someone offered a life fish to Zichan, the prime minister of Zheng, he ordered his pond keeper to release it in a pond. The pond keeper then ate the fish but reported to Zichan that the fish had at first appeared to be embarrassed but later had swum away joyfully, whereupon Zichan exclaimed: "It had found its element!"

104 Although primarily known as a famous Confucian statesman and poet, Su Shi (1036–1101), also known as Su Dongpo (1036–1101) was also very interested in Buddhism.

105 The famous Tang dynasty poet Bai Juyi (Letian) (782–846) was a devout Buddhist in his private life.

106 The grammar of this line is clear, but the meaning is not. Does the author want to state that while Confucius dwells in heaven, Zichan, Su Shi, and Bai Juyi serve as judges in the Underworld? The Chinese tradition knows numerous stories of officials who, upon their deaths, were appointed as judges in the Underworld because of their probity. The famous Judge Bao was even said to serve as a judge of the living during the day and as a judge of the dead during the night.

107 The life of a person who is controlled by his passions may be compared to a spring dream, as he is unaware of the true nature of his existence.

108 Ever since the end of the first millennium, a common conception of the Underworld held that it was administered by ten courts, each with its own presiding judge. Sinners passed before each of these judges, among whom King Yama held the highest position (see the introduction in this volume).

109 "Cinnabar Hill" is one of the many names of the world of the immortals.

110 Cf. *Analects* 4.15. "The Master said, '. . . There is one single thread binding my way together.'" One of the best-known and most widespread sectarian religions in modern China is known as Single-Thread Way (Yiguandao).

245 | Notes to *The Precious Scroll of the Three Lives of Mulian*

111 A dharma is a thing that the mind perceives as an object, and the "myriad dharmas" refers to all the physical elements that make up the world we live in.

112 Confucianism, Buddhism, and Daoism.

113 "The Dipper" is the Chinese name for Ursa Major.

114 In other words, they were too afraid to go back to King Yama and report their failure.

115 The title of Ksitigarbha (Dizang).

116 In imperial China, salt was a government monopoly, and salt merchants, who bought and sold salt in bulk, as a rule were very wealthy.

117 The bodhisattva referred to here most likely is Guanyin, who was widely venerated for her ability to grant children.

118 As an easy birth often is a sign that the child is destined for greatness, a difficult birth may be a sign of great evil.

119 The seven stars are the stars of the Dipper (Ursa Major).

120 In Chinese, the "Chao" in the name Huang Chao is written with the character for "nest" (*chao*).

121 The Ming and Qing dynasties conducted both literary examinations for the selection of civil officials and military examinations for the selection of military officers.

122 To "leap across the Dragon Gate" means to pass the examinations.

123 Emperor Xizong of the Tang dynasty reigned from 874 to 889.

124 "The Yellow Way" refers to the ecliptic, or, more broadly, the zodiac. A lucky day may also simply be referred to as "a Yellow Way day."

125 This refers to students recommended by their local prefecture.

126 The obvious meaning of the name Liaokong is "Understanding Emptiness," but the name can also be construed to mean "Meeting His End in a Hollow [Tree]."

127 "Amituofo" is the standard way to recite the name of the Buddha Amitabha, who promises rebirth in his Western Paradise to whosoever sincerely calls on him.

128 The earlier text makes no mention of any specific taboo, except that Huang Chao will first have to kill the monk Liaokong before he can use the sword. It may be that it was considered inauspicious for a warrior's first victim to be a defenseless monk.

129 Zhu Wen (852–912) would become one of the most powerful generals of the final years of the Tang dynasty. Eventually he would accept the abdication of the last Tang emperor and found the Later Liang dynasty (907–922). Li Cunxiao was a fierce general serving under Li Keyong, the leader

of the Shatuo Turks. Li Keyong's son would eventually topple the Liang regime and found the Later Tang dynasty (923–935).

130   The Hegemon-King is Xiang Yu (232–202 B.C.E.), a nobleman of the ancient state of Chu, who rose in rebellion following the death of the First Emperor in 210 B.C.E. Despite initial successes, he finally lost out against Liu Bang, the future founder of the Han dynasty (206 B.C.E.–220 C.E.). When Xiang Yu had been utterly defeated, a ferryman offered to row him across the river, suggesting that he might levy new troops and continue the battle, but Xiang Yu replied that he did not have the courage to face the parents of the soldiers he had led into battle earlier and who all had died. He then committed suicide.

131   The Three Terraces is a Chinese asterism that is said to correspond to the three "cinnabar fields" in the human body of the mystic. This line can therefore be understood as "When will my body be filled with brightness?"

132   The Five Elements (or Five Phases) are metal, wood, water, fire, and earth. All material things are composed of one or more of these five elements.

133   A kalpa is an immeasurably long period between the generation of a world-system and its destruction (which will then be followed by the generation of a new world-system).

134   Chang'an (modern-day Xi'an) was the capital of both the Han and Tang dynasties. Later, the name was also used to refer to the capital of the reigning dynasty.

135   This is a euphemism for death, as the crane is a symbol for immortality.

136   A wooden fish is a hollowed-out block of wood in the shape of a fish that is beaten rhythmically in accompaniment to the recitation of the sutras.

137   A life deluded by passion is compared to a house on fire in the Lotus Sutra.

138   In popular prints, Guanyin in her female manifestation was often surrounded by Weituo, a fierce-looking warrior-god whose job it is to protect Buddhism; Good-in-Talent (also known as Sudhana and Shancai); a granddaughter of the dragon king of the Eastern Ocean; and a parrot.

139   The festival of Double-Fifth, best known for its dragonboat races, is celebrated on the fifth day of the Fifth Month.

140   The *Rites* (which includes the *Liji*, *Yili*, and *Zhouli*) is counted as one of the Five Classics, traditionally believed to have been edited by Confucius. The *Rites* lays out in great detail rules for proper behavior in all social situations.

141   Xiao He was one of the advisers of Liu Bang, the founder of the Han dynasty. The law code Xiao He drafted when the Han dynasty was established was renowned for its simplicity and severity.

142 The "Golden Placard" refers to the list of those who passed the triennial metropolitan examinations for the selection of candidates for office.

143 Lingyan Tower (Tower That Soars Above the Mists) had been erected by Taizong (Li Shimin) and housed the portraits of twenty-four ministers and generals who had played a major role in the founding of the Tang dynasty.

144 According to popular belief, the Dragon-Flower Assembly will take place at the foot of the Dragon-Flower Tree, the tree under which Maitreya, the future buddha, will achieve enlightenment and where he will preach the Dharma.

145 The Queen Mother of the West is the ruler of all female immortals and lives atop the mythical Mount Kunlun in the far west. The peaches of immortality grow in her garden.

146 "Ridge" (*ling*) and "numinosity" (*ling*) are homophones.

147 Please keep in mind that Bodhisattva Guanyin has taken on the guise of a monk!

148 The surname Jia has the same pronunciation as the word *jia*, which means "false," "fake," or "feigned."

149 Here the term "bodhisattva" is used to address a patron, the widowed mother of the two girls.

150 An arhat is a person who has been enlightened by hearing the Buddha's words.

151 "Yellow Springs" is an ancient designation of the realm of the dead.

152 The Fruit of Truth refers to the final enlightenment.

153 The Eastern Land is China, as opposed to India.

154 That is, Dark Clouds Palace, the abode of Ksitigarbha.

155 Of past, present, and future.

156 Ordinary people, who do not adhere to a vegetarian diet, will be punished for their sins and have only themselves to blame.

157 Rebirth Tales are tales about people who, because of their piety, have been reborn in the Pure Land of the Buddha Amitabha. The Heart Sutra is a very short and extremely popular Buddhist text, believed by some to have actually been composed in China. It belongs to the general category of Buddhist wisdom texts, which emphasize the fundamental emptiness of all phenomena.

158 "One" refers to the final truth of the fundamental unity of the cosmos.

159 "The Land of the Springs" refers to the world of the dead.

Woman Huang Recites the Diamond Sutra

1   Pangu, according to Chinese mythology, was born from a huge cosmic egg, after which he embarked on the task of creating the world by separating yin and yang with his giant ax to create the earth and the sky. Another legend has it that he actually created the world out of his own body.

2   The Five Thearchs are the five rulers who, according to legend, preceded the Three Emperors. The last of the Three Emperors traditionally is regarded as the founder of the Xia dynasty (first half second millennium B.C.E.).

3   According to popular belief, a record of the good and bad deeds of every person is kept in the Underworld and serves as the basis for judging punishment or reward after death. These records are referred to as the "ledgers of life and death" in the Mulian story.

4   The term "sutra" refers generally to any scripture or text attributed to the Buddha. The term "Western Heaven" (Xitian) was one of many used to refer to India, which was located to the west of China (the most common land route from China to India passed through Central Asia).

5   An arhat (lohan) is someone who has attained enlightenment under the guidance of the Buddha and thus no longer needs to be reborn into the suffering world. The eighteen arhats were said to represent the enlightened disciples of Sakyamuni Buddha. In China, the eighteen arhats, each with his own particular character and quirk, were often depicted in both painting and sculpture, with distinctively non-Chinese features.

6   These include, among other things, garlic, leeks, and onions, all of which are said to encourage aggressive and lustful behavior and thus are to be avoided by the pious and good.

7   By boiling the water—to be used for scalding the butchered pigs—Woman Huang becomes an accomplice in the killing.

8   Chinese traditionally use the number 72 or 360 (72 multiplied by 5) to refer to all the possible professions and occupations.

9   The second-century He Jin was born into a butcher's family but rose to political power when his half sister was inducted into the palace and became a favorite consort of Emperor Ling of the Eastern Han. When the emperor died in 189, He Jin and his sister served as regents for a short while until He Jin was killed by an assassin, and the country was plunged into chaos once again.

10   Oxhead and Horseface are the Underworld demons primarily responsible for fetching sinners and bringing them to the Underworld and of overseeing, and often inflicting, the punishments these sinners receive.

11 As will soon become clear, "Alas Bridge," "Spear Mountain," and "Sword Mountain" all refer to specific sites in the Underworld where sinners are forced to undergo various types of rather gruesome punishments.

12 Silk is made from threads produced by silkworms, which are killed when the cocoons are plunged into boiling water in order to harvest the threads. Thus any person who wears silk contributes indirectly to the killing of animals.

13 These are the five grains or crops that have long been considered sacred in China. They usually include wheat, two types of millet, rice, and soybeans.

14 That is, within three days following delivery. A new mother is supposed to keep to her bed for one full month. While such a rule may be inspired by the fear of pollution, it also has the practical effect of protecting the new mother.

15 The Kitchen God (which we also occasionally translate as Stove God) is the most important of the Chinese domestic gods. He keeps an eye on all household activities, and, according to popular belief, on the twenty-third day of the twelfth lunar month, he goes up to heaven and reports on the activities of the household to the Jade Emperor, who then hands out rewards or punishments accordingly.

16 Every body of water—lake, river, sea, or ocean—has its own dragon king. According to popular Chinese tradition, these dragon deities reside in great palaces under the water. They are responsible for bringing much-needed rain and thus must be kept happy.

17 That is, the moon and the sun.

18 The white beads (pearls in the original) are the pearl-like beads of her Buddhist rosary.

19 This is a reference to the marriage ritual.

20 In elite circles, the ideal marriage was considered to be that between a talented man (usually a student or scholar with poetic gifts) and a beautiful woman.

21 "The Senluo Hall" refers to the court of King Yama, which is usually, although not always, said to be the fifth of the Ten Courts of Hell. As described in the introduction to this volume, the Chinese Buddhist Underworld is composed of eighteen hells and subhells, each characterized by a different type and intensity of suffering. The soul must also pass through the Ten Courts of Hell, ruled by the Ten Kings, sometimes called the Yama Kings, where the type and length of punishment are determined according to the soul's good and bad actions while alive.

22 The Maitreya Buddha is believed to dwell in the Tushita Heaven, awaiting his final rebirth as the next buddha of this world.

23   The Purple Bamboo Grove was believed to be the domicile of the bodhisattva Guanyin, located on Mount Putuo (Putuoshan), a small island off the coast of Ningbo.

24   In Chinese popular as well as Daoist mythology, the Jade Emperor is the supreme ruler of heaven, earth, and hell.

25   Master Li is the sage Laozi, said to have left China for the West (that is, India), but not before he was persuaded to write down the nearly five thousand characters of the famous Daoist classic sometimes translated as the *Classic of Power and Virtue* but more often referred to by its Chinese name, the *Daodejing*.

26   The Eight Immortals (Baxian) are the legendary eight Daoist transcendents (seven men and one woman). They frequently appear in Chinese popular literature and are often depicted in Chinese popular arts and crafts.

27   The attendants of Daoist deities are often referred to as "Golden Lads" and "Jade Maidens."

28   By reciting the sutra just as it is written, Woman Huang will demonstrate that she has fully memorized it and mastered its contents.

29   That is, the border between the Underworld, or World of Darkness (Yin), and the World of Light (Yang).

30   The god of the soil (*tudi gong*), which we also occasionally translate as "earth god," is an important village deity, often described as a kind of heavenly low-level bureaucrat responsible for dealing with agriculture-related affairs. Even today, many Chinese keep a small earth god shrine under the main altar or below the main door.

31   In Confucianism, the Three Obediences (Sancong) are a woman's obedience to her father, her husband, and her son. The Four Virtues (Side) are the virtues a woman was expected to embrace and embody, specifically, proper behavior, proper speech, proper demeanor or appearance, and proper work.

32   Emperor Taizong (599–649) of the Tang dynasty is said to have honored his two loyal generals Qin Shubao and Yuchi Jingde by hanging their portraits on his front door. These became the door gods, colorful prints that, even today, ordinary Chinese people hang on their doors to keep out evil spirits and bring good luck.

33   The Three Officials (of heaven, earth, and water) are Daoist deities said to be responsible for keeping records of people's deeds on earth and determining the length of a person's life span and his or her fate after death.

34   "Fengdu" (Opulent Metropole) is another name for the Underworld. It is often used in Daoist mythology.

35   The city god, as the name implies, was the deity responsible for the super-natural well-being of the city as whole, the divine counterpart of the human district magistrate (like the human official, the city god was changed every three years). Among his various responsibilities, the city god sent the souls of the dead in his area to the Underworld.

36   It is unclear which patriarchs are being referred to here. Leaders of popular religious sects such as the Way of Former Heaven (see introduction) sometimes sought to bolster their legitimacy by claiming the first several patriarchs of Chan Buddhism (including the legendary Indian master, Bodhidharma) as their own and adding their lineage patriarchs and teachers to the group.

37   The Heavenly Guardians, sometimes known also as the Four Heavenly Kings, are four guardian gods, each of whom watches over one cardinal direction of the world. Their fearsome images are often displayed in the gate buildings of a Buddhist monastery.

38   The future buddha, Maitreya, is said to have come to the world to scout out the situation in the form of the big-bellied monk Budai, who is nearly always portrayed as laughing or smiling, which is why he is popularly known as the Laughing Buddha.

39   In China, a person's birth is calculated from the month of conception rather than that of birth, and at the beginning of every new year, everyone is automatically a year older. Changshou is three *sui*, which could mean that he was only two or even just one year old, depending on when he was born. The name Changshou means "Long Life," which is one of the things Woman Huang seeks for both herself and her family through her pious activities.

40   The Clear and Bright (Qingming) Festival falls on the 104th day after the winter solstice. It was—and for many Chinese people continues to be—the custom for families to sweep the graves of and make offerings to their deceased relatives while enjoying the first days of spring weather. The Double-Ninth Festival, as its name indicates, falls on the ninth day of the ninth lunar month. It was an occasion for climbing to a high spot where one could enjoy the moon with family and friends and also a time for visiting the graves of the departed.

41   As becomes clear later on, Woman Liu is Woman Huang's sister-in-law. She is an impious and selfish woman and, as such, represents the direct opposite of the good Woman Huang.

42   Controller of Fate is yet another title of the Stove God, or Kitchen God.

43   In elite Buddhism, an eminent master carried a fly whisk as a sign of spiri-

tual authority; here, it is used, together with the rosary beads, as a symbol of Woman Huang's religious renunciation.

44   The meaning of these two lines is very unclear. They may reflect a conflation of two different legends. The Lustrous Emperor (Minghuang), also known as Xuanzong, reigned from 713 to 756. According to one story, he once had a dream in which a thieving imp was captured by a large and ugly fellow who explained that his name was Zhong Kui, that he had taken part in the examinations but had been rejected by the examiners because of his ugliness, and that upon his suicide the Underworld authorities had appointed him to be a demon catcher. The emperor thereupon ordered Zhong Kui's picture displayed on every gate at the midsummer festival of Double-Fifth (Duanwu) in order to ward off ghosts. There are no stories, however, about the Lustrous Emperor visiting the Underworld. The emperor who visited the Underworld is Emperor Taizong (r. 627–49). This story was quite popular, also because it was retold in great detail in chapters 9–11 of the sixteenth-century novel *Journey to the West* (Xiyou ji). In the story, the emperor has failed to protect the dragon king of the Jing River. When he is summoned to the Underworld, one of his ministers provides him with a letter to his good friend Cui Jue, who, since his death, has been serving as a judge in the World of Darkness. Cui Jue obligingly grants the emperor another twenty years of life. Before the emperor returns to the World of Light, he liberates many sinners from hell by borrowing money from the ample treasure of a couple from Kaifeng (who, he finds out later, are virtuous beggars who have laid up a great store of merit in the world below).

45   This is a hollow wooden drum in the shape of a fish (chosen, according to one explanation, because a fish supposedly never sleeps). Buddhists use these drums, both in the temple and at home, to mark time for recitation and chanting.

46   Traditional Chinese copper coins are round and have a square hole in the middle.

47   We may see here a trace of the early sectarian versions of the Woman Huang story, in which Maitreya played a central role as the future buddha who would usher in a new age of peace and prosperity.

48   The yamen is the residence of an official.

49   A general's pillar is the tall sturdy pole erected outside a government office to which condemned criminals were bound and then executed.

50   "Amituofo" is the Chinese pronunciation of the name of Amitabha, the buddha who presides over the Western Pure Land. According to Pure

Land belief, sincere repetition of Amitabha's name will ensure rebirth in this Pure Land. In the case of a woman, rebirth in the Pure Land would also mean leaving behind her female body, since one of the primary characteristics of this buddha realm is that there are no women (and, by implication, none of the types of sufferings to which women are subject in the ordinary world).

51 The court-sponsored Hanlin Academy was one of the most prestigious institutions of traditional China.

52 "Lotus feet" is a euphemism for tiny bound feet.

53 According to popular belief, each of the ten courts of the Underworld is presided over by a Yama King; they are not to confused with King Yama, who is the ruler of the entire Underworld.

54 Bodhidharma is the semilegendary Indian monk said to have introduced Chan (Zen) Buddhism into China.

55 Although the original text was not divided into chapters, the Chinese translation of this sutra traditionally was divided into thirty-two sections or divisions.

56 This is a reference to the story of Princess Miaoshan, who, after disobeying her father's order to marry, fled to Fragrant Mountain (Xiangshan), where she engaged in spiritual cultivation. Later, when her father, afflicted with a horrific disease, came to seek the help of the Great Master of Fragrant Mountain (unaware that she was his daughter), Miaoshan sacrificed her hands and eyes for him. This led to his cure and, ultimately, her apotheosis as Guanyin, the Bodhisattva of Compassion.

57 Bodhidharma is said to have transmitted the truth of Chan Buddhism to the Chinese monk Shenguang Huike (487–593), who then became known as the Second Patriarch of Chan Buddhism.

58 The lineage gets a little garbled here and may refer to a separate lineage transmission associated with the sectarian religious group that made use of the Woman Huang story for purposes of conversion. Traditionally, the Third Patriarch of Chan Buddhism is said to have been Sengcan (d. 606), and it was the Fourth Patriarch, Daoxin (580–651), who is said to have taught for thirty years on Double Peak Mountain (Shuangfengshan), after which he is said to have passed on the lineage to the Fifth Patriarch, Hongren (601–673). The Sixth Patriarch, said to be Huineng (638–713), is the author of the Platform Sutra. He was indeed said to have first achieved enlightenment upon hearing the Diamond Sutra being recited (he supposedly was illiterate and so could not read it himself). There is much dispute over which monk could lay claim to be the Seventh Patriarch. The impor-

tant thing to note is that the Way of Former Heaven sect sought to establish its legitimacy by referring to its founder, Huang Dehui (1684–1750), as the Ninth Patriarch.

59   Note that one of the many benefits and blessings to be derived from the recitation of this particular sutra is rebirth as a male.

60   One of the duties of the emperor, or Son of Heaven, was to ensure, through rituals and his own upright and moral behavior, that the country did not suffer drought, thereby endangering the harvest. If, however, there was a bad dry spell, the emperor would then pray for rain.

61   The Underworld was sometimes also referred to as "the Yellow Springs."

62   The term "samadhi" refers both to actual trance meditation and to the highest enlightened wisdom achieved while in that state.

63   Normally the Yama King of the Tenth Court is distinguished from King Yama, the overlord of the Underworld whose residence is the Fifth Court, Senluo Hall. Here, the two figures (and locations) appear to be conflated. For the sake of clarity, we refer to him as "King Yama," as he appears to be the one who has assembled all the other kings in the hall in order to pass final judgment on Woman Huang.

64   One *zhang* measures ten feet.

65   The term "Eastern Land" refers to the continent of Jambudvipa (in other words, the dwelling place of human beings) on which the historical Buddha Sakyamuni preached the Law. Here, it also refers more specifically to China itself.

66   The four holy mountains of Chinese Buddhism are Mount Wutai in Shaanxi, Mount Emei in Sichuan, Mount Jiuhua in Anhui, and Mount Putuo in Zhejiang.

67   The Buddhist bodhisattva Ksitigarbha (Dizang) is responsible for bringing relief to souls suffering in hell. Since the Ming dynasty, his name has been popularly associated with Mount Jiuhua in Anhui.

68   Lü Dongbin is the most famous of the Eight Immortals. He also played an important role in many religious sects, including the Way of Former Heaven.

69   Although the original has Xuandu, we are reading it here as Xuandi, which makes more sense. Xuandi, or the Dark Thearch, is the god of the north and is better known as the Dark Warrior (Xuanwu) or the True Warrior (Zhenwu). He, too, played an important role in many religious sectarian movements.

70   Guanshiyin is another name for the bodhisattva Guanyin.

71   Wen Qiong and Zhao Gongming are two of the four celestial marshals

who protect the Daoist ritual arena. Wen protects against epidemics, and Zhao is widely revered as a god of wealth.

72 The Avici Hell is the lowest and hottest of the Buddhist hells. The Thearch on High (Shangdi) is the supreme god of ancient Chinese religion.

73 In other words, her body had already decomposed and could not be revived.

74 The Chinese title *yuanwai* was popularly used to refer to a rich man, often a wealthy landowner.

75 Presumably, these years are added to those originally allotted by fate (the specifics of which are not provided), not to the current ages of Woman Huang's husband, Lianfang, and their three children.

76 In Buddhism, much as there are many hells at different levels, so are there many heavens inhabited by beings who have achieved various levels of spiritual attainment. "The Ten Heavens" refers generally to the realms inhabited by gods, who are ranked above humans but below buddhas and bodhisattvas.

77 As a ghost, Woman Huang must depart before the break of day, or she will remain in the world of Yin, unable to be reborn as a human being.

78 Kaifeng, the capital of the Northern Song dynasty (960–1126), was officially known as the Eastern Capital. Luoyang was the Western Capital.

79 Here, they are placing cups of tea on the ancestral altar.

80 The Three Mothers are the three goddesses of conception and childbirth.

81 Traditionally, the birth of a child was not formally announced until three days afterward. A month later, the birth would then be celebrated in grand style, especially if the child was a boy.

82 These refer to the *Classic of Odes* (Shijing), also known as the *Classic of Poetry*, and the *Book of Documents* (Shujing), two ancient texts that all boys from elite families traditionally were expected to master.

83 "Flourishing talent" (*xiucai*) is the name given to someone who has passed the prefecture-level exams, the lowest of the three levels in the traditional examination system. The other two are the provincial and the metropolitan exams.

84 Students who passed the metropolitan examinations and the palace examinations achieved the degree of "presented scholar" (*jinshi*).

85 The Eastern Floriate (Donghua) Gate was located on the east side of the Imperial Palace; the Dragon-Phoenix (Longfeng) Gate also was one of the palace gates. In popular literature, one also encounters the expression Eastern Floriate Dragon-Phoenix Gate.

86 As on other important dates in the calendar, the magistrate is expected, in his role as a representative both of the emperor and of the people he

governs, to offer incense to all the major deities revered in his district.

87   The Astral Deity of the Great White (Venus) is an important Daoist deity. As the planet Venus corresponds to the element metal, he is also designated as the Metal Star or the Gold Star. In popular ballads, this Astral Deity of the Great White often appears in the guise of a friendly old man.

88   Presumably, the second sister has also been sent for so that all of Woman Huang's children are assembled together.

89   As noted in the introduction to this volume, the story of Woman Huang is very popular to this day among the Bai ethnic minority of Yunnan.

90   In traditional China, the night was divided into five watches of equal length. The emperor received his officials in audience at dawn, meaning that the officials were required to assemble at court before daybreak, which corresponds to the fifth watch.

91   One sign of a good official (or a good ruler, for that matter) is good weather, which of course meant good crops.

92   *Qian* and *kun* are two trigrams in the *Classic of Changes* (Yijing), the former embodying the masculine (yang) and the second the feminine (yin). According to Daoist inner alchemical theory, their union creates the elixir of eternal life.

93   From this point onward, there are clear traces of the early association of this story with the teachings of the Way of Former Heaven (also known as the Great Way of Former Heaven).

94   The detached and blissful state of mind that is said to be the result of religious self-cultivation.

95   When the Maitreya Buddha descends to earth from Tushita Heaven as promised, all of the gods, bodhisattvas, and devoted followers will assemble together at the base of the Dragon-Flower Tree, where they will listen to Maitreya preach the Dharma. This notion of a gathering of the faithful at the coming of Maitreya is found in the teachings of many sectarian religious sects.

96   This is a reference to one of Confucius' most famous sayings: "If a man in the morning hear the Way, he may die in the evening without regret" (*Analects*, 8.8).

97   The Three Refuges are Buddhism's Three Jewels (the Buddha, the Dharma [or Teaching], and the Sangha [or monastic community]), in which believers take refuge, and the Five Precepts (to abstain from killing, lying, stealing, sexual impropriety, and mental intoxication).

98   The general meaning is that, as a result of self-cultivation, one will become eternally youthful, a primary goal of many Daoist schools.

99   The Six Thieves are the six senses, which are said to cause people to become attached and, ultimately, to create all manner of negative karma.

100   These lines, like the ones in the following section, refer to the process of Daoist cultivation, or inner alchemy, which is described in terms of nurturing the embryo of a spiritual body with the goal of giving birth to an immortal body and shedding the physical body.

101   The notion that ultimate truth is beyond words is common to both Daoism and Chan Buddhism. However, the notion of a wordless sutra appears to have been appropriated by popular religious sects for their own purposes. Even today, the popular syncretic religious sect Single-Thread Way, or Yiguandao (a modern-day offshoot of the Way of Former Heaven), refers to the second of its Three Treasures as both the "True Sutra" and the "Wordless Sutra."

102   Bodhidharma is said to have sat for nine years in meditation facing the wall of his cave on Mount Song.

103   The meaning here is not completely clear; however, "lotus lamps" may refer to those who illuminate the truth (symbolized by the lotus) for others to see.

104   This refers to a special plaque denoting marital as well as familial peace and harmony. Such a plaque, especially if inscribed with the calligraphy of the emperor, was a sign of great honor.

105   In the Chinese patrilineal society, the ideal was to have a long-lived patriarch overseeing the flourishing of a household composed of several generations. While a two- or three-generation household would not be too unusual, a five-generation household would be quite rare.

GLOSSARY OF CHINESE CHARACTERS

A

Amituofo　阿彌陀佛
Anhui　安徽

B

Bai (zu)　白 (族)
Bai Juyi (Letian)　白居易 (樂天)
Banjie　半姐
Bao (Judge)　包
Bao Shuya　鮑叔牙
baojuan　寶卷
baxian　八仙
bianwen　變文
Budai　布袋

C

Can Tang Wudai shi yanyi zhuan　殘唐五代史演義傳
Caodong　曹洞
Caozhou　曹州

Chang'an　長安
Changshou　長壽
chanlin　禪林
Chen　陳 (Man of the Way)
Chen Ruihong　陳瑞鴻
Chenhe　辰河
Chu　楚
chuanqi　傳奇
Chunyin shuzhuang　春陰書莊
Cu hulu　醋葫蘆

D

Da Muqianlian mingjian jiumu bianwen　大目揵連冥間救母變文
Dao　道
Dao qing　道情
Daodejing　道德經
Daoxin　道信
Daxue　大學
Dequan　德全
diyu　地獄
Dizang　地藏
Dizang pusa benyuan jing　地藏菩薩本原經
Donghua　東華
Dou E yuan 竇娥冤
Dunhuang 敦煌

E

Emei　娥眉

F

Fakong　法空
Fengdu　酆都
Foshuo Dazang zhengjiao xuepen jing　佛說大藏政教血盆經
Foshuo fumu en zhong nan bao jing　佛說父母恩重難報經
Foshuo Mulian jiumu jing　佛說目連救母經

Fu Xiang　傅相

fuquan　腹泉

G

gaoqiang　高腔

Gaoseng zhuan　高僧傳

Guan Hanqing　關漢卿

Guan Zhong　管仲

Guangmu　光目

Guanshiyin　觀世音

Guanyin　觀音

Guixiang　桂香

H

Hanlin　翰林

Hanyang　漢陽

He (shi)　何 (氏)

He Jin　何進

He Wenxiu　何文秀

He Xiang　賀祥

He Yin　賀因

Hongmen　洪門

Hongren　弘忍

Houqi　侯七

Huaiyin shanfang　槐蔭山房

Huang Baiwan　黃百萬

Huang Chao　黃巢

Huang Dehui　黃德惠

Huang Junda　黃俊達

Huang Zongdan　黃宗旦

Huangshi nü dui Jingang　黃氏女對金剛

Huangshi nü youyin　黃氏女遊陰

Huijiao　慧皎

Huineng　惠能

Huizhou　惠州

J

jia 假

Jia 賈

Jiang Gong 姜肱

Jiangyong 江永

Jiaogu 姣姑

jie 戒

Jin ping mei 金瓶梅

Jingang jing 金剛經

Jingang jing zhengguo: Sanshi xiuxing Wangshinü bairi shengtian 金剛經證
果三世修行王氏女白日升天

Jingjiang 靖江

Jinnu 金奴

Jinshan 金山

jinshi 進士

jiu 酒

Jiuhua 九華

K

Kaifeng 開封

Kong 孔 (Master)

kun 坤

L

Laiguo 來果

Lao Laizi 老來子

Leishen 雷神

li 禮

Li Baihua 李百花

Li Cunxiao 李存孝

Li Keyong 李克用

Li Shimin 李世民

Liang 梁

Liang Hong 梁鴻

Liaokong 了空

Liji 禮記

ling　岭

ling　靈

Lingdi　靈帝

Lingyan　凌煙

Linji　臨濟

Liu (shi)　柳 (氏)

Liu Bang　劉邦

Liu Jia　劉賈

Liu Qingti　劉青提

Liu Xiang baojuan　劉香寶卷

Longfeng (men)　龍鳳 (門)

Lü Dongbin　呂洞賓

Luo Menghong　羅孟洪

Luo Qing　羅清

Luobo　蘿蔔

Luoyang　洛陽

Luxi　泸溪

M

Ma　馬(Man of the Way)

Mashan　馬山

Meng　孟 (Granny)

Meng Guang　孟光

Miaoshan　妙善

Mulian　目連

Mulian jiumu chu diyu shengtian baojuan　目連救母出地獄升天寶卷

Mulian jiumu quanshan ji　目連救母勸善記

Mulian jiumu youming baozhuan　目連救母幽冥寶傳

Mulian quanzhuan　目連全傳

Mulian sanshi baojuan　目連三世寶卷

Muqianlian zunzhe jiumu chuli diyu shengtian baojuan　目揵連尊者救母
出離地獄升天寶卷

N

Namo Jile du Pusa Mohesa　南無極樂度菩薩摩訶薩

Nanhua　南華

neidan 內丹
Ningbo 寧波
nüshu 女書

P

Pangu 盤古
Putuo (shan) 普陀 (山)

Q

qian 乾
Qin Shubao 秦叔寶
Qingming 清明
Qingping 青平
Quanzhen 全真

R

rou 肉

S

Sancong 三從
Sengcan 僧璨
Senluo baodian 森羅寶殿
Shancai 善才
Shangdi 上帝
Shen Wenbao 沈文寶
Shenguang Huike 神光慧可
Shijing 詩經
Shiwang jing 十王經
Shiyue huai 十月懷
Shouxiang 壽香
"Shuahai'er" 耍孩兒
Shuangfeng (shan) 雙峰 (山)
Shujing 書經
Side 四德
Su Shi (Dongpo) 蘇軾 (東坡)

sui 歲

Suwenxue congkan 俗文學叢刊

T

Taizong 太宗

tanci 彈詞

Tian (shi) 田 (氏)

Tiantai 天台

Tianzhu 天朱

Tongcheng 桐城

tudi gong 土地公

W

Wan Zhang 萬章

Wang 王

Wang Dalin 王大林

Wang Mingda 王明大

Wang Shan 王善

Wei 衛

Weituo 韋陀

Wen Qiong 溫瓊

Wu 武

Wu Dougui 吳斗鬼

Wuchang 無常

Wudi 五帝

Wuji zulai tuohua Wangshi xiannü linmingzhong libie kuquanhua zhongsheng
無極祖來托化王氏賢女：臨命終離別哭勸化眾生

Wutai 五台

Wuwei jiao 無為教

X

Xiang Yu 項羽

Xiangshan 香山

Xiangshan baojuan 香山寶卷

Xiantian (da) dao 先天 (大) 道

Xiao (shi)　蕭 (氏)

Xiao He　蕭何

Xinmin (lu)　新民 (路)

Xitian　西天

xiucai　秀才

Xizong　僖宗

Xu Wenpu　許文溥

Xuandi　玄帝

Xuandu　玄都

Xuanwu　玄武

Xue　薛

xuehu　血湖

Xuepen baojuan　血盆寶卷

Xuepen jing　血盆經

Y

yang　陽

Yangtai　陽臺

Yanluo Wang　閻羅王

Yidi　儀狄

Yiguandao　一貫道

Yijing　易經

Yili　儀禮

Yili　益利

yin　陰

Yinniuxi　銀紐系

yinyuan　因緣

Youyuan　有緣

Youzhou　幽州

Yu　禹

Yuanshi tianzun jidu xiehu zhengjing　元始天尊濟度血湖真經

yuanwai　員外

Yuchi Jingde　尉遲敬德

Yue Dili　悅帝利

Yulanpen hui　盂蘭盆會

Yulanpen jiangjingwen　盂蘭盆講經文
Yulanpen jing　盂蘭盆經
Yuyuan　遇緣

Z
Zhabei　閘北
zhai　齋
Zhang Jinda　張進達
Zhang Shouxiang　張壽香
Zhao Jinbang　趙金榜
Zhao Lianfang　趙連芳
Zheng Zhizhen　鄭之珍
Zheng Zichan　鄭子產
Zhenwu　真武
Zhongguo Xinan wenxian congshu　中國西南文獻叢書
Zhongyang yanjiuyuan Lishi yuyan yanjiusuo　中央研究院歷史語言研究所
Zhouli　周禮
Zhu Wen　朱溫
Zhu Xi　朱熹
Zichan　子產
Zongbao　宗保

SELECTED BIBLIOGRAPHY

Adler, Joseph. 2002. *Chinese Religious Traditions.* Upper Saddle River, N.J.: Prentice Hall.

Ahern, Emily M. 1975. "The Power and Pollution of Chinese Women." In *Women in Chinese Society,* edited by Margery Wolf and Roxane Witke, 269–90. Stanford, Calif.: Stanford University Press.

Anonymous. 1983. *Can Tang Wudai shi yanyi zhuan* 殘唐五代史演義傳 (Historical romance of the destruction of the Tang and Five Dynasties). Beijing: Baowentang.

Anonymous. 1999. *Cu Hulu* 醋葫蘆, in *Zhongguo fenjin wenxue mingzhu* 中國焚禁文學名著, Vol. 5. Beijing: Zhongguo xiju chubanshe.

Bai Ruosi 白若思 (Rostislav Berezkin). 2008. "Lishi chuanshuo zai Zhongguo tongsu shuochang wenxue zhongde yanbian<—>Huang Chao qiyi de chuanshuo zai *Wudaishi pinghua* yu *Mulian baojuan* zhongde liuchuan" 歷史傳說在中國通俗說唱文學中的演變—黃巢起義的傳說在五代史平話與目連寶卷中的流傳 (The development of the historical tale in Chinese popular prosimetric literature: The legend of the Huang Chao rebellion in *Plain Tale of the Five Dynasties* and *Precious Scroll of Mulian*). In *Guoji qingnian xuezhe Hanxue huiyi lunwenji—Minjian wenxue yu Hanxue yanjiu* 國際青年學者漢學會議論文集—民間文學與漢學研究 (Collected papers from the International Conference of Young Sinologists: Popular literature and sinological study), 401–17. Taipei: Wanhualou.

Baptandier, Brigitte. 2008. *The Lady of Linshui: A Chinese Female Cult*. Translated by Kristin Ingrid Fryklund. Stanford, Calif.: Stanford University Press.

Bender, Mark. 2001. "A Description of *Jiangjing* (Telling Scriptures) Services in Jingjiang, China." *Asian Folklore Studies* 60: 101–33.

Berezkin, Rotislav. 2010. "The Development of the Mulian Story in Baojuan Texts (14th–19th Century) in Connection with the Evolution of the Genre." Ph.D. Dissertation, University of Pennsylvania.

———. 2011. "Scripture-telling (*jiangjing*) in the Zhangjiagang Area and the History of Chinese Storytelling." *Asia Major 36*, 1–43.

Bray, Francesca. 1997. *Technology and Gender: Fabric of Power in Late Imperial China*. Berkeley: University of California Press.

Brokaw, Cynthia J. 1991. *The Ledgers of Merit and Demerit: Social Change and Moral Order in Late Imperial China*. Princeton, N.J.: Princeton University Press.

Cabezón, José Ignacio, ed. 1992. *Buddhism, Sexuality, and Gender*. Albany: State University of New York Press.

Chan, Alan L. 2004. *Filial Piety in Chinese Thought and History*. London: Routledge/Curzon.

Che Xilun 車錫倫. 1997. *Zhongguo baojuan yanjiu lunji* 中國寶卷研究論集 (Collected studies on Chinese precious scrolls). Taipei: Xuehai chubanshe.

———. 2000. *Zhongguo baojuan zongmu* 中國寶卷總目 (Complete catalogue of Chinese precious scrolls). Beijing: Beijing Yanshan chubanshe.

———. 2009. *Minjian xinyang yu minjian wenxue* 民間信仰與民間文學 (Popular religious belief and popular literature). Taipei: Boyang wenhua shiye youxian gongsi.

Chen Fangying 陳芳英. 1983. *Mulian Jiumu gushi zhi yanjin jiqi youguan wenxue zhi yanjiu* 目連救母故事之演進及其有關文學之研究 (A study of the tale of Mulian rescuing his mother and its related literature). History and Literature Series, no. 65. Taipei: Guoli Taiwan daxue.

Ch'en, Kenneth K.S. 1973. *The Chinese Transformation of Buddhism*. Princeton, N.J.: Princeton University Press.

Chu, Cordia Ming-Yuek. 1980. "Menstrual Beliefs and Practices of Chinese Women." *Journal of the Folklore Institute* 171: 38–55.

Cohen, Myron L. 1988. "Souls and Salvation: Conflicting Themes in Chinese Popular Religion." In *Death Ritual in Late Imperial and Modern China*, edited by James L. Watson and Evelyn S. Rawski, 180–202. Berkeley: University of California Press.

Cole, Alan. 1998. *Mothers and Sons in Chinese Buddhism*. Stanford, Calif.: Stanford University Press.

———. 2006. "Buddhism." In *Sex, Marriage, & Family in World Religions*, edited by Don S. Browning, M. Christian Green, and John Witte, Jr., 299–366. New York: Columbia University Press.

Dauth, Ursula. 1996. "Sichuan Mulianxi in Mianyang (in September 1993)." In *The Bamboo-Leaf Boat: The Magic of the Chinese Theatre*, edited by Dana Kalvodová, 185–205. Acta Universitatis Carolinae. Philosophica et Historica 5–1994 Theatralia X. Prague: Univerzita Karlova.

Despeux, Catherine, and Livia Kohn. 2003. *Women in Daoism*. Cambridge, Mass.: Three Pines Press.

Donnelly, Neal. 1990. *A Journey through Chinese Hell: "Hell Scrolls" of Taiwan*. Taipei: Artist Publishing.

Duan Ping 段平, comp. 1992. *Hexi baojuan xuan* 河西寶卷選 (Selected precious scrolls from western Gansu). 2 vols. Taipei: Xinwenfeng chubanshe.

Dudbridge, Glen. 1978. *The Legend of Miao-shan*. London: Ithaca Press. Revised edition. London: Oxford University Press, 2004.

Eberhard, Wolfram. 1967. *Guilt and Sin in Traditional China*. Berkeley: University of California Press.

Eoyang, Eugene, trans. 1978. "The Great Maudgalyayana Rescues his Mother from Hell: From the Tun-huang *Pien-wen* Manuscript P2319." In *Traditional Chinese Stories: Themes and Variations*, edited by Y.W. Ma and Joseph S.M. Lau, 443–53. New York: Columbia University Press.

Fan Jinshi and Lin Mei. 1996. "An Interpretation of the Maudgalyayana Murals in Cave 19 at Yulin." *Orientations* 27.10: 70–75.

Faure, Bernard. 1998. *The Red Thread: Buddhist Approaches to Sexuality*. Princeton, N.J.: Princeton University Press.

———. 2003. *The Power of Denial: Buddhism, Purity, and Gender*. Princeton, N.J.: Princeton University Press.

Furth, Charlotte. 1999. *A Flourishing Yin: Gender in China's Medical History, 960–1665*. Berkeley: University of California Press.

Goodrich, Anne Swan. 1981. *Chinese Hells: The Peking Temple of the Eighteen Hells and Chinese Conceptions of Hell*. Sankt Augustin, Germany: Monumenta Serica Institute.

Goossaert, Vincent. 2005. *L'interdit du boeuf en Chine: Agriculture, éthique et sacrifice*. Paris: Collège de France.

Grant, Beata. 1989. "The Spiritual Saga of Woman Huang: From Pollution to Purification." In *Ritual Opera, Operatic Ritual: "Mu-lien Rescues His Mother" in Chinese Popular Culture*, edited by David Johnson, 224–311. Publications of the Chinese Popular Culture Project 1. Berkeley: University of California.

———. 1995. "Patterns of Female Religious Experience in Qing Dynasty Popular Literature." *Journal of Chinese Religions* 23: 29–58.

———. 2008a. "Women, Gender, and Religion in Premodern China: A Brief Introduction." *Nan Nü* 10, no. 1: 2–21.

———. 2008b. "Women, Gender, and Religion in Premodern China: A Selected Bibliography of Secondary Sources in Chinese and Western Languages." *Nan Nü* 10, no. 1: 152–75.

Guang, Xing. 2005. "Filial Piety in Early Buddhism." *Journal of Buddhist Ethics* 12: 82–106.

Guo, Qitao. 2005. *Ritual Opera and Mercantile Lineage: The Confucian Transformation of Popular Culture in Late Imperial Huizhou.* Stanford, Calif.: Stanford University Press.

Hansen, Valerie. 1995. *Negotiating Daily Life in Traditional China: How Ordinary People Used Contracts, 600–1400.* New Haven, Conn.: Yale University Press.

He Fang 何芳 et al. 2008. "Anhui sheng Huangshanshi Qimen xian Mashan Mulian lianxi xianzhuang diaocha" 安徽省黃山市祁門縣馬山目連連戲現狀調查 (An investigation into the current state of the Mulian plays of Mashan in Qimen county of Huangshan city in Anhui province). *Huangshan xueyuan xuebao* 黃山學院學報 1: 18–21.

Hou Jie. 2002. "Mulian Drama: A Commentary on Current Research and Source Materials." In *Ethnography in China Today: A Critical Assessment of Methods and Results,* edited by Daniel Overmyer, 23–48. Taipei: Yuan-Liou Publishing.

Hsiung, Ping-chen. 1994. "Constructed Emotions: The Bonds between Mothers and Sons in Late Imperial China." *Late Imperial China* 15, no. 1: 87–177.

Huijiao 慧皎. 1992. *Gaoseng zhuan* 高僧傳 (Biographies of eminent monks). Annotated by Tang Yongtong 湯用彤, edited by Tang Yixuan 湯一玄. Beijing: Zhonghua shuju.

Idema, W. L. 2004. *Boeddha, hemel en hel: Boeddhistische verhalen uit Dunhuang.* Amsterdam: Atlas.

———. 2008. *Personal Salvation and Filial Piety: Two Precious Scroll Narratives of Guanyin and Her Acolytes.* Honolulu: University of Hawai'i Press.

———. 2009a. *Heroines of Jiangyong: Chinese Narrative Ballads in Women's Script.* Seattle: University of Washington Press.

———. 2009b. *The White Snake and Her Son.* Indianapolis: Hackett.

———. 2010. "Prosimetric and Verse Narrative." In *The Cambridge History of Chinese Literature,* edited by Kang-i Sun Chang and Stephen Owen. Vol. 2, 343–412. Cambridge: Cambridge University Press.

Idema, Wilt L., and Beata Grant. 2004. *The Red Brush: Writing Women in Imperial China*. Cambridge, Mass.: Harvard University Press.

Iovene, Paola. 2010. "Chinese Operas on Stage and Screen: A Short Introduction." *The Opera Quarterly* 26, nos. 2–3: 181–99.

Johnson, David, ed. 1989. *Ritual Opera Operatic Ritual: "Mu-lian Rescues His Mother" in Chinese Popular Culture*. Berkeley, Calif.: Chinese Popular Culture Project.

———. 1992–93. "Report on the International Conference on Chinese Southern Opera (Nanxi) and Mulian Opera." *Chinoperl Papers* 16: 207–14.

———. 1995. "Mu-lien in *Pao-chüan*: The Performance Context and the Religious Meaning of the *Yu-ming pao-ch'uan*." In *Ritual and Scripture in Chinese Popular Religion: Five Studies*, 55–103. Berkeley, Calif.: Chinese Popular Culture Project.

Jordan, David K. 2004. "Pop in Hell: Chinese Representations of Purgatory in Taiwan." In *The Minor Arts of Daily Life, Popular Culture in Taiwan*, edited by David K. Jordan, Andrew D. Morris, and Marc L. Moskowitz, 90–118. Honolulu: University of Hawai'i Press.

Judd, Ellen R. 1994. "Mulian Saves His Mother in 1989." In *Memory, History, and Opposition under State Socialism*, edited by Rubie Watson, 105–26. Santa Fe, N.Mex.: School of American Research Press.

———. 1996. "Ritual Opera and the Bonds of Authority: Transformation and Transcendence." In *Harmony and Counterpoint: Ritual Music in Chinese Context*, edited by Bell Yung, Evelyn S. Rawski, and Rubie Watson, 226–46. Stanford, Calif.: Stanford University Press.

Kang Xiaofei. 2009. "Rural Women, Old Age, and Temple Work." *China Perspectives*, 442–53.

Kapstein, Matthew T. 2001. "A Dunhuang Tibetan Summary of the Transformation Text on Mulian Saving His Mother from Hell." In *Dunhuang wenxian lunji* 敦煌文獻論集 (Studies of Dunhuang documents) , edited by He Chunwen 郝春 文, 235–47. Shenyang: Liaoning renmin chubanshe.

———. 2007a. "Mulian in the Land of Snow and King Gesar in Hell: A Chinese Tale of Parental Death in Its Tibetan Transformation." In *The Buddhist Dead: Practices, Discourses, Representations*, edited by Bryan J. Cuevas and Jacqueline I. Stone, 345–77. Honolulu: University of Hawai'i Press.

———. 2007b. "The Tibetan *Yulanpen jing*." In *Contributions to the Cultural History of Early Tibet*, edited by Matthew T. Kapstein and Brandon Dotson, 211–38. Leiden: Brill.

Kieschnik, John. 2005. "Buddhist Vegetarianism in China." In *Of Tripod and*

Palate: Food Politics and Religion in Traditional China, edited by Roel Sterckx, 186–212. New York: Palgrave Macmillan.

Kikkawa Yoshikazu 吉川良和. 1991. "Guanyu Riben faxian de *Foshuo Mulian jiumu jing*" 关于日本发现的佛说目连救母经 (On the discovery in Japan of *The Scripture of Mulian Rescues His Mother Spoken by the Buddha*). *Xiqu yanjiu* 37: 177–206.

———. 2003. "*Kyūbokyō to Shōten hōkan* no Mokurenbutsu ni kansuru sesshō geinōteki shikiron*" 救母經と升天寶卷の目連物に關する說唱藝能旳試論 (A preliminary essay on the *Scripture of Mulian Rescues His Mother* and the *Mulian Precious Scroll* from the perspective of prosimetric storytelling). *Hitotsubashi daigaku kenkyū nempō shakaigaku kenkyū* 41: 61–135.

———. 2005. "*Kyūbokyō to Shōten hōkan* no seisho nendai shōkaku" 救母經と升天寶卷の成書年代商榷 (On the dates of the completion of the *Scripture of Mulian Rescues His Mother* and the *Mulian Precious Scroll*). *Shinagawa daigaku jimbungaku kaishi* 155: 9–43.

Ko, Dorothy, JaHyun Kim Haboush, and Joan R. Piggott, eds. 2003. *Women and Confucian Cultures in Premodern China, Korea, and Japan*. Berkeley: University of California Press.

Konami Ichirō 小南一郎. 2003. "*Urabon kyō* kara *Mokuren hembun* e—Kyōkō to kataribungei to no aida I" 盂蘭盆經から目連變文へ—講經と語り物文藝とのあいだ上 (From the Yulan Bowl Sutra to the Mulian transformation text: Between sutra explanation and the art of storytelling: Part 1). *Tōhō gakuhō* 75: 81–122.

———. 2004. "*Urabon kyō* kara *Mokuren hembun* e—Kyōkō to kataribungei to no aida II" 盂蘭盆經から目連變文へ—講經と語り物文藝とのあいだ下 (From the Yulan Bowl sutra to the Mulian transformation text: Between sutra explication and the art of storytelling: Part 2). *Tōhō gakuhō* 76: 1–84.

Lai, Shufen Sophia. 1999. "Father in Heaven, Mother in Hell: Gender Politics in the Creation and Transformation of Mulian's Mother." In *Presence and Presentation: Women in the Chinese Literati Tradition*, edited by Sherry J. Mou, 187–213. New York: St. Martin's Press.

Lee, Jen-der. 2003. "Gender and Medicine in Tang China." *Asia Major*, 3rd ser., 16.2: 1–32.

———. 2005. "Childbirth in Early Imperial China." *Nan Nü* 7: 216–86.

Legge, James. 1974. *The Chinese Classics with a Translation, Critical and Exegetical Notes, Prolegomena and Copious Indexes*. Vols. 1 and 2. Reprint. Taipei: Wenshizhe chubanshe.

Levering, Miriam L. 1982. "The Dragon Girl and the Abbess of Mo-shan: Gender and Status in the Ch'an Buddhist Tradition." *Journal of the International Association of Buddhist Studies* 5.1: 19–35.

Lhamo, Yeshe Choekyi. 2003. "The Fangs of Reproduction: An Analysis of Taiwanese Menstrual Pollution in the Context of Buddhist Philosophy and Practice." *History and Anthropology* 14.2: 157–98.

Li Ang. 1986. *The Butcher's Wife: A Novel.* Translated by Howard Goldblatt and Ellen Yeung. San Francisco: North Point Press.

Li, Chengyang, ed. 2000. *The Sage and the Second Sex: Confucianism, Ethics, and Gender.* Chicago: Open Court.

Lin Xinyi 林欣儀 2008. *Shehui guizhen: Zhonggu Handi Fojiao famieguan yu funü xinyang* 捨穢歸真：中古漢地佛教法滅觀與婦女信仰 (Abandoning Pollution and Returning to Purity: Women's Religious Belief and the Concept of the Decline of the Dharma in Medieval Chinese Buddhism). Taibei: Daoxiang chubanshe.

Liu Xun. 2004. "Visualizing Perfection: Daoist Paintings of Our Lady, Court Patronage, and Elite Female Piety in the Late Qing." *Harvard Journal of Asiatic Studies* 64, no. 1: 57–115.

Liu Zhen 刘祯. 1997. *Zhongguo Mulian minjian wenhua* 中国目连民间文化 (The popular culture of Mulian in China). Chengdu: Ba Shu shushe.

Lopez, Donald S., ed. 1995. *Buddhism in Practice.* Princeton, N.J.: Princeton University Press.

———, ed. 2004. *Buddhist Scriptures.* London: Penguin Books.

Lu Yongfeng 陆永峰 and Che Xilun. 2008. *Jingjiang baojuan yanjiu* 靖江宝卷研究 (A study of the precious scrolls of Jingjiang). Beijing: Shehui kexue wenxian chubanshe.

Mair, Victor H. 1983. *Tun-huang Popular Narratives.* Cambridge: Cambridge University Press.

———. "Notes on the Maudgalyayana Legend in East Asia." *Monumenta Serica. Journal of Oriental Studies* 37 (1986–87): 83–93.

———. 1996. *The Columbia Anthology of Traditional Chinese Literature.* New York: Columbia University Press.

———. 1997. "The Prosimetric Form in the Chinese Literary Tradition." In *Prosimetrum: Cross-Cultural Perspectives on Narrative in Prose and Verse*, edited by Joseph Harris and Karl Reichl, 365–85. Cambridge: D. S. Brewer.

Mann, Susan, and Yu-yin Cheng, eds. 2001. *Under Confucian Eyes: Writings on Gender in Chinese History.* Berkeley: University of California Press.

Mark, Lindy Li. 1995a. "Food, Political Satire: Two Themes in Sichuan Mulian

Ritual Drama; The 1993 Symposium Performance." *Chinoperl Papers* 18: 95–114.

———. 1995b. "Legends of the *The Original Vow of the Bodhisattva of the Earth Sanctuary.*" In *Hawai'i Reader in Traditional Chinese Culture*, edited by Victor H. Mair, Nancy S. Steinhardt, and Paul R. Goldin. Honolulu: University of Hawai'i Press.

Maspero, Henri. 1963. "The Mythology of Modern China." In *Asiatic Mythology: A Detailed Description and Explanation of the Mythologies of All the Great Nations of Asia*, edited by J. Hackin et al., 252–384. New York: Crescent Books. (Orig. pub. 1932.)

Minford, John, and Joseph S.M. Lau, eds. 2002. *Classical Chinese Literature: An Anthology of Translations.* New York: Columbia University Press.

Moerman, D. Max. 2005. *Localizing Paradise: Kumano Pilgrimage and the Religious Landscape of Premodern Japan.* Cambridge, Mass.: Harvard University Press.

Moskowitz, Marc L. 2004. "Yang-Sucking She-Demons: Penetration, Fear of Castration, and Other Freudian Angst in Modern Chinese Cinema." In *The Minor Arts of Daily Life, Popular Culture in Taiwan*, edited by David K. Jordan, Andrew D. Morris, and Marc L. Moskowitz, 204–17. Honolulu: University of Hawai'i Press.

Mu Soeng. 2000. *The Diamond Sutra: Transforming the Way We Perceive the World.* Boston: Wisdom Publications.

Mugitani, Kunio. 2004. "Filial Piety and 'Authentic Parents' in Religious Daoism." In *Filial Piety in Chinese Thought and History*, edited by Alan L. Chan, 110–21. London: Routledge/Curzon.

Nadeau, Randall L. 1993. "Genre Classification of Chinese Popular Literature: *Pao-chüan.*" *Journal of Chinese Religions*, 121–28.

Overmyer, Daniel L. 1991. "Women in Chinese Religion: Submission, Struggle, Transcendence." In *From Benares to Beijing: Essays on Buddhism and Chinese Religion*, edited by Koichi Shinohara and Gregory Schopen, 91–120. New York: Mosaic Press.

———. 1999. *Precious Volumes: An Introduction to Chinese Sectarian Scriptures from the Sixteenth and Seventeenth Centuries.* Cambridge, Mass.: Harvard University Press.

Pas, Julian F. 1989. "A New Report of Shamanistic Travel to the Courts of Hell." *Journal of Chinese Religions* 17: 43–60.

Paul, Diana Y. 1979. *Women in Chinese Buddhism: Images of the Feminine in Mahâyâna Tradition.* Berkeley: University of California Press.

Peng, Fei, and Gary Seaman. 1994. *Chinese Mulian Plays: Resources for Studies of Ritual and Performance.* Los Angeles: Ethnographic Press, University of Southern California.

Poo, Mu-chou. 1998. *In Search of Personal Welfare: A View of Ancient Chinese Religion.* Albany: State University of New York Press.

Red Pine. 2001. *The Diamond Sutra: The Perfection of Wisdom.* Washington, D.C.: Counterpoint.

Rosenlee, Li-Hsiang Lisa. 2006. *Confucianism and Women: A Philosophical Interpretation.* Albany: State University of New York Press.

Roy, David Tod, tr., 2011. *The Plum in the Golden Vase* or, *Chin P'ing Mei*: Volume Four: The Climax: 4 (Princeton Library of Asian Translations). Princeton, N.J.: Princeton University Press.

Sangren, P. Steven. 1983. "Female Gender in Chinese Religious Symbols: Kuan Yin, Ma Tsu, and the 'Eternal Mother.'" *Signs: Journal of Women in Culture and Society* 9, no. 1: 4–25.

———. 1994. "Gods and Familial Relations: No-chia, Miao-shan and Mu-lien." *Minjian xinyang yu Zhongguo wenhua guoji yantaohui lunwenji*, 民間信仰與中國文化國際研討會論文集 (Collected papers of the International Conference on Popular Belief and Chinese Culture), 22–74. Taipei: Hanxue yanjiu zhongxin.

Sawada, Mizuho澤田瑞穂. 1968. *Jigokuhen: Chūgoku no meikaisetsu.* 地獄変：中国の冥界說 (Hell transformations: Chinese discourse on the afterlife). Kyoto: Hōzōkan.

———. 1975. *Hôken no kenkyu* 寶卷の研究 (A study of precious scrolls). Rev. ed. Tokyo: Kokusho kankokai.

Schopen, Gregory. 1984. "Filial Piety and the Monks in the Practices of Indian Buddhism: A Question of Sinicization Viewed from the Other Side." *T'oung Pao* 70: 110–26.

Schmid, David Neil. 2008. "Revisioning the Buddhist Cosmos: Shifting Paths of Rebirth in Medieval Chinese Buddhism." *Cahiers d'Extrème Asie* 17: 293–325.

Seaman, Gary. 1975. "The Sexual Politics of Karmic Retribution." In *The Anthropology of Taiwanese Society*, edited by E. M. Ahern and Hill Gates. Stanford, Calif.: Stanford University Press.

See, Lisa. 2005. *Snow Flower and the Secret Fan.* New York: Random House.

Seiwert, Hubert, in collaboration with Ma Xisha. 2003. *Popular Religious Movements and Heterodox Sects in Chinese History.* Leiden: E. J. Brill.

Shek, Richard H. C. 1980. "Religion and Society in Late Ming: Sectarianism and Popular Thought in Sixteenth and Seventeenth Century China." Ph.D. diss., University of California, Berkeley.

Somers, Robert M. 1979. "The End of the T'ang." In *The Cambridge History of*

China. Vol. 3, *Sui and T'ang China 589–906*, Part 1, edited by Denis Twitch-ett, 682–789. Cambridge: Cambridge University Press.

Sponberg, Alan. 1992. "Attitudes towards Women and the Feminine in Early Buddhism." In *Buddhism, Sexuality, and Society*, edited by Jose Ignacio Cabezon, 3–36. Albany: State University of New York Press.

Strong, John. 1983. "Filial Piety and Buddhism: The Indian Antecedents to a 'Chinese' Problem." In *Traditions in Contact and Change*, edited by Peter Slater and Donald Wiebe, 171–86. Waterloo, Ont.: Wilfred Laurier University Press, 1983.

Takemi, Momoko. 1983. "'Menstruation Sutra' Belief in Japan." *Japanese Journal of Religious Studies* 10, nos. 2–3: 229–46.

Teiser, Stephen F. 1988. *The Ghost Festival in Medieval China*. Princeton, N.J.: Princeton University Press.

———. 1994. *The Scripture of the Ten Kings and the Making of Purgatory in Medieval Chinese Buddhism*. Honolulu: University of Hawai'i Press.

———. 2006. *Reinventing the Wheel: Paintings of Rebirth in Medieval Buddhist Temples*. Seattle: University of Washington Press.

Tian, Min. 2003. "Chinese Nuo and Japanese Noh: Nuo's Role in the Origina-tion and Formation of Noh." *Comparative Drama* 37, nos. 3–4: 343–61.

Topley, Marjorie. 1963. "The Great Way of Former Heaven: A Group of Chinese Secret Religious Sects." *Bulletin of the School of Oriental and African Studies* 26: 362–92.

Tong Guangxia 童光俠. 1990. "Foshuo yulanpen jing yu Mulian jiumu bian-wen" 佛说玉兰盆经与目连救母变文 (The *Scripture of the Yulan Bowl as Spoken by the Buddha* and the *Mulian Rescues His Mother Transformation Text*). *Dunhuang jikan* 17: 100–104.

Valussi, Elena. 2003. "Beheading the Red Dragon: A History of Female Inner Alchemy in China." Ph.D. diss., University of London.

Waley, Arthur. 1960. *Ballads and Stories from Tun-huang*. London: George Allen and Unwin.

Wang Mingda 王明達. 1984. "Huangshi nü de beiju xingxiang yu Baizude zongjiao xinyang" 黃氏女的悲劇形象與白族的宗教信仰 (The tragic image of Woman Huang and the religious beliefs of the Bai people). *Shancha* 1: 52–54.

Wilson, Liz. 1996. *Charming Cadavers: Horrific Configurations of the Feminine in Indian Buddhist Hagiographic Literature*. Chicago: University of Chicago Press.

Wood, Frances and Mark Barnard 2010. *The Diamond Sutra: The Story of the World's Earliest Dated Printed Book*. London: The British Library.

Xiao Dengfu 蕭登福. 1996. *Dao Fo shiwang diyu shuo* 道佛十王地獄說 (The ten kings and their hells in Daoism and Buddhism). Taipei: Xinwenfeng chuban gongsi.

Yifa and Peter M. Romaskiewicz, trans. 2008a. *The Sutra on the Past Vows of Kṣitigarbha Bodhisattva*. Taiwan: Buddha's Light Publishing.

——, trans. 2008b. *The Yulan Bowl Sutra and Collection of Filial Piety Sutras*. Taiwan: Buddha's Light Publishing.

Yong You. *The Diamond Sutra in Chinese Culture*. Los Angeles: Buddha's Light Publishing, 2010.

You Hong 尤紅, ed. 2007. *Zhongguo Jingjiang baojuan* 中国靖江宝卷. 2 vols. Nanjing: Jiangsu Wenyi chubanshe.

Young, Serinity. 2004. *Courtesans and Tantric Consorts: Sexualities in Buddhist Narrative, Iconography, and Ritual*. New York: Routledge.

Yü, Chün-fang. 2001. *The Chinese Transformation of Avalokiteśvara*. New York: Columbia University Press.

Zhang Zong. 2008. Translated by François Lachaud and Kuo Li-ying. "Comment le bodhisattva Dizang est parvenu a gouverner les Dix Rois des Enfers." *Cahiers d'Extrème Asie* 17: 265–91.

Zheng Zhenduo 鄭振鐸. 1959. *Zhongguo suwenxue shi* 中國俗文學史 (The history of Chinese popular literature). Reprint. Beijing: Wenxue guji chubanshe.

Zhiru. 2007. *The Making of a Savior Bodhisattva*. Honolulu: University of Hawai'i Press.

Zhongguo Heyang Baojuan ji 中国河阳宝卷集 (Collected precious scrolls from Heyang). 2007. 2 vols. Shanghai: Shanghai wenhua chubanshe.

Zhou Yiqun. 2003. "The Hearth and the Temple: Mapping Female Religiosity in Late Imperial China." *Late Imperial China* 24: 109–55.

Zhu Hengfu 朱恒夫. 1993. *Mulianxi yanjiu* 目连戏研究 (A study of the Mulian plays). Nanjing: Nanjing daxue chubanshe.

——. 2001. "Chenhe gaoqiang Mulian xi di wuben Wang Guixiang sanshi xiu gushi wei 'Dou'e yuan' de fangzuo" 辰河高腔目连戏第五本王桂香三世修故事为窦娥冤的仿作 (The story of the three lives of Wang Guixiang in the fifth section of the Gaoqiang Mulian drama from Chenhe and its indebtedness to *Injustice to Dou E*). In *Yishu baijia*, 159–61.